New Destinations of Empire

GEOGRAPHIES OF JUSTICE AND SOCIAL TRANSFORMATION

SERIES EDITORS

Mathew Coleman, *Ohio State University*
Ishan Ashutosh, *Indiana University Bloomington*

FOUNDING EDITOR

Nik Heynen, *University of Georgia*

ADVISORY BOARD

Deborah Cowen, *University of Toronto*
Zeynep Gambetti, *Boğaziçi University*
Geoff Mann, *Simon Fraser University*
James McCarthy, *Clark University*
Beverley Mullings, *Queen's University*
Harvey Neo, *Singapore University of Technology and Design*
Geraldine Pratt, *University of British Columbia*
Ananya Roy, *University of California, Los Angeles*
Michael Watts, *University of California, Berkeley*
Ruth Wilson Gilmore, *CUNY Graduate Center*
Jamie Winders, *Syracuse University*
Melissa W. Wright, *Pennsylvania State University*
Brenda S. A. Yeoh, *National University of Singapore*

New Destinations of Empire

MOBILITIES, RACIAL GEOGRAPHIES, AND CITIZENSHIP IN THE TRANSPACIFIC UNITED STATES

EMILY MITCHELL-EATON

THE UNIVERSITY OF GEORGIA PRESS
Athens

CONTENTS

List of Figures vii

List of Abbreviations ix

Acknowledgments xi

CHAPTER 1. Mapping Imperial Migrations from the Pacific to the United States 1

CHAPTER 2. How Free Is Freely Associated Statehood? The Compact of Free Association and Its Colonial Past 32

CHAPTER 3. "We Are Here Because You Were There": War, Labor, Migration, and Empire in the Natural State 72

CHAPTER 4. "Of All Places!": Springdale, Arkansas, as a New Destination of Empire 106

CHAPTER 5. "No Such Thing as an Illegal Marshallese": COFA Status as Imperial Citizenship 150

CHAPTER 6. New Transpacific Destinations and the Future of Imperial Mobilities 189

Notes 203

References 211

Index 229

FIGURES

FIGURE 1. Chart of Pacific Island political, citizenship, and U.S. immigration statuses, rev. 1998   11
FIGURE 2. Map of author's research sites   23
FIGURE 3. U.S. troops with American flag on Kwajalein Atoll, Marshall Islands, World War II   42
FIGURE 4. Official map, UN Trust Territory of the Pacific Islands, 1962   46
FIGURE 5. Arrival of UN Visiting Mission, Majuro, Marshall Islands, 1978   56
FIGURE 6. Marshall Islanders in line to vote in plebiscite, Majuro, Marshall Islands, 1983   58
FIGURE 7. Nose art of the Arkansas traveler razorback on B-24 bomber, ca. 1943   81
FIGURE 8. Nose art of the Arkansas traveler on P-38 fighter aircraft, 1944   81
FIGURE 9. Map of War Relocation Authority Relocation Centers, 1942–1946   89
FIGURE 10. Map of Fort Chaffee, Camp Dermott, and Camp Robinson   91
FIGURE 11. Mural, *Local Industries*, Springdale, Arkansas, ca. 1940   108
FIGURE 12. Map of Northwest Arkansas   113
FIGURE 13. The Apollo on Emma Theater, downtown Springdale, Arkansas   139
FIGURE 14. Map of requests for Republic of the Marshall Islands Consular services   191

ABBREVIATIONS

ACA	Affordable Care Act
ARKids	Arkansas Children's Health Insurance Program
BIPOC	Black, Indigenous, and People of Color
CBP	Customs and Border Protection
CIMT	crime involving moral turpitude
CNMI	Commonwealth of Northern Mariana Islands
COFA	Compact of Free Association
DACA	Deferred Action for Childhood Arrivals
DHS	Department of Homeland Security
ESG	Education for Self-Government program
ESL	English as a Second Language
FAS	Freely Associated States
FSM	Federated States of Micronesia
GAO	Government Accountability Office
ICE	Immigration and Customs Enforcement
INS	Immigration and Naturalization Services
IPA	Independent Practice Association
MONAH	Museum of Native American History
NDE	new destination of empire
NID	new immigrant destination
NWACC	Northwest Arkansas Community College
RMI	Republic of the Marshall Islands
TTPI	Trust Territory of the Pacific Islands
USCIS	U.S. Citizenship and Immigration Services

ACKNOWLEDGMENTS

This book began as a dream, one that has taken years to decipher. Dreams are never products of isolation, of course, although they are borne out of darkness and a kind of solitude. Even while we dream alone, dreams tether us through invisible fibers to loved ones, those sleeping silently under our own roof and those moving about in daylight on the far side of the earth. Dreams assemble ghosts and memories, endless arrivals and departures, a thousand possible destinations. In dreams, we long for—and sometimes manage to manifest—connections across great, sprawling distances. Other times, our dreams present connections—odd pairings of places, people out of context—that we labor in vain to interpret. Here, I hope to make visible all of the filaments of community that made this dream of a book possible.

Mobility, itinerancy, and contingency—themes that thread through all the stories in this book—also defined my early academic career and the conditions under which I completed this project. Across six universities and five U.S. states, this book has been my main intellectual project, a cross to bear at times and a life raft at others. This project first took root in the Syracuse University Geography (now Geography and the Environment) Department under the superlative guidance of my dissertation advisor, Jamie Winders, who believed in and guided its unfolding. Anyone who has worked with Jamie knows that to have her on your side is to be fiercely mentored, expertly advised, and constantly compelled to ask the most challenging and necessary questions of your own work. Thank you. The other members of my dissertation committee also shepherded this project's early development: they include Don Mitchell, Jackie Orr, Matt Huber, Gretchen Purser, and Natalie Koch. A more generous group of interlocutors would be hard to imagine. A debt of gratitude is owed to the administrative staff of the Syracuse Geography and the Environment Department and to Joe Stoll at the Syracuse University Cartographic Laboratory for lending his cartographic skills to this book. Early mentorship, training in collaborative qualitative research, and fieldwork opportunities in Guåhan and Saipan came from Alison Mountz and our wonderful team of research collaborators on the Island Detention Project, funded by Alison Mountz's NSF CAREER Grant, "Geographies of Sovereignty: Global Migration, Legality, and the Island Index," award #0847133. At Syracuse University, research funding was generously provided by the Moynihan Institute of Global Affairs, the David E. Sopher Memorial Award, the Roscoe-Martin Dissertation Award, and the Geography and Women & Gender Studies Departments.

At the University of California at Santa Cruz, a postdoctoral fellowship in the Mellon Sawyer Seminar Workshop on Non-Citizenship (2016–2017) allowed me the breathing room to gestate many beings, including my first child and the creature that would become this book. Deep thanks are due to Catherine Sue Ramírez, my postdoctoral advisor, and to the other faculty conveners of the Sawyer Seminar. A Research Cluster grant from UCSC's Chicano Latino Research Center (now the Dolores Huerta Research Center for the Americas) provided additional funding and a fertile intellectual space, which I shared delightedly with Claudia López and Tsering Wangmo Dhompa. Claudia and Tsering, you made that year between the ocean and the redwoods magical. I will cherish it always.

At Trinity College (2017–2018), the Patricia C. and Charles H. McGill III '63 Distinguished Lecturer and Visiting Assistant Professor of International Studies provided space and support for this book's research. Zayde Antrim mentored with kindness first and always, and Garth A. Myers was a joy and an ally. Vijay Prashad kindly lent me his office for writing. Teresa Davis wore a thousand hats, all beautifully: among them were coconspirator, interlocutor, office mate, travel companion, and friend.

A move to southwestern Vermont (2018–2020) brought into formation new constellations of scholarly and personal ties. At Bennington College, John Hultgren was a comrade, a collaborator, and a friend, and Kate Paarlberg-Kvam kept the fight alive in all of us. My students at Bennington were some of the most incredible humans I have ever known: they taught me, through their own doing, how to lean into political conviction and radical vulnerability simultaneously. At Williams College (2020–2021), additional support came from a Faculty Research Grant, and Greg Mitchell and Kiaran Honderich in the WGSS program made sure I had everything else I needed. Greta Snyder and Elizabeth Iams Wellman were consummate cheerleaders, encouraging my persistence in the project (and the academic job market) in a COVID- and postpartum-inflected year.

Finding a scholarly home in Colgate University's Geography Department has been a dream come true. I want to thank each one of my colleagues there for the support, intellectual and personal as well as financial, that allowed me to conduct this research. Special thanks to mentors Pete Scull, Peter Klepeis, Maureen Hays-Mitchell, and Ellen Percy Kraly. Thanks, also, to Maura Tumulty and Jill Harsin for extradepartmental mentorship. The administrative support I received from Sarah Hughes and Erin Conroy was indispensable. Funding was generously provided by the Colgate University Research Council.

Across these institutional contexts, I have been lucky to have many opportunities to workshop and receive feedback on portions of this book. For inviting me to present early versions of various chapters and portions of this book, I am indebted to the Dartmouth Society of Fellows workshop and Yui Hashimoto; the Center for Cultural Studies Colloquium at UC Santa Cruz; the Social Sciences Brown Bag lecture series at Colgate University; the Center for Australian, New Zealand & Pacific Studies at Georgetown University (CANZPS); the Earth and Environmental Sciences Colloquium at the CUNY Graduate Center; the McGill Annual Lecture in International Studies at Trinity College; and the Shiloh Museum of Ozark History in Springdale, Arkansas. Additional chapter feedback, including insights on how to write (de)colonial histories with care and from below, came from Glenn Petersen as well as from Claudia López and Joaquín Villanueva, who also offered constant support and encouragement for this project. Thank you.

Exceptional editorial support and guidance for this project came from the University of Georgia Press, where my editor Mick Gusinde-Duffy has been a delight and an advocate for this project from the beginning, and where my project editor Jon Davies has attentively shepherded this book to completion. Thanks, also, to the Geographies of Justice and Social Transformation series editors, Mat Coleman, Sapana Doshi, and Ishan Ashutosh, and to the University of Georgia Press's top-rate editorial and production staff, including Jared Kazik Asser, Elizabeth Adams, Jason Bennett, Christina Cotter, Stacey Hayes, and Bethany Snead. This manuscript was greatly improved by five anonymous reviewers who gave feedback on the prospectus and manuscript; by Zubin Meer, who provided impeccable copyediting; and by Shazia Iftkhar and Rachel Fudge at *Ideas on Fire*, thanks to their exceptional developmental editing. Thanks, too, to Eldes Tran and Cathy Hannabach at *Ideas on Fire* for the book's index. Special thanks to Craig Gilmore for his comprehensive advice on book marketing and promotion. Any remaining errors are my own.

My greatest gratitude goes to the many people I interviewed for this book.

To respect their anonymity, I mostly do not name them individually here but honor and cherish each of the experiences, insights, and memories they shared with me for this book's research. I appreciate the time and support lent to this project by the staff of the Marshallese consulates in Honolulu, Hawai'i; Springdale, Arkansas; and Washington, D.C.; and to the embassies of the Republic of the Marshall Islands (RMI) and the Federated States of Micronesia (FSM) in Washington, D.C. Thanks in particular to staff at the Marshallese Educational Initiative (MEI), Arkansas Coalition of Marshallese (ACOM), the RMI consulates in Arkansas, D.C., and Hawai'i, the Northwest Arkansas Workers' Justice Center (NWAWJC), the OMNI Center for Peace, Justice & Ecology, and the Gaps in Services to Marshallese Task Force, organizations whose social activism is grounded in Northwest Arkansas but whose dreams and efforts for justice extend far beyond that space.

Early research conversations and insights into decolonial organizing across Oceania (2011–2013) came from Kyle Kajihiro, Michael Lujan Bevacqua, and staff members at We Are Guåhan, as well as from Sasha Davis, who generously provided early feedback on this book project. Preliminary fieldwork in Arkansas was made possible by John Treat and by my uncle and aunt, Courtney Alan Mitchell and Susan Jackson, who warmly hosted me in their homes and indulged my rapid-fire questions and excited musings after research interviews. Several Pacific Islands scholars and analysts offered guidance on policy issues and enthusiasm for this project during and after my trips to Washington, D.C.; they include Emil Friberg, Alan Tidwell, Al Stayman, and Al Short, as well as many others. They were generous with their time, materials, and insights, and this book benefited from both. Carol Fitch Baulos, Cheryl and Randy Kruid, Berni Peñaflor, and Ladd and Fran Baumann provided housing, travel support, and good conversation.

Librarians and archivists are too often the unsung heroes of research. This book would have been impossible without their knowledge and expertise. In particular, I want to thank the Shiloh Museum of Ozark History in Springdale, Arkansas, who provided me not only with working space, field contacts, and near-constant research support but also with their warm companionship for several months. Special thanks go to Marie Demeroukas, for her extraordinary archival skills, and to Susan Young, whose love of local history is born out of, and matched by, a love for the people around her and a genuine curiosity in their stories. Every research project should be so lucky to have a Susan. Thanks also to then-director Allyn Lord for her enthusiastic support and for access to the museum. Additional thanks for research support go to the staff of the Pacific Collection at the University of Hawai'i at Mānoa in Honolulu, especially Eleanor Kleiber; the Micronesian Area Research Center (MARC) at the University of Guam; the Clinton Presidential Library in Little Rock, Arkansas; the Reagan Presidential Library in Simi Valley, California; the Special Collections at the University of Arkansas in Fayetteville, Arkansas; and to Guy Lancaster and Michael Keckhaver at the Encyclopedia of Arkansas History & Culture in Little Rock.

This book would never have been dreamed into being without three incredible people on Saipan. Agnes McPhetres offered up her home and shared delicious meals. Her patio was a fertile space of grounded theorizing on Chamorro and Pacific Islander education and self-determination, in the broadest sense possible. Sam McPhetres Jr. was an excellent travel companion and a treasured friend. And finally, Sam McPhetres Sr. (1938–2021): So much of this book exists thanks to you. I'm sorry it took me so long to write it—I wish I could hand you a copy. Hope you're enjoying the next adventure, dear friend.

Friend-colleague-comrades: You are many. Jenna M. Loyd and Lisa Bhungalia offered comradery, support, and conference selfies over the past decade. Kate Coddington and Nancy Hiemstra have been wonderful feminist coconspirators, generously sharing advice, insights, and time. Jacque Micieli understood the twin hopes and tolls of mobility, and Mitul Baruah was a cherished writing partner and friend since the early days. Dana Olwan's integrity was paralleled only by her overflowing generosity. Mazen Labban shared many gifts, among them the conviction to make this book my own. Maddy Hamlin has been a dream colleague, confidante, and copy editor, especially in the book's final stages. To Rich Nisa and Ben Rubin I owe a great debt: in our "digital space of love" meetups during lockdown, and through countless group texts, readings of chapter drafts, and pep talks, they nourished me and this book in ways large and small.

In March 2020, as the COVID-19 pandemic enveloped the United States, my childhood Quaker friends started meeting for weekly Zoom calls, and these calls continue four years later. These friends keep me grounded, connected, and laughing. In Hamilton, New York, Christine Moskell and Ángela Carrizosa Aparicio helped me strategize during the book's final stages, and Rachel Newman and Anne Valente wrote alongside me in our dreamy mini–writing retreats on Colgate's campus. The Academic Mamas with Babies Born in 2017 group has been a constant support in all things professional and personal. The completion of this project would have been impossible without the many childcare providers who cared for my children since 2017, including the staff at CNS, WCP, Oak Hill, BECC, and TC4 as well as Gegia.

Finally, I thank my family. My mother and father, Remegia Mitchell and

Wade Eaton, never stopped believing in this book and seemingly never tired of hearing about it. Aidan Mitchell-Eaton, my brother and oldest friend, has been a sounding board and confidante throughout this book's gestation. Nora and Theo, my niece and nephew, have been beloved playmates. Erika Halvorsen taught me about bringing new beings into the world with vulnerability and strength. My sister, Jackie Kohn (1957–2014), both in her life and in her dying during the fieldwork for this book, taught me to not go gently but to keep looking for a new way forward.

To my two children, Ciaran Hanul and Malcolm Taeyang, you are my sky and my sun, my day and my night, my playful curiosity and my desire to persist. Your love, and my love for you, made this book possible.

Lastly, to my partner, Sung, I owe everything, though he would be first to say that I was the one who made this book happen. For over ten years, he marshaled every personal and family resource—time, thought, project-planning skills, intellectual curiosity, childcare, culinary labor and meal preparation, diaper changes and nighttime wakings, and space for writing retreats—in support of this project. His belief in it and in me was unflagging, even when my own belief wavered. Sung, we did it.

Sections of this book draw on research published previously in the works listed below. While the material in this book has been heavily revised, some content is based on those works. Thank you to the editors and anonymous reviewers of these pieces for facilitating their publication.

> Mitchell-Eaton, E. (2021). Imperial citizenship: Marshall Islanders and the Compact of Free Association. In C. S. Ramírez, S. M. Falcón, J. Poblete, S. C. McKay, and F. A. Schaeffer (Eds.), *Precarity and belonging: Labor, migration, and noncitizenship*. New Brunswick, N.J.: Rutgers University Press.
>
> Mitchell-Eaton, E. (2021). No island is an island: COVID exposure, Marshall Islanders, and imperial productions of race and remoteness. *Society & Space*. https://www.societyandspace.org/articles/no-island-is-an-island.
>
> Mitchell-Eaton, E. (2023.) Compact of Free Association (COFA) status: An imperial status on the move. *Asian-Pacific Law & Policy Journal*. http://manoa.hawaii.edu/aplpj/wp-content/uploads/sites/120/2023/05/APLPJ_24.3_MitchellEaton_JM.pdf.

New Destinations of Empire

CHAPTER 1

Mapping Imperial Migrations from the Pacific to the United States

In the early 1980s, Springdale, Arkansas, was a small town in the Ozark Mountains whose population of twenty-four thousand was almost exclusively white, due in large part to a long history of racialized dispossession and resettlement. A site on the Trail of Tears, Springdale witnessed the forcible relocation of the Cherokee population in the 1830s, followed by repopulation by white settlers from the northeastern United States. Springdale was also a "sundown town" during the Jim Crow era:[1] by the mid-1920s and until as late as the 1970s, it, like many towns in the region, had expelled or excluded any Black people from residing there. Since the 1980s, however, an influx of immigrants from Latin America and the Pacific has earned Springdale a reputation as Northwest Arkansas's "immigrant town" in the eyes of many white residents in the area.[2] Due largely to this migration, the city's population nearly tripled over the course of four decades (1980–2020), and it shows no signs of slowing down. The transformations of race, citizenship, labor, and politics that have taken place there over the past forty years—and, indeed, over the last century—have remade place and space in Springdale and beyond.

While many sites in the U.S. South have been studied as new destinations for Latinx immigrants, Springdale as a new destination has a different face: it is now home to up to twelve thousand Marshall Islanders, or Marshallese, making it the single largest Marshallese population outside the Marshall Islands. Arriving in unprecedented numbers, Marshallese residents now make up more than 10 percent of the city's population of nearly ninety thousand. According to 2020 U.S. census figures, there are approximately sixty-five hundred Native Hawaiʻian and Pacific Islanders living in Springdale, the vast majority of whom are Marshallese. However, the Marshallese Consul and other community sources estimate the Marshallese population to be closer to twelve thousand. Marshallese migrants arrived in Springdale on the heels of Latinx migrants, primarily Mexicans, Salvadorans, and Guatemalans, who began to settle there in the early 1980s. Together, these two groups—Marshallese and Latinx residents—now constitute more than 45 percent of Springdale's population. Although it is uncommon for rural Arkansas to be thought of as a hub of Pacific Islander diasporas, Marshallese settlement there has put Springdale on the map of the transpacific (Hoskins and Nguyen 2014) in an unexpected way.

How did Marshall Islanders end up in Northwest Arkansas, "of all places"?[3] The historical roots of Marshallese migration to the United States are based in a 1986 agreement between the United States and the Marshall Islands known as the Compact of Free Association. The Compact signaled the formal end of U.S. colonial administration over the islands, a control which dated back to 1947, with the UN-led creation of the U.S.-administered Trust Territory of the Pacific Islands (TTPI). The 1986 Compact, in addition to safeguarding long-term U.S. military access to the Marshall Islands, established a unique caveat to U.S. immigration law: it granted citizens of the Marshall Islands the right to travel to, reside in, and work in the United States without a visa. This caveat created a unique legal status, which I refer to as COFA status, for Marshallese, Micronesians, and Palauans—citizens of U.S. Freely Associated States (FAS) and former TTPI residents—living in the United States. This unique legal status has created new Pacific diasporas across the United States over the past four decades, remaking the landscape of immigrants' rights and (non)citizenship everywhere COFA migrants settle.

As a result of the Compact, Marshallese migration to the United States has skyrocketed. Since 1986, Marshall Islanders have resettled in growing numbers in the U.S.-affiliated (or U.S.-occupied) Pacific Islands of the Commonwealth of Northern Mariana Islands (CNMI), Guåhan, and Hawai'i.[4] In slightly smaller numbers, and in less geographically concentrated patterns, Marshallese immigrants have also resettled on the U.S. West Coast, in places such as Salem, Oregon, and Orange County, California (Nero, Burton, and Hess 2001). In this way, the Compact's migration provision has dramatically reshaped Pacific diasporas, etching new lines of migration, labor streams, and social networks between former U.S. territories and the U.S. mainland. Marshallese migrants' arrival in Springdale thus conjures up an old refrain of postcolonial and imperial migrants in Britain: "We are here because you were there."

While perhaps uncommonly heard in the United States, migrants' use of this imperial adage elsewhere is clarifying, as it forefronts the role of empires in global migration. Empires, as political and territorial systems wherein a sovereign state or leader exerts power over populations without their formal consent, necessarily impede the sovereignty of other peoples and places. At times (and in places), empires wield this power through direct, frequently militarized control and formal governance—often referred to as colonialism; and at others, they do so through more indirect or less formal forms of influence, coercion, and control—often referred to as imperialism. The uneven power relations that characterize empires are also (re)produced through the migration of imperial subjects; the production of their second-class citizenship status through racialized, classed, and gendered processes; and those subjects' challenges to subjugation, including through rights-based and decolonial struggles and everyday assertions of autonomy and agency. As such, empires are rife with dynamic tensions, and their constituent players and parts are constantly in motion.

As this book argues, COFA status and COFA migrants in the U.S. embody the tension between two conflicting desires always churning within empires: first, the desire of dominant (in this case, U.S.) political and military actors to maintain and expand global hegemony through military, economic, and political access to sites around the globe, while managing imperial populations' access to the metropole; and second, the desire of imperial migrants, people from those far-flung sites of empire, to *maintain access* to the metropole, including through citizenship rights, and to leverage their mobility to seek new places and ways of living. The tension between these two desires, the mobilities they engender, and the politics that animate them resonates throughout this book.

These conflicting tensions and desires were also structured by power disparities between the United States and the Marshall Islands over several decades of U.S. military, economic, and political control over the islands, dynamics that themselves built on and reworked much older and deeper colonial dynamics in the region. In this way, the *historical legacy* of U.S. imperialism in the Pacific is a crucial part of the story of the *ongoing* U.S. military presence there, as is the longer history of colonizing attempts in the region. The U.S.-affiliated Pacific Islands currently bear the greatest concentration of military bases in the world, some of the most intensive and invasive U.S. military training and testing, and among the highest military enlistment rates in the United States. Imperial political formations such as the TTPI and the Compact of Free Association laid the groundwork for ongoing and future U.S. influence in the Pacific, what U.S. secretary of state Hillary Clinton heralded in 2011 as "America's Pacific Century" and what would inaugurate the U.S. military's strategic "pivot to Asia."

Just as U.S. militarism has profoundly influenced Pacific Islands' political status, it has also been central to the formation of Pacific Islanders' citizenship and, thus, to the conditions of their mobility. The story of Compact migration, this book shows, is the story of how a policy provision once viewed by U.S. government officials as "relatively minor in the grand scheme of things" (interview, senior U.S. policy official, Washington, D.C., 2014) became a central tenet in the lives of Marshallese migrants in diaspora, their families and friends in the islands, and receiving communities in other Pacific Islands and the U.S. mainland. As Kristina Stege, climate envoy for the Marshall Islands, has written, "The Compact of Free Association colors nearly every story on the Marshall Islands" (2004, 127). Its effects, however, have also spread well beyond the Marshall Islands themselves, through COFA migrants. This policy is part of their history as well.

To narrate that history, *New Destinations of Empire* examines U.S. empire through three interrelated lenses: through an imperial policy, the Compact of Free Association; through the imperial diaspora—the Marshallese diaspora—that the policy produces; and through the town of Springdale, Arkansas, a new immigrant destination (NID) that has also become a new destination of empire (NDE). These three lenses reveal how empire's interrelated workings—migration, militarization, capitalism, racialization, labor, and citizenship, among others—inform one another to uphold U.S. imperial power and how U.S. empire both engenders and constrains mobility for its subjects.

New Destinations of Empire:
Geographies of Transit, Arrivals, and End Points

What makes a new destination of empire (NDE) different from a new immigrant destination (NID), the latter defined broadly as a place experiencing major migration for the first time (Marrow 2011)? Rather than providing readers with a typology of what is (and isn't) an NDE, I offer new destinations of empire as a conceptually expansive analytical framework that allows for multiple understandings of both destinations *and* empire through a focus on migration. Broadly, I define new destinations of empire as sites where migrants from former or current U.S. territories are arriving for the first time, bringing with them the embodied histories of U.S. occupation, militarization, and outsized political and economic influence in its nonsovereign territories. New destinations of empire are created through a double movement: as agents of empire seek out new sites in which to consolidate economic markets, maintain a military foothold, and impose their political will, so, too, will empire's subjects continue to move to new destinations, expanding beyond preliminary sites of settlement to places off the beaten path, ones usually understood as "remote."

This framework, thus, asks not, Which NIDs are NDEs and which are not?—arguably, empire touches *all* sites of immigrant settlement in the United States—but, rather, What can we see about an immigrant destination and its historical and contemporary dynamics, including other places and geographic scales it connects to, when we use a lens that brings empire into focus? In asking this question, the NDE framework expands both the *political* project of NID scholarship, which has largely overlooked imperialism and colonialism's effects on immigration (but see D. Robinson 2010; Carneiro, Fortuna, and Varejão 2012; Winders 2014), and its *geographic* scale of analysis, by examining how imperialism and colonialism shape ostensibly "new" immigrant destinations while forging their connections to other places across empire. In doing so, this book offers a capacious and broadly applicable analytical framework—one that can enrich theories of political geographies and imperial mobilities at a range of sites and scales—rather than a simple case study of Marshallese migration or a single "immigrant town."

Empire shapes the geography of diasporas worldwide: Migrants do not resettle simply *anywhere*, and migration patterns are never arbitrary. Rather, for many migrants, their ability (or need) to resettle in certain places is largely an outcome of imperial dynamics (Atkinson 2016). Yet despite empires' overwhelming influence on both contemporary and historical migration worldwide, studies of this phenomenon, while well developed in the context of European empires, have been quite limited in the context of U.S. empire until recently (and have focused almost exclusively on Puerto Rico and the Philippines; see García-Colón 2020; Findlay 2018; Baldoz 2011; McGreevey 2018). Additionally, scholarship on imperial migration has focused primarily on migrants from former colonies to major cities in colonial metropoles; for example, South Asian and West Indian migration to London (Ball 2004) or West African resettlement to Paris (Thomas 2007). Far less attention has been paid to migration, imperial or otherwise, to rural areas, though NID scholars are challenging this rural bias (Lichter and Johnson 2006). As Marshall Islander and other COFA migrant communities expand throughout the rural U.S. South and Midwest in record numbers, however, they present a vital and exciting opportunity to study new dimensions and geographies of U.S imperial migration.

New destinations of empire are created in part by migration policies that enable people to migrate from former or current territories to new sites across the United States. In the case of the Compact migration provision, a policy "on the move," such sites proliferate endlessly, created each time COFA migrants move to new destinations. As imperial diasporas—populations dispersed from an original homeland by empire's effects—spread geographically, migrants increasingly settle in new destinations, seeking jobs and more affordable housing or following family and friends. When we "follow the policies" that create these migration streams (Peck and Theodore 2012), they lead us to these new sites of immigrant settlement, tracing a novel cartography of empire that differs from imperial geographies historically mapped around military bases and camps, occupied islands, militarized borders, and Native reservations.

COFA status also creates ambiguities and uncertainties in NDEs, where the lived realities of what I call imperial citizenship—a liminal, exceptional, and exclusionary legal status held by subjects of empire that is determined and enforced by the imperial power—materialize in migrants' interactions with local state actors. Since imperial migrants' unique legal statuses—and, often, their places of origin—are often unfamiliar to residents and public actors in NDEs, imperial migrants are "hard to place" for many in these new destinations, both literally and figuratively. Imperial migrants bear the deleterious effects of that unintelligibility: uncertainty about their eligibility for public services and benefits, friction with other immigrant groups, and a lack of existing social infrastructure for advocacy (e.g., in the form of community organizations, interpreters and translators, institutional liaisons, and, in Springdale's case, even a local consulate). As a result, imperial migrants such as Marshallese COFA migrants, despite their slightly privileged legal status as compared with "nonimperial migrants," often fall through the cracks as they attempt to access services, benefits, and protections to which they are legally entitled, exacerbating their precarity and vulnerability.

Additionally, in NDEs, new formulations of race and racism, identity, and belonging get worked out in migrants' encounters with long-term residents and public actors. This book shows that empire fundamentally shapes those formulations, both in the past and the present. A closer look at Arkansas's racial, colonial, and militarized history shows that there is nothing new about empire bringing people into the state and giving contour to their reception there; moreover, as chapter 3 documents, empire has long sutured Arkansas to the Pacific. In the present, as long-term residents in NDEs encounter new neighbors they cannot make sense of—ones who don't fit into readily available narratives of immigration—they make *new* sense, reaching for the logics and histories they have at hand. Through these sense-making processes, old imperial mobilities and geographies are dredged to the surface, often in ways that, paradoxically, occlude the very fact of U.S. empire.

To make sense of the geographies and mobilities of U.S. empire, I engage multiple meanings of the word "destination" in the book's title, *New Desti-*

nations of Empire. This book and its inquiries are animated by these many meanings of destination—as journey, place of arrival, purpose, terminus, and destiny—as they illuminate the various ways in which empire produces and constrains mobilities and the ways in which people pursue, resist, experience, and understand their own mobility—and futurity—under empire. The word "destination" is most commonly used to mean a location to which one journeys, a place of arrival. Rather than think about destinations exclusively as end points, however, I want to retain the sense of mobility in the term "destination," its forward-looking and aspirational quality. This latter sense of destination implies an ever-expanding (and -contracting), ever-mobile geography of empire and its constituent parts and processes. I highlight this dynamism in this book to show empire's contingency or indeterminacy, which is to say, its impermanence.

While "destination" is also used to refer to "the purpose for which something is predetermined or destined" (or, more simply, "one's fate"), this book actively challenges such meanings of destination that predetermine and foreclose futures. What are the destinies of small island nations in the Pacific Ocean? What is their political fate? Their predetermined purpose? For much of the twentieth century and into the twenty-first, Pacific Islanders across thirty thousand islands and sixty million square miles of ocean—over 30 percent of the Earth's surface—have fought to determine their own political futures—their destinations—and the paths they would follow to get there. At every step of this process, empires have conspired to foreclose or predetermine Indigenous political futures, and imperial actors (state administrators, yes, but also journalists, policy analysts, and academics) have circulated discourses presenting small island nations as politically destined for external control because of their so-called scattered, remote, and underpopulated nature. But islanders' political imaginaries have always resisted enclosure, embracing instead the vastness of Oceania, that which Tongan-Fijian anthropologist Epeli Hau'ofa (1994) referred to as "our sea of islands" and its nurturance of both roots and routes.

Despite the sense of certainty conveyed in the term "destiny" and its derivative "destination," the histories this book narrates and the geographies it maps have always been tinged with indeterminacy and contingency. My aim in emphasizing this contingency is not to present a story of empire unmoored from its historical materialism—quite the contrary—but, rather, to imagine a plurality of stories of empire, empires with multiple possible centers and pathways toward multiple possible destinations. Contingency matters because freedom lies precisely in those undetermined possible futures and destinations, in that "multitude of alternative political spaces" (Villanueva and Lebrón 2020, n.p.). Such spaces have been charted in the decolonial geographical imaginaries of Puerto Rican Studies, Indigenous geographies (Daigle and Ramírez 2019), and Black and abolition geographies (Eaves 2020; McKittrick 2006), all radical geographic traditions that build liberatory futures by imagining "freedom as a place" (Gilmore 2022), one outside or beyond empire and white supremacy. I join these conversations here, offering that what happens in "small" and "remote" places can change the course of global history, remaking the course of empires and the struggles against them. Indisputably, the world has already been made and remade by movements against empire, in two senses: both by social movements for self-determination and by physical human movement, or migration, against the restraints imposed by empire. Recognizing this, *New Destinations of Empire* writes against the idea of destination as *determination*, contending that there is nothing predetermined about islands in the Pacific or Caribbean being subjugated to colonization, just as there is nothing inevitable about immigrants settling in cities such as New York City, Chicago, or Los Angeles. We might say that it is just as *natural*—though we may resist that word, and well we should—for Pacific Islanders to journey to Northwest Arkansas, "of all places," and just as logical for a grand story of empire to begin or end there.

Two NDE Encounters

What does it mean to understand a place such as Springdale, Arkansas, as a new destination of *empire*, not just as a site of new immigrant settlement? The two anecdotes I will recount shortly reveal two key dimensions of new destinations of empire: first, the *unintelligibility* of imperial migrants and geographies to state actors in NDEs (and state actors' efforts to render imperial migrants intelligible), and second, the *precarity* that such unintelligibility produces in the lives of COFA migrants. In the first encounter I share, we will see one common phenomenon in NDEs: public actors trying to make *geographic* sense of the Pacific Islands and *legal* sense of Pacific Islanders. In the second encounter, we will see Marshall Islanders traveling hundreds of miles, from Arkansas to the U.S.-Mexico border, just to maintain their precarious legal status, one that is still unfamiliar to many state actors. Both encounters show how COFA migrants' legal ambiguity—paired with state actors' geographical ignorances—can have dramatic and deleterious effects on Marshallese lives.

During my first research trip to Northwest Arkansas in 2013, I met with a U.S. Customs and Border Protection (CBP) officer working at the Rogers Municipal Airport, one of two U.S. ports of entry in Arkansas.[5] Greeting me at her office, Officer Lynn (a pseudonym) handed me a piece of paper.[6] "You might be interested in this," she said. The document, a chart presumably given to CBP officers to aid them in processing Pacific Islander arrivals to the United States (figure 1), reads, "There are hundreds of islands in the Pacific Ocean and during the inspection process, many questions arise regarding the status of citizens of these islands. A list of the major island groups was developed to assist inspectors in determining the citizenship and U.S. immigration status of these persons." In the original document, reformatted here for legibility, palm trees appeared over a sandy beach, overlooking an ocean. The document appeared to have been photocopied repeatedly, and the text at the top of the page was blurred nearly to the point of being undecipherable, implying many years of use and circulation. Dated January 21, 1998, the document was already fifteen years old when it reached me in 2013, having traveled from its site of production—somewhere in Washington, D.C., sometime in the mid-1980s?, to this rural Arkansas airport (did its creator ever imagine its destination being here?)—where it was still being used by state officials in everyday border policing.

As soon as the CBP officer handed me this document, I realized I held in my hands something incredible: something like an abbreviated field guide to islands, empire, and citizenship. So simple and yet so dense, it contains thick layers of information, histories of imperial occupation and decolonial struggle, contested geographies of territory, and wily, defiant histories of human movement and settlement, of entries and departures. These histories and geographies are all inelegantly wedged into a frame of neat legal categories for the purposes of the U.S. immigration system. At once, this form speaks to the unintelligibility of these imperial cartographies and the jigsawed nature of the political statuses within them, while promising a geography of U.S. immigration status that can be made intelligible to imperial state officials.

Producing intelligibility through geographic knowledge, of course, is an essential role of the imperial state, whether it is at work in an office in Washington, D.C., at a U.S. border, or in a field office in a "remote" site nestled in an empire's hinterlands. This chart, like so many government documents and maps, has a power that is both *descriptive*—as it produces, through description, a kind of geographic knowledge about imperial places and subjects—and *prescriptive*—as it aims to determine or dictate a set of state actions toward imperial subjects and their homelands. It conveys a simple yet powerful geographical imaginary: that the Pacific Islands are remote and scattered, tantalizingly tropical, and easily confused for one another. In other words, the document implies, U.S. immigration inspectors are right to be befuddled by the vast Pacific Ocean and its "hundreds of islands," but their befuddlement need not impede their work of managing human flows from such distant shores. These same geographical ideas or imaginaries (D. Gregory 1995)—of the Pacific Islands as remote and distant—profoundly shaped twentieth-century U.S. imperialism in the Pacific and continue to pervade geographic sense-making by public actors and residents in NDEs such as Springdale. This chart drives home that both political status and immigration status are constructs deeply entrenched in geography and born out of geographic ideas or imaginaries, demonstrating the importance of studying the *material effects* of geographical imaginaries that might at first glance seem abstract or inconsequential.

In simplifying such complex dynamics, this chart omits just as much as it reveals. The chart neglects to show, for example, where the imperial political statuses it outlines are contested by Indigenous inhabitants (as is the U.S. territorial status of Guam, known locally as Guåhan) or regularly subject to renegotiation, as is Freely Associated Statehood in the Republic of the Marshall Islands (RMI), Federated States of Micronesia (FSM), and Palau. It also says nothing about whether people classified as "aliens" need a visa to enter the United States (most do, but residents of U.S. FAS do not). These omissions naturalize imperial imaginaries of Pacific space while producing potentially deleterious effects for Pacific Islanders arriving at U.S. borders. By omitting complexities such as the ones named above, this guide is likely to produce ambiguity (or an erroneous sense of clarity) in state actors referencing it for the purposes of border enforcement, thus jeopardizing rights to which COFA migrants are legally entitled.

Finally, this chart says nothing of the people who experience COFA status's precarity daily, who *live* in the fine print. The chart, in categorizing Marshall Islanders as "aliens," greatly misrepresents the legal experiences of COFA migrants, who hold (at least on paper) many rights not granted to other foreign populations in the United States. The very conditions of COFA migrants' lives—their eligibility for employment or housing, their ability to migrate with their children or visit their elderly parents back home—are glossed over in the blurred details of this handout.

I now turn to a second field encounter, described below, which reveals how U.S. state actors' unfamiliarity with both the imperial *legal status* of COFA migrants and the imperial *geography* of the United States can produce precarity and uncertainty for COFA migrants, even to the point of jeopardizing their right to remain in the United States. During a summer 2019 trip to Northwest Arkansas, I met with a Marshallese organizer, John, whom I had gotten to know in previous years through various community meetings, site visits, and

Mapping Imperial Migrations   11

THE PACIFIC ISLANDS — There are hundreds of islands in the Pacific Ocean and during the inspection process many questions arise regarding the status of citizens of these islands. A list of the major island groups was developed to assist inspectors in determining the citizenship and U.S. immigration status of these persons.

U.S. IMMIGRATION STATUS	ISLAND GROUPS	POLITICAL STATUS	
U.S. CITIZENS	Guam	Territory of the U.S.	
	Hawaii	State of the U.S.	
	Northern Mariana Islands	Commonwealth of the U.S.	
U.S. NATIONALS	American Samoa, Swains Is.	Outlying possession of the U.S.	
ALIENS	Cook Islands	Free Association with New Zealand	
	Federated States of Micronesia	Free Association with the U.S.	(CFA/FSM)
	Fiji	Independent	
	French Polynesia	Territory of France	
	Kiribati	Independent	
	Marshall Islands	Free Association with the U.S.	(CFA/FSM)
	Nauru	Independent	
	New Caledonia	Territory of France	
	Niue	Free Association with New Zealand	
	Norfolk	Territory of Australia	
	Palau (Belau)	Free Association with the U.S.	(CFA/FSM)
	Papua new Guinea	Independent	
	Pitcairn	Dependency of Britain	
	Rapa Nui (Easter Island)	Dependency of Chile	
	Solomon Islands	Independent	
	Tokelau	Free Association with New Zealand	
	Tonga	Independent	
	Tuvalu	Independent	
	Vanuatu	Independent	
	Wallis and Futuna	Territory of France	
	Western Samoa	Independent	

FIGURE 1. U.S. port-of-entry inspection document showing the citizenship or U.S. immigration status and political status of people in the major Pacific Island groups. U.S. federal government, chart recreated by author.

interviews. That summer, immigrants in Springdale and across the U.S. South were on edge due to a spate of recent Immigration and Customs Enforcement (ICE) raids and deportations. I had planned this research trip to meet with Marshallese and Latinx community leaders to find out how Northwest Arkansas immigrants were experiencing this uptick in anti-immigrant hostility and policing.

Chapter One

At my companion's suggestion, we met for lunch at a Marshallese convenience store, one that served Hawai'ian food in Styrofoam containers. As we found a table and sat down, our conversation turned to the I-94, a small paper stub that is given to foreign entrants by CBP agents during processing at a port of entry, such as the one in Rogers. Since 2013, the U.S. DHS has issued I-94s electronically, so newly arriving COFA migrants no longer must keep a paper stub as proof of legal entry. However, any COFA migrant who last entered the United States before 2013 must still retain the paper I-94 for legal purposes. John elaborated:

> **John:** The I-94 is a big issue for COFA [migrants]. If you don't have it, you cannot go to work, you cannot do anything.
>
> **EME:** But it's easy to get again, right?
>
> **John:** There are three ways you can get it. Either go back to your country, pay the $445 filing fee, and wait six months, or cross the [U.S.-Mexico] border. So I've been taking Marshallese and FSM citizens to the border. Those people were really giving us a hard time. There were two times that we were stuck there from, like, 8 a.m. until 8 p.m. They held us there.
>
> **EME:** So are they really issuing the I-94s, and just being a pain about it?
>
> **John:** They don't know the Compact. They don't know shit about it. So I called [the Marshallese Consul in Springdale], and he's good about responding. He yelled at that lady there, and she was really mad. It was back and forth. We were really tired—we did not eat lunch.
>
> **EME:** So that's basically what you can do, right? You get [the consul] on the phone with them, and have him explain it?
>
> **John:** Yeah, and we had to fax a lot of paper.
>
> **EME:** This is one of the things that always surprises me: [COFA status] is written into law, but it's like a footnote. People just don't know.
>
> **John:** She was really about to deport all of us! She thought we were from South America. Then she looked up the Marshall Islands. She said, "Never mind, it's too far." But she was about to send us back! We were like, "Oh, shit." And she went to Google the Marshall Islands, and she read it out loud, about the COFA. Even though she read it, she was like, "Yeah, you made that up."

In revisiting this story, I imagine the utter exhaustion that must have plagued John's travel companions, driving thirteen hours to the border in a packed van, then waiting in line for twelve hours more. Then, the fear, anxiety, and uncertainty they must have felt when a government agent told them that she had never heard of their islands and was planning to deport them. Those emotions likely turned to frustration, as the agent had to be convinced by the consul of the travelers' federally recognized legal status, and then to relief, when she finally located their islands on a map. During the long drive home, the travelers, finally succumbing to fatigue, might have felt resentment creeping in. *She thought we made it up*, they might have thought angrily, *and she didn't even know where our islands were*. Each of these emotions—fear, uncertainty, frustration, relief, incredulity, fatigue, resentment, and anger—were shared with me by Marshall Islanders I met and interviewed during this research. Throughout the book, I have attempted to interweave Marshall Islanders' frustrations with their desires for more just conditions of migration to the United States.

I open the book with these two encounters to show how an imperial policy such as the COFA migration provision "travels" to new places, touching down in sites where its beneficiaries settle and changing those places in the process. These encounters offer a glimpse of how policies, too, change as they land, through the interpretations and case-by-case implementations of immigration officials, social service providers, and other local actors. Perhaps most strikingly, both encounters reveal that not even the state actors in charge of monitoring COFA migrant flows understand their obscure legal statuses. These two vignettes provide a window into the book's larger methodology: What does it look like to "follow a policy" (Peck and Theodore 2012) as a geographic methodology? What can such an approach reveal about the interconnections between distant and "remote" sites in empire, and, thus, about empires themselves? What can it tell us about the lives of the people it affects most intimately? *New Destinations of Empire* brings together the interpretations of both COFA's migration policy's administrators—those who put it into effect—and the people who hold COFA migration status—those who *live* its effects daily—to answer these questions.

Theoretical and Methodological Contributions: Geographies of Empire and Migration

In examining two spatial processes—empire and migration—as mutually constituted, *New Destinations of Empire* develops a theory and methodology of imperial migration centered on three geographic tenets, each developed below: mobility, remoteness, and multiscalarity. Its (inter)disciplinary contributions are twofold. First, it pushes geography as a discipline toward a more sustained and critical engagement with empire and migration *together*, two areas richly developed independently within geographic scholarship but less frequently analyzed in their coproduction. Second, it argues that a more rigorous *geographic* analysis can enrich studies of imperial migration in other disciplines, particularly migration and diaspora studies, American Studies, and Asian American Studies. As I argue in this book, focusing on imperial diasporas and NDEs reveals the mobilities and flows within empire and empire's multiscalar processes, pushing our geographic understandings of empire beyond oversimplified spatial binaries of metropole/colony and core/periphery.

MOBILITY: PEOPLE AND POLICIES ON THE MOVE

Why study empire through mobility? Empires constrict, facilitate, and often necessitate the mobility of their most legally liminal subjects, including through forms of imperial citizenship. Imperial subjects have always moved within empires, and that movement has always been surveilled, controlled, and fretted over by imperial powers (Mongia 1999). Imperial migrants' mobility, even their *attempts* at mobility, threaten to disrupt imperial distinctions between here and there, home and abroad, and colony and metropole—the very constructs on which empire itself depends. Attention to mobility allows us to pay close attention to where people move and why, how empires *move* people and why, and which methods and mechanisms (including policies) imperial states use to manage the mobility of people, things, resources, and geographic ideas. This book adds to the now well-established "mobilities turn" in geography and elsewhere (e.g., Sheller and Urry 2006), bringing mobility studies into direct engagement with political geographies of empire.

Studying empire through mobility also enables us to see how diasporas such as the Marshallese diaspora are shaped by U.S. empire. What makes the Marshallese diaspora imperial? First, its geographic dispersion is largely contained by the territorial outlines of U.S. empire: overwhelmingly, when Marshall Islanders move out of the RMI, they move to other sites in the United States and its territories. Second, Marshallese migration is fundamentally governed by U.S. laws, policies, and borders. In other words, while the RMI is formally sovereign, and though Marshall Islanders hold RMI citizenship, their diasporic movement and settlement outside the islands is overwhelmingly shaped, geographically and territorially, by the United States. This dynamic implicates Marshall Islanders as migrants *within* U.S. empire and as *imperial* migrants. Third, Marshall Islanders' diasporic mobility is imperial because it is legally made possible by a U.S. legal status: COFA status. Characterized by its liminal, exceptional, and exclusionary nature, COFA status as a form of imperial citizenship creates illegibility and precarity for its holders (as seen in the two anecdotes presented earlier), even as it partially enables Marshall Islanders' mobility *within* the United States. As Jodi Byrd (2011, xv) writes in *The Transit of Empire: Indigenous Critiques of Colonialism*, "What it means to be in transit, then, is to be in motion, to exist liminally in the ungrievable spaces of suspicion and unintelligibility. To be in transit is to be made to move." Seeing COFA migrants' double-edged, precarious, and often unintelligible mobility as explicitly *imperial* enables a deeper understanding of the interrelation between empire and mobility and its effects on empire's legally liminal subjects.

In addition to tracing human mobilities, this book also attends to policy mobilities, engaging a "follow the policy" approach (Temenos and McCann 2013; Peck and Theodore 2012) to examine the Compact and its effects as they "travel" to new destinations such as Springdale. "Following the policy" helps us to trace policies' circulation between different sites, examine how and where policies (and people) are stopped, interrupted, rerouted, or (mis)interpreted, and expose the power relations that enable or impede that movement (Cook and Harrison 2007). Following the Compact to Springdale also reveals the embodied linkages the Compact creates between apparently disparate and supposedly "remote" sites in U.S. empire, such as Arkansas and the Marshall Islands, though a kind of transnational policy ethnography (Hiemstra 2019). In NDEs such as Springdale, the Compact's "ripple effects" radiate out from COFA migrants to other residents, policymakers, and social service providers, creating new interactions between policies and policy beneficiaries in areas of health, housing, education, and immigration that reshape landscapes of rights and rightlessness there.

Examination of imperial policies, especially those as topically broad-reaching in their provisions as the Compact, reveals that imperial powers such as the United States attempt to manage populations in semi- or nonsovereign territories by harnessing migration-based policies to economic, political, and military ones. *New Destinations of Empire* analyzes the costs and contingencies of seemingly benevolent provisions such as visa-free migration—namely, their enmeshment with military and economic imperatives of the more powerful signatory nation—to examine their larger geopolitical implications. As it argues, the Compact's provisions ultimately shored up expansive and enduring U.S. influence in the Marshall Islands, Micronesia, and Palau, even as it enabled COFA migrants' mobility and ushered in the RMI's formal sovereignty.

REMOTENESS: CENTERING AND CONNECTING THE PERIPHERIES

New Destinations of Empire, in its focus on NIDs in the U.S. South and on Pacific Islands at the geographic edges of U.S. empire, also centers an analysis of remoteness and "remote" places. It takes seriously places commonly understood as remote, or distant and far removed—primarily by people other than their own inhabitants—as well the discursive and material processes through which places are *made* remote (Loyd and Mountz 2018; Ybarra 2021). Such productions emerge through always relational geographical imaginaries that frame some places (such as the U.S. South and the Pacific Islands) as remote, backward, racist, or unable to self-govern in order to hold up others (such as the United States writ large) as central, modern, and nonracist, a theme that threads throughout this book. "Remoteness" is integral to U.S. exceptionalism as its flip side: the concept of remoteness is commonly used to justify a U.S. imperial presence in the Pacific and to make sense of experiences of racism and immigrant reception in small-town Arkansas. Remoteness, thus, is one thread that produces a relational geography between the Pacific and the U.S. South. Imperial notions of race (and racist places) and remoteness work in tandem, a point central to my arguments in both chapters 2 and 3.

But racism is no more "natural" in the U.S. South than immigrants are "unnatural" there, as recent work has made clear (Desai and Joshi 2013; Quraishi 2020). Since the mid-2000s, scholars of the U.S. South have increasingly highlighted the region's global and transnational dimensions, positioning the U.S. South as dynamic, complex, and interconnected (Regis 2006; Woods 2017). Countering long-standing notions of the U.S. South as provincial (Kolchin 2009), such approaches frame the U.S. South not only as recipient of "the global" but also as a global producer and exporter of ideas, people, and commodities, as well as a region where colonial formations and racial logics are produced (and resisted; see Kelley 1990) and from whence they are exported (Domosh 2023). One need simply look to the global reach of Tyson Foods, a Springdale-based company, or of Walmart, headquartered in neighboring Bentonville, for evidence of Arkansas's global presence in the present. Works such as Gavin Wright's *Old South, New South* (1986) and more recent scholarship on the "plantationocene" (Davis et al. 2019) help to situate the U.S. South's contemporary interconnectedness within a longer history, showing how "the southern experience has fit into national and international economy currents over the past two centuries" (Wright 1986, vi).

New Destinations of Empire extends global and transnational U.S. South studies by sharpening our focus on empire, and, in turn, broadening the kinds of questions we can ask about a place such as Arkansas. Seeing the U.S. South as not only global and transnational but also as *imperial* in its globality makes clear that Marshallese migrants, as subjects of empire, are not "out of place" in Arkansas, no more so, at least, than are U.S. American tourists in Waikiki,

Hawai'i, or U.S. military contractors in Vieques, Puerto Rico. The very idea of being out of place springs from a geographic imagination that understands regions as bounded spatial containers, an imagination—if it can be called that—that is as erroneous as it is incurious about connections. This incuriosity kneecaps critical geographical inquiry: as Julie Weise (2015) warns, "When narratives of region and nation structure not only our answers but also our questions, they limit our ability to comprehend the complex dynamics of history" (13). For too long, the questions geographers have asked about empire and migration have been limited by this container-like view of regions and nations, one that unnaturally isolates social, political, and economic phenomena to certain spatial scales. This book counters that container-like view, aiming to cultivate instead a critical geographic imagination of "remote" and "provincial" places in its readers. My hope is that such an imagination might prompt one, instead of merely shrugging at the "unlikely" presence of Pacific Islanders in a place like Arkansas—or the "out-of-place" presence of a U.S. military intercontinental ballistic missile–site in Kwajalein—to get curious about the particular sinews of empire and capital, of race and labor, that tether those places together.

A focus on the connections between understudied, "remote," and "peripheral" sites of empire also reveals new countertopographies of empire, material connections across and between sites forged by empire and global racial capitalism (Katz 2001). By examining Northwest Arkansas and the Marshall Islands as coproduced, *New Destinations of Empire* extends the study of imperial migrants beyond colonial metropoles, unearthing connections not only between the local and the *global*—a more common analytical structure in geographies of empire—but also between the local and the *local*. It takes inspiration from Puerto Rican scholar Jose Fusté, who writes that "relational historiography traces causal interrelationships through time between seemingly disconnected peoples and places. It resists either generalizing or particularizing excessively. Instead, it pinpoints linkages while remaining attuned to situatedness and contingency" (2017, 93). Similarly, attending to multiple "remote" places requires a multisited and relational-geographic approach, a way of pivoting between sites and storylines that readers will find throughout this book. The work of the pivot is to reveal existing grappling hooks and the latticework of lifelines between seemingly unconnected sites, to shine a light on the spiderweb's infrastructure, to refocus our eyes to be able to see it. This pivoting approach highlights U.S. empire's ability to link seemingly unrelated, if not "unimportant," sites.

Multisited methodologies in and across "remote" sites also reveal the contingency of U.S. empire, the nonuniversality of how it operates (i.e., how empire governs, racializes, utilizes and produces space, responds to resistance, etc.) and its varying effects on places and people. This nonuniversality or *particularity* results from the uneven social topography of the places U.S. empire touches and the material, social, political, and economic relations of the people(s) living there. In short: when we want to study *how* U.S. empire operates, it matters *where* we study it.

When we take seriously the concept of remoteness and its effects, the importance of "remote" places, and the possibility of multiple geographic centers of empire, we also reconsider which archives matter to the stories we tell. This reconsideration can, as a result, shift the *geography* of where we conduct archival research on empire. For a geographer in pursuit of empire's mobile subjects and effects, locating the archives of (U.S.) empire raises the questions of *where* the colonial past resides and where the imperial—or decolonial—present and future are located. Yet seeing colonialism and imperialism as deeply interrelated allows us to also see key continuities and similarities between these systems. Assumptions about the temporal beginning and end of political systems can affect where we anticipate finding the "right" archival sources, where what Ann Stoler (2008) calls "paper empires" will reside.

Multisited archival research can serve as a rich method for studying complex temporalities and geographies, fleshing out (often unexpected) connections between places in larger systems such as empires (McClintock 1995), allowing us to trace intimate links between seemingly disparate sites of empire, their multiple, partial pasts and their possible futures. These histories, in refusing to be absorbed quietly into capital-H History, also migrate and morph, melding into other local and regional histories of the United States. Through my archival analysis, detailed further in subsequent chapters, I show that it is possible to have an "authoritative" archive of U.S. imperialism in a small town in Arkansas or on a small island in the Pacific. This book's methodology brings together the archival history of Arkansas's "colonial present" (D. Gregory 2006) with contemporary encounters between immigrants and long-term Arkansans, as well as the policies that have brought the Pacific to this new destination of empire.

MULTISCALARITY: MOVEMENT(S) ACROSS GEOGRAPHIC SCALES

New Destinations of Empire employs a multiscalar structure, methodology, and analysis, meaning that it is simultaneously attentive to processes playing out locally, regionally, nationally, and globally. Multiscalarity thus shapes both the book's geographic scope and its analytical scope—the kinds of questions it asks of geographic processes. Most significantly, a multiscalar analytical framework (and its corresponding methodology) enables me to situate immigrant resettlement sites as nested within a larger scale of U.S. empire. This approach places migration patterns—movements between individual sites—within larger processes, revealing how contemporary human mobility is structured by militarization, global capitalism, colonialism, and imperialism. In other words, by using a multiscalar lens, this book presents a thicker relationality between places migrants move *from* and places they move *to*. As such, *New Destinations of Empire* blurs distinctions between sites of immigrant origin and settlement, showing how human and policy movement between them, and processes across them, coproduce these sites over time. Migration studies that frame geographic movement between "sending" and "receiving" sites risk presuming an ontological fixity in these sites as separate. However, as this book shows, the notion of separate "sending" and "receiving" sites begins to fall apart when we look at intra-empire migration, or migration *within* an empire.

New Destinations of Empire, by focusing on movement at, across, and within different geographic scales—from distant atolls to small towns, between two independent countries, and across the vast expanse of U.S.-occupied territory—emphasizes that empires have multiple centers and peripheries, and that movement between them is never singular, simple, or unidirectional. In doing so, it undertakes a key challenge of mapping imperial migration and diasporas: representing the complex relationships between the local and the global and the scales nested in between, a challenge with which other geographers have also grappled (Katz 2001; Pain and Staeheli 2014; Swyngedouw 1997). Geographers Mary Gilmartin and Lawrence D. Berg (2007), in addressing the need to weigh the colonial local against the global, call for a "double movement" that balances the globalizing tendencies of grand theory with the local, site-specific histories of the places that colonialism partially reconstitutes. Feminist geographers have also engaged the methodological dilemmas of balancing the particular and the universal (e.g., Nast 1994; Staeheli and Lawson 1994), linking "smaller scale methodologies to larger-scale political concerns [to] reveal how power is distributed between macro and micro scales" (Mullings 1999, 348). This book studies the *macro* scale of U.S. empire through the *micro* scale of Springdale, Arkansas, examining how politics and space are produced contingently by processes and events happening at these different scales. The following chapters, thus, devote extensive space to Springdale and Northwest Arkansas and the historical, political, and geographical reasons that Springdale isn't just *anywhere*. They map out the particular social dynamics that make Springdale a *new destination of empire*, dynamics which in turn reverberate throughout other sites of empire across Arkansas, the U.S. South, and the Pacific.

More broadly, study of imperial policies at a range of geographic scales and sites simultaneously affords a key vantage point on shifting modes of global domination and territorial power. By analyzing contemporary geopolitical agreements and bilateral accords *as imperial* policies, this book shows how such policies re-entrench hegemonic power relations between two (or more) nations while ostensibly existing outside, or beyond, formal colonial occupation. While the global political system has largely, though not entirely, shifted away from formal colonial rule in recent decades, key elements of colonial systems—external control over population movement, economic development, and militarization of territories—are retained and re-entrenched through new modes of global hegemonic governance. A *multisited* analysis of imperial policies, then, sheds light on shifting worldwide geographies of (non)sovereignty, illuminating how the formal UN-recognized sovereignty of formerly colonized countries is often eroded by policymaking at other geographic scales.

Finally, in theorizing the multiscalar dimensions of race and racism, *New Destinations of Empire* contributes to a growing body of geographical scholarship on white supremacy (Pulido 2017; Bonds and Inwood 2016; Daigle and Ramírez 2019), adding an explicit focus on imperial migration and imperial migrants in the production of racial geographies. Chapter 2 examines racialized geographical imaginaries in U.S. imperial policymaking across Micronesia during the post–World War II period. Chapter 3 then traces similar racialized geographical imaginaries and xenophobic practices across the state of Arkansas, showing how they buttress empire-making during and after wars. Chapters 4 and 5 zoom in on Springdale, attending to how "race" informs and is informed by place-based meanings, landscapes, and formulations of citizenship. These processes not only make empire but also, foundationally, make race *in* place, while tugging on threads that stretch *beyond* that place.

In theorizing these processes, I return to Ruth Wilson Gilmore's definition of racism as "the state-sanctioned or extralegal production and exploitation of group-differentiated vulnerability to premature death *in distinct yet densely interconnected political geographies*" (2002, 261, emphasis added).[7] By examining race and racism in the "distinct yet densely interconnected political geographies" of the transpacific U.S. South, I show how white supremacy is produced *through* U.S. empire, and how empire is simultaneously central to understanding racialized place-making in Arkansas. I also draw on Omi and Winant's (1994, 2014) theorization of racial formations to examine the entanglements between discourses of race and the material processes that shape those discourses *in place*. As I show, Springdale was constructed as a white settler town, and, later, as an "immigrant town," through various interrelated processes of white supremacy. At the same time, racialized geographic discourses of islanders' incapacity to govern have facilitated U.S. military imperialism in "distinct yet densely interconnected political geographies" from the Pacific to the Caribbean for over a century. This book attends carefully to these racialized discourses at various scales while examining their importance and utility for white supremacy.

Last, *New Destinations of Empire* brings to life the historically racialized landscape of small-town Northwest Arkansas, displacing the commonly held idea that Springdale was rendered "racial" with the arrival of immigrants in the 1980s. It does so by positioning the town's centuries-long "whitening" process as a longer process of racialization *through* U.S. empire. In other words, by explicitly theorizing whiteness as ongoing settler colonialism, I show settler colonialism as a violent, structural place-making process that is at once constitutive of U.S. empire and obscured by place-based discourses of whiteness and practices of whitening.

RESEARCH AND METHODS

In conducting the research for this book, I sought to answer three questions: (1) How were the terms of the 1986 Compact of Free Association, particularly its immigration provisions, negotiated, contested, and enacted? (2) How is COFA status, the exceptional legal status of Marshallese immigrants in the United States, produced in law and policy, and how does it take shape on the ground in Northwest Arkansas? And (3) how does the racial history and present of Springdale, a new destination of empire, shape contemporary reception of Marshall Islanders and social justice movements in Northwest Arkansas? Addressing these questions required conducting research in multiple field sites across the U.S.-affiliated (or U.S.-occupied) Pacific, including Saipan, Tinian, Guåhan, and Hawai'i, and the U.S. mainland, including Northwest Arkansas, Little Rock, Arkansas, and Washington, D.C. (figure 2).[8] My research brings together a range of qualitative methods, including archival research, textual and policy analysis, semistructured interviews, informal meetings, and participant observation, which I describe in greater detail below.

The Pacific node of my fieldwork began in the summer of 2013, when I traveled to Saipan (CNMI), the historic TTPI headquarters. While there, I researched the history of the TTPI and the Compacts under the expert and enthusiastic guidance of former TTPI archivist Samuel McPhetres, whose personal archives spanned decades of U.S. and UN political involvement in the region. As I embarked on this first trip, I was confronted for the first time in my life with the sheer geographic spread of the U.S. territorial system: To reach Saipan, I flew from Syracuse to New York City to Tokyo to Guåhan. Without passing through customs on the ground, I left U.S. jurisdiction and then re-entered it upon arrival in Guåhan, an unincorporated U.S. territory. I then flew northward to Rota, the southernmost island in the CNMI, before finally arriving at Saipan International Airport, twenty-eight hours after leaving home.

As my island hopping illuminates, the fieldwork for this book, particularly that which was conducted in the Pacific, was enabled by my own hypermobility. A white settler with full U.S. citizenship by birth, I had easy legal access to all the sites I needed to visit, due not only to my U.S. passport (and my whiteness) but also with my travel and research *within* the territorial expanse of U.S. empire. Thus, my own legal, racial, and settler status within the United States allowed me the immense privilege of virtually unfettered movement between my field sites. This was an ease of movement not always afforded to the also mobile, but legally more precarious, COFA migrants who became my research subjects, as I discuss in later chapters.

During the six weeks I spent in Saipan, Guåhan, and Hawai'i, I analyzed archival documents related to the historical political relationship between the United States and the Marshall Islands, focusing on negotiations over the Compact of Free Association. I also interviewed state and community actors who had been involved in island and regional politics during the Micronesian political-status negotiations and the Compacts' enactment. I concluded this field visit with a short stop in Guåhan for the 2nd Annual Marianas History Conference, followed by a week in Honolulu, where I conducted archival research at the University of Hawai'i at Mānoa's Pacific Collection, seeking additional documents on the political-status negotiations from the Congress of Micronesia, the region's legislative body from 1964–1979.

Washington, D.C., was another important field site for researching the Compact's ongoing implementation, negotiation, and analysis. During two weeklong research trips there in 2014 and 2019, I interviewed policy officials, Compact negotiators, and RMI and FSM embassy staff about the events preceding the Compact's passage and debates around its migration provision. Their perceptions helped shed light on U.S. and FAS interests during and after Compact negotiations. Later, my interviews with senior representatives of the Office of Insular Affairs, Government Accountability Office (GAO), and FAS embassies focused on Marshallese and Micronesian interests since the Com-

Mapping Imperial Migrations   23

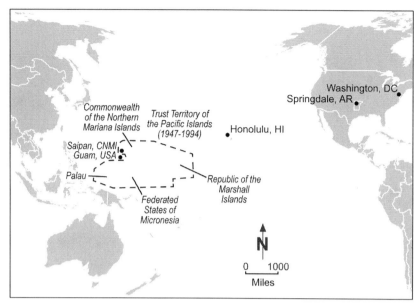

FIGURE 2. Key locations in the Pacific and the United States discussed in the book. Map by the Syracuse University Cartographic Laboratory.

pact's initial negotiation and their visions for the Compact's future. While in Washington, D.C., I also analyzed policy documents, including the Compact and its corollary documents, U.S. federal policies, and congressional hearing transcripts, which pertained broadly to the U.S.-Marshall Islands' political relationship.

Fieldwork in Springdale, and in the broader Northwest Arkansas region, was conducted over five months (March–July 2014), with subsequent visits in 2016 and 2019. There, I interviewed state actors and policymakers, social service providers, immigrants' rights activists, and long-term residents to understand the Compact's various impacts on Springdale. I also attended regular meetings of immigrants' rights' coalitions, Springdale County Court sessions, and local cultural events to gain a sense of social dynamics in the town and interactions between new immigrants and long-term residents. Finally, I analyzed local and state historical archives, including news articles; promotional brochures from area organizations and companies; city planning documents and maps; oral histories collected by local historians; constituent letters to state politicians; and other publications on Springdale's growth and development. Archival research was primarily conducted at the Shiloh Museum of Ozark History in Springdale, the University of Arkansas Special Collections in

Fayetteville, and the Clinton Presidential Library in Little Rock. In 2019, two years into the Trump administration and four years before Compact renegotiations were set to begin, I returned to Northwest Arkansas to interview Marshallese community leaders and activists about the local and diasporic effects of the Trump administration's anti-immigrant policies (including ICE raids across the region that summer) and the emboldening of white supremacists, as well as Marshall Islanders' concerns about the Compact's extension; I discuss these findings in chapter 5.

In addition to conducting formal and informal interviews in Arkansas, I also conducted site visits and attended public events at a number of locations. I attended several sessions of Springdale County Court, which met weekly and frequently included Marshallese defendants. These sessions gave me a partial window into the workings of the local legal system and the ways in which Latinx and Marshallese residents, as well as white (and occasionally Black) residents, were drawn into it. I also visited a number of more quotidian sites across Northwest Arkansas: local restaurants and cafés, gas stations, public buildings, city administrative offices, Walmart stores, poultry plants (though I was never able to gain internal access to these, despite repeated attempts), grocery stores, and libraries, among others. These visits allowed me to flesh out a more detailed view of daily life in Springdale and the sites and spaces where Springdale residents, new and old, interacted, and how structures of race, citizenship, and belonging got remade or reworked in the process.

My early field interviews in Arkansas targeted two main groups: key actors (of various racial, ethnic, and immigration backgrounds) and long-term (primarily white) residents of Springdale.[9] This decision was strategic: I wanted to become as immersed as possible in local discourses and conversations about Marshallese resettlement in Springdale, and as informed as possible about local immigration, labor, and racial justice issues, before conducting interviews with Marshallese residents. Before long, however, I began to perceive tensions among Marshallese community leaders about the presence of external researchers studying Springdale's Marshallese community. From my fieldnotes: "Met with Deb tonight. She recounted her initial meeting with the Marshallese Consul General of Arkansas, who, when Deb told her she was planning to do some research with the Marshallese community, said: 'Oh, no, don't tell me you're going to do another survey. *We are so tired of surveys!*'" (Springdale, June 2014). As a result of this conversation and others, I chose not to insert myself directly into Marshallese community groups to solicit interviews with Marshall Islanders who had not actively sought a public-facing role. Instead, I moved intentionally toward a focus on key actors and on the reception side of

Marshallese resettlement. During my return trip in 2019, I focused exclusively on Marshallese key actors to determine their perspectives on the shifting legal landscape of COFA status, as I discuss in chapter 5. This shift admittedly created somewhat of an absence around "everyday" Marshall Islanders' lived realities of race, class, mobility, and citizenship in Springdale, which readers will note. However, this approach enabled me to ask different kinds of questions about how U.S. empire becomes visible (or not) in NDEs by seeking insights from Marshallese figures most familiar on a *policy* level with COFA status as it operated on the ground. More importantly, it allowed me to limit potential harm and "research fatigue" caused by outsider—and particularly white/settler—researchers (Tuck and Yang 2014).

Altogether, I conducted sixty-five formal semistructured interviews and about sixty informational meetings for this book. Along the way, my interviewees, colleagues, new friends, and travel companions thought aloud with me about the logics underlying dynamics we observed, the structures guiding social, racial, economic, and political relations, and the histories they dragged behind them, carving trenches in the ground. These were everyday analyses and analyses of the everyday, geographic sense-making on the fly, grounded theorizing to make sense of our small lives dropped down within grand histories of empire, racial capitalism, and global migration.

Empire's Global Mobilities:
"We Are Here Because You (Are) There"

Marshallese migrants to Arkansas were not the first imperial migrants, nor are they the most well known. In 1948, a ship named the HMT Empire Windrush departed Trinidad, destined for the Tilbury docks in Essex, UK, another island. It carried nearly five hundred passengers, gathered from ports in Trinidad, Jamaica, the Gulf Coast of Mexico, and Bermuda. These passengers carried with them the refrain of what would become known as the Windrush generation, migrants who moved to Britain from Caribbean islands formerly (or still, at the time) under British control: "We are here because you were there."

We are here. You were there. This phrase does so much: it demands accountability, naming the complicity and culpability of the intended listener. It identifies a logical sequence, a historical cause and effect. It is a reminder of Britain's imperial history. It is also a rejoinder to xenophobic nationalists indignant at the arrival of Black and Brown immigrants from the Caribbean, from South Asia, who came to Britain in search of livelihoods and inclusion in the operations center of the British Empire, an empire that had, decades or centuries before, enveloped their own homelands like a dark specter. But the phrase also does something more: it maps a *double movement* of empire, a geography continuously forged through the expand-and-recede pattern of imperial territorial power and the seeking-and-settling tendencies of those living under its dark shadow. "We are here because you were there" labors against occlusion, working instead to reveal the hidden histories, human geographies, and political machinations of empire that propel—and sometimes obstruct—migration flows. This book aims to do something similar.

While Britain's Windrush generation is the most well known, postcolonial migrations also characterized other declining European empires: after World War II, many waning empires' colonial subjects circulated in diaspora, some settling in colonial metropoles. At the dusk of French empire, between 1963 and 1982, the French government recruited approximately a hundred and sixty thousand people from the French Caribbean islands of Guadeloupe, Martinique, Réunion, and French Guiana to fill jobs in France's service and construction industries. While these islands were no longer French colonies—they had become "overseas departments" by 1946—their tenuous yet enduring legal ties to the imperial power channeled people between the postcolonial Caribbean and Europe, carving migration routes that still exist today. Similarly, Britain made appeals to the inhabitants of former colonies—islands, primarily, scattered across the Caribbean and off the southeast coast of Africa—to relocate to their former imperial metropole to fill labor shortages that had caused economic losses compounded by the wartime costs after World War II. In other words, the Windrush migrations were propelled by both the desires of formerly colonized peoples to move freely and the postwar labor demands of empires in decline.

The postwar period inaugurated a new phase of global mobility, as former subjects of European empires continued to migrate. As they did, they often acquired a new (and often precarious, liminal, and exclusionary) legal standing upon arrival to the metropole, a legal formation I theorize in this book as imperial citizenship. Between 1948 and 1970, nearly half a million people took advantage of the rights outlined in the British Nationality Act of 1948, which granted British citizenship to anyone born in the United Kingdom or its colonies. Imperial and postcolonial subjects' citizenship and immigration rights came into question as these subjects moved and as the ground shifted beneath them. Solicited workers traveled long distances by boat, then were subjected to trainings meant to turn them into "modern," "civilized" subjects; such trainings included language classes, physical examinations, and other investigations into migrants' suitability for life on a new island.

At the same time, new geographies of empire were being carved out across the Pacific region of Micronesia, though the United States' Pacific Windrush era was still four decades away. 1947 brought the creation of the TTPI, a political entity defined and overseen by the UN and to be administered by the United States. The TTPI's ostensible purpose, one it shared with the ten other trust territories patchworked across the Global South, was to transition its residents, under the colonial tutelage of a colonial administrator from the Global North (in this case, the United States), into either self-government or a more formalized political status under U.S. governance. The TTPI's premise, and the four decades of geopolitical negotiations, island militarization, and fierce contestation that followed its creation, fundamentally circumscribed the possibilities for Micronesian political status and the legal conditions of Micronesians' mobility after 1986. Studying this history reveals surprising insights about the scale at which postcolonial and imperial citizenship is produced: While citizenship is often understood as something *internal* to nation-states, chapter 2 shows just as much that Freely Associated Statehood, and by relation, COFA status, has been forged at the *international* scale. This process played out with the involvement of the UN and the League of Nations, through transnational and global conflicts such as the world wars and the Cold War, and through the transnational operations of the U.S. military-base empire, which touches ground on foreign countries and nonsovereign or occupied territories in every corner of the globe.

The postwar era of formal decolonization also produced an abundance of new geopolitical and legal entities—among them, trust territories, commonwealths, and freely associated states—all of which made geographic analyses of empires, and migration within them, more complex and challenging. While this book argues that the Marshall Islands exist in an imperial relationship with the United States, with a political status that is unique to Pacific Islands under the Compact of Free Association, I do not wish to delegitimize or diminish Marshallese struggles for formal independence and broader visions of self-determination. Yet I recognize that mapping and naming imperial geographies conjures fraught questions: *Where* is the (post)colonial? *Where* is the imperial? (I play here on Stuart Hall's 2002 provocation, "When was 'the postcolonial'?") The difficulty in resolving these questions, and the resulting tensions, remain throughout this book largely because they are inherent in studies of—and experiences of—imperial migration.

Here and throughout the book, I want to emphasize COFA migrants' agency to determine the conditions of their own mobility, their citizenship status, and their islands' political status, often amid intensely challenging political conditions. COFA migrants and FAS citizens in the islands must confront not only the whims of U.S. geopolitical interests, which drive U.S. efforts to maintain exclusive military access to the islands, but also contentious and xenophobic immigration debates in the United States. Across the broader region of Micronesia, and in COFA diaspora sites from Arkansas to Hawai'i to Oregon, COFA status acquires its meaning not only from the top down, by state actors and U.S. geopolitical interests, but also from the bottom up, by activists organizing for more just forms of mobility and a more robust set of rights for people on the move.

The Chapters: An Overview

To tell that story, the book proceeds in the following way. Chapter 2 turns to the policy dynamics between the United States and RMI, arguing that the Compact is an imperial document forged between the two entities, but also an agreement shaped at every stage by islanders' decolonial desires and political visions for self-determination. In this chapter, I contend that the migration provision established by the Compact for Marshallese citizens creates a type of *imperial citizenship* for Marshall Islanders in diaspora, one informed by racialized geographic imaginaries about islanders as incapable of self-government. The chapter lays out a twentieth-century history of U.S. colonialism and imperialism in the Pacific Islands to show that the current political relationship between the United States and the RMI—defined as Freely Associated Statehood between two formally sovereign nations[10]—emerged from and itself reproduces a long trajectory of colonial and imperial relations. This chapter expands on this history to show how militarism and migration can become enmeshed in imperial policymaking, as the U.S.-RMI Compact does by marrying exclusive U.S. military access to the Marshall Islands while enshrining migration rights for RMI citizens.

Chapter 3 pivots the storyline from the Marshall Islands to the state of Arkansas, examining how U.S. war-making abroad has funneled different populations into Arkansas since World War II, as well as connecting Arkansas to the Pacific through military service and wartime federal investments. In doing so, it aims to disturb clean distinctions between home and abroad, and domestic and foreign, distinctions that are blurred by the movements spurred by empire. The histories it documents reveal Arkansas, and Springdale within it, as a *long-standing* destination of empire.

To develop this argument, the chapter first examines how World War II forged an early transpacific link between Arkansas and the Pacific, when Arkansan veterans deployed to military engagements in the Pacific Islands returned with recollections of the region and its people. These veterans constitute one of many human links between Arkansas and the Pacific, links created through U.S. military imperialism during war, and their wartime memories continue to mobilize militarized imaginaries of the Pacific across Arkansas and elsewhere. The chapter then traces wartime and postwar imperial arrivals to Arkansas, from the World War II internment of Japanese Americans and German prisoners of war (POWs), to the arrival and detention of Vietnamese war refugees after the Vietnam War, to the detention of Haitian and Cuban refugees and asylum-seekers during the 1980s, when the U.S. government was deeply involved in (often violent) regime change in the Caribbean as a means to shore up its economic and political influence there. Each of these population movements was in some way produced by U.S. military engagements "abroad," and these groups' migration to Arkansas, whether forced, coerced, or chosen, brought the effects of U.S. military imperialism "home" to the U.S. mainland.

Finally, the chapter turns to contemporary Arkansan reception of Marshall Islanders, analyzing "imperial sense-making," or the logics long-term residents use to make sense of Marshall Islanders' right of visa-free migration to the United States. As it shows, long-term Springdale residents make sense of Marshallese migration by interpreting Marshallese as *refugees* resettled by the United States or by assuming that their right to visa-free migration has been granted as U.S. *reparations* for nuclear testing. Both logics—the refugee logic and the reparations logic—rely on notions of U.S. exceptionalism,[11] upholding the good name of the United States as either as a benevolent provider of safe haven or a liberal, progressive democracy that eventually rights past wrongs. Neither explanation, however, understands the United States as an *imperial* power that continues to exert control over the RMI and other Pacific Islands. In this way, long-term residents' interpretations of why COFA status exists exemplify and perpetuate an occlusion of U.S. empire, as did framings of previous arrivals to the state.

Chapter 4 zooms in on Springdale, a small town in Northwest Arkansas, showing how the arrival of Latinx and Marshallese immigrants to this once virtually all-white town radically changed Springdale's population and, in some ways, its residents' understanding of the town's racial identities. As it argues, long-standing geographical ideas about Springdale (and Arkansas) as remote and racist—juxtaposed with emerging understandings of neighboring Fayetteville (and Northwest Arkansas) as progressive by comparison—shape local and regional discourses about how Springdale became an immigrant destination, however an unlikely one. The chapter then turns to the racial histories and racial geographies that formed Springdale's "racial present" in both discursive and material ways. While the town's formation through settler colonialism, Black exclusion, and immigration was in some ways particular to Springdale, these processes are also central to the formation of empire and racial capitalism (C. J. Robinson 1983) at larger scales. For this reason, I argue, Springdale can serve as a site *through which* to tell larger histories of empire. These histories of racialized exclusion and conditional inclusion, condensed into the site and scale of Springdale, shape local narratives of race, identity, and belonging in ways that profoundly affect immigrant reception, forging Springdale as a new immigrant destination (NID) but also as a new destination of empire (NDE).

Chapter 5 returns to the concept of imperial citizenship, first outlined in chapter 2, to show how COFA status, a liminal, exceptional, and exclusionary legal status, produces precarity and uncertainty in subjects on the legal, political, and geographic margins of U.S. empire. First, the chapter examines the production of the COFA migrant's legal status in law and policy, situating it as a form of imperial citizenship. As it argues, COFA status is a U.S. imperial status that is both novel—nothing else like it exists within U.S. immigration law—and long-standing, taking precedent from other types of imperial citizenship granted to subjects of U.S. empire since 1898. The chapter then turns to the production of COFA status on the ground in Northwest Arkansas, examining encounters between Marshallese migrants and key actors (white, Latinx, and Marshallese) in three contexts: 1) law, policing, and immigration enforcement, (2) social services, advocacy, and benefits, and (3) activism and social justice organizing. As I argue, each of the three contexts reveals and produces a different dimension of Marshallese COFA status's liminal, exceptional, and exclusionary character. At the same time, each of these three contexts also impedes local actors from seeing the *imperial* dimensions of COFA status—including its production through U.S. imperialism in the RMI—dimensions which Marshallese key actors clearly identify.

Finally, chapter 6 returns to the Compact's significance for studies of U.S. empire and imperial migration more broadly, as well as its broader significance for decolonial, immigrants' rights, and racial justice movements in the

U.S. South, the Pacific, and elsewhere. Looking ahead to the upcoming Compact renegotiations in 2023 and 2024, and with an eye to the groundswell of racial justice and immigrants' rights organizing across the United States, it shows that the U.S. South and the Pacific are anything but remote: instead, they are in many ways at the center of the United States' most pressing political and geopolitical issues. Finally, the chapter, and the book, ends by mapping out how climate change, border policing and militarization, and empire—as well as people's negotiated resistance to these processes—are likely to shape global migration and mobility in the years to come.

CHAPTER 2

How Free Is Freely Associated Statehood?

The Compact of Free Association and Its Colonial Past

Marshall Islanders can migrate to Arkansas, and to the United States more broadly, because of a unique policy provision that grants them visa-free migration into the country, a kind of provision that does not exist anywhere else in U.S. immigration law. This provision was enshrined by the 1986 Compact of Free Association, an agreement elaborated between the United States and the Republic of the Marshall Islands (RMI) to formalize Marshallese independence from U.S. colonial administration, which began immediately after World War II. At the same time, the 1986 Compact also ushered in a new phase of U.S. imperialism in the Marshall Islands, establishing a new political relationship between the Marshall Islands and the United States: that of Freely Associated Statehood.[1] Simultaneously, the United States formed political relationships of Free Association with two other new states in the broader Micronesian region—the Federated States of Micronesia (FSM) and Palau—as they gained formal independence from the United States.

As this chapter argues, Freely Associated Statehood (FAS) is in many ways just the latest mechanism of long-standing U.S. political, economic, and military influence in the islands, as it upholds asymmetrical power dynamics established during formal U.S. colonialism in the islands. The Compact of Free Association thus, rather than being a simple bilateral agreement between two formally sovereign states, functions more as an *imperial* agreement between the United States and the Marshall Islands—one that upholds U.S. imperial control over the Marshall Islands through economic and military means, thus diminishing the Marshall Islands' sovereignty. Negotiations for the 1986 Compact, and the 2003 Amended Compact, were shaped by extreme power disparities between the negotiating parties, which curtailed Marshallese efforts to assert and protect their sovereignty *through* the Compact.

Most centrally to this book's argument, the Compact linked Marshall Islanders' migration and citizenship rights in the United States with restricted sovereignty and ongoing militarization in the Marshall Islands. As such, the Compact's geopolitical history provides a crucial foundation for my argument that contemporary Marshallese political status, citizenship, and mobility in the U.S.-based diaspora are profoundly imperial. But all imperialisms are negotiated, contested, and challenged from below and through those challenges are forged into something different. By asserting their visions for self-determination over the quarter century it took to forge their political status and demands, Marshallese and other Micronesian leaders and activists managed to heave the hulking body of U.S. empire and its designs on the Pacific region in a slightly different direction, pointing, perhaps, toward a different destination. That direction is spelled out, at least for now, in the three Compacts. As such, the Compacts are also a reflection of Micronesian efforts over four decades to resist full incorporation by the United States and to defend their own political autonomy.

This chapter traces the genealogy of U.S. imperial geographic practice and thought in the Pacific, which laid the foundation for current political configurations across Micronesia. Each imperial project in the Pacific during the twentieth century was shaped by both the territoriality of previous projects and the geographic ideas or imaginaries that motivated them (Said 1994). Moreover, both would fundamentally shape how U.S. migration policies, Marshallese political status, and the Marshallese diaspora took form in the 1980s and beyond, cementing the profound linkages between empire, migration, and citizenship.

In the Marshall Islands, imperial geographic ideas about islands (and, by extension, about islanders) have directly shaped both U.S. practices and international oversight of colonial systems, with long-lasting effects on Marshallese sovereignty and citizenship. These ideas, based in Western colonialist notions of place and space, have been remarkably consistent across the twentieth and twenty-first centuries, revealing a continuity of colonial policy, thought, and geopolitical strategy in the Pacific region. Among them, three main ideas have been repeated: the Pacific Islands are (1) remote (or distant); (2) small; and (3) sparsely populated (or, having a low population density). Since World War I, the United States and other Western actors have presented these three (real or presumed) characteristics as evidence of islands' and islanders' lack of centrality, civilization, and capacity for self-government. Collectively, these ideas project the image of a static, unchanging people in a region "trapped in time," underdeveloped, or a "deficit area" (an actual term used by U.S. political actors to describe Micronesia; see Solomon 1963), an image that would motivate some of the most long lasting, geographically expansive, and environmentally devastating colonial experiments of the twentieth century. Analysis of the particular geographic ideas that the United States used to rationalize its policies in the Pacific reveals how geographical imaginaries animate and perpetuate empires.

Colonial and imperial ideas about space are also ideas about race, which necessarily color notions of sovereignty and political subjectivities (Gilmore 2002). Racist notions of Pacific Islanders as dependent, unmotivated, premodern, and lazy were understood by many U.S. actors to be self-evident and inherent qualities, and, moreover, a product of islanders' *environmental* conditions. These racial and spatial ideas profoundly shaped what U.S. political actors thought about Pacific Islanders' right to be sovereign: how capable they were of self-government, how much they needed protection or custodial care, and how effectively they might mount an independence campaign. This last question vexed many U.S. state actors, and, much as they labored to present islanders as meek, directionless, and willful beneficiaries of U.S. aid, they were unable to rest easy in the belief that this was the case.

In tracing the long lives of these racial and spatial ideas, this chapter documents a history of how such ideas materialized in global governance and U.S. colonial policy during a period of formal decolonization, complicating the possibilities of true self-determination for islanders worldwide. Racialized ideas about Indigenous people's incapacity to self-govern did not disappear in the United States' outward turn to advancing global democracy and a liberaldemocratic order, as Simeon Man (2018) and Nikhil Singh (2017) have examined. Instead, such notions have only become more insidious, reworked to frame the United States as a protectionist and benevolent custodian responsible for "integrating the Micronesian people into the strenuous political and economic conditions of the modern world" (Solomon 1963, n.p.). These same ideas persist into the twenty-first century, trailing Marshallese COFA migrants into the U.S. mainland and coloring policy debates about Marshall Islanders' rights to citizenship, sovereignty, and quality of life in the diaspora.

However, nothing about the way U.S. empire grew and materialized in the Pacific was inevitable—*nor was it perceived that way* by either U.S. or Pacific Islander political actors during Micronesia's decades-long transition from colonialism to formal independence. As soon as the United States began to expand its influence in the Pacific, it was threatened by growing independence movements and international pressures to support decolonization. As early as 1946, U.S. politicians anticipated the loss of key bases in the Philippines due to

Philippine independence and activist pressure and anxiously labored to shore up future military access to the region. U.S. political actors also anticipated Micronesian resistance to ongoing U.S. political control in the islands, which motivated further U.S. attempts to delimit the possible outcomes of plebiscite votes on political status in the late 1970s and early 1980s. Finally, the United States experienced consistent and mounting pressure for decolonization from the UN and other international actors, as it was the last Western power to relinquish control of a UN trust territory. In other words, the twentieth century is anything but a simple story about the United States easily gaining territory in the Pacific.

What would all this mean for the colonized and soon-to-be-formerly colonized peoples of the world? At what geographic scale would their rights and citizenship be determined and overseen, and what opportunities—or imperatives—would they have to migrate in the coming decades? While rights of citizenship and immigration are often understood as being determined at the national level or scale, this chapter shows how, for a key group of Pacific Islander migrants, such rights have been fundamentally defined at the geographic scale of empire. As this chapter demonstrates, however, the policymaking and territoriality of the twentieth century, with its imperial and decolonial tensions playing out at multiple scales, would lay a crucial groundwork for the citizenship-based and racialized struggles of Indigenous peoples and colonized subjects in diaspora after formal decolonization. These diasporas would materialize in their own dispersed and "far-flung" geographies, both for the postcolonial migrants of the Windrush generation and for islanders across the U.S.-occupied Pacific. While the 1986 Compact did not create Marshallese migration to the United States, it kicked off a new phase of emigration, with a new legal status for FAS citizens—COFA status—that, despite its legal formalization, would usher in new forms of liminality, precarity, and exclusion for its holders in diaspora.

Just as the modern history of the Marshall Islands and the Marshallese people should be understood for its historical, geographical, and political specificity, it is also a story that can and should be read as a transnational history of twentieth-century imperialism and its adversaries. While much attention has been paid to the global significance of liberation movements in the Caribbean, Africa, and Southeast Asia, much less focus has been put on the Micronesian independence struggles of the 1960s and 1970s, the Pacific Islands' significance for U.S. Cold War geopolitics and strategy, and the subsequent ramifications for global mobility in a formally postcolonial world. To rectify this oversight, this chapter places the Marshall Islands firmly at the center of a global history of the twentieth century, in the multiple territorial scales in which it has been mapped, understood, and lived. Centering the Marshall Islands, and the larger region of Micronesia, in this global history reveals just how *central* the Marshall Islands were (and are) to U.S. empire, as a site where key U.S. imperial geographical imaginaries were honed and then weaponized and where new imperial legal formations enabled the expansion of U.S. military hegemony in the late twentieth and early twenty-first centuries. Woven throughout this history are Marshallese and Micronesian people's own histories of resistance to U.S. imperialism and nuclear testing and their countries' transformation through decades of mass emigration. In other words, the islands, despite being portrayed as remote or peripheral by key U.S. political actors, were and continue to be central sites of U.S. empire's expansion *and* contestation.

Moreover, as this chapter shows, the mobilities of empire—the circulation of its subjects, its policies, its nuclear fallout, and even its geographic ideas across space—necessitate a multiscalar geographical analysis, one I engage explicitly in this chapter. While I focus primarily on what is now the Republic of the Marshall Islands (RMI), the Marshall Islands forms part of the larger geographical region of Micronesia, much of which was encompassed under the TTPI and, perhaps more importantly, was the regional scale at which Micronesian political actors—*including* those from the Marshall Islands and Palau—worked to forge a political identity and future for their islands. Therefore, I use the term "Micronesia" in this chapter to refer to the geographic region (again, the region that includes the Marshall Islands), which I distinguish from the Federated States of Micronesia (FSM), a contemporary country *within* the Micronesian region. My aim in discussing the Marshall Islands within the context of Micronesia and the broader Pacific is not to collapse cultural and political differences among and between these places—differences that both precede and extend beyond U.S. colonial rule—but to emphasize the significance of the Marshall Islands to politics playing out at larger geographic scales, and to show how, in turn, global political dynamics shaped politics on the islands and in the COFA diasporas.

This chapter develops these arguments in four parts. The first section demonstrates that the political sovereignty of the RMI, and the other U.S. Freely Associated States, are historically and inextricably rooted in imperialism and militarization. It documents how Western actors constrained Pacific Islanders' sovereignty through the League of Nations Mandate system (1918–1945) and the TTPI (1947–1986), justifying external military occupation in the Pacific through geographic ideas about islands as vulnerable and islanders as incapable of self-government. The TTPI, one of eleven UN trust territories established after World War II and the only one designated a "strategic trust," enabled expansive U.S. military uses of the islands, including a massive nuclear testing campaign from 1946–1958. The TTPI, in place for four decades before the Compact's passage, also set the stage for the Compact's negotiation and eventual passage as well as for the formalization of an ongoing U.S. political and military presence in the Pacific. In this way, earlier colonial and military projects—and their attendant geographies and geographic ideas—laid the way for subsequent ones.

The chapter's second section examines the period of Micronesian political-status negotiations (1961–1986), arguing that the Pacific Islands, and the TTPI in particular, were crucial to the United States' Cold War geopolitical strategy and to the United States' global image during a period of formal decolonization. Yet both were jeopardized by Micronesian efforts for self-determination and the protracted TTPI political-status negotiations (1969–1986), as they threatened to destabilize U.S. political control in the Pacific—a key site of U.S. military expansion—and distort the United States' desired global image as a liberal-democratic power. U.S. administrators were eager to maintain a strong economic, political, and military presence in the Pacific and to exclude other superpowers from this region, as they had done elsewhere (Mason 1989). However, they also wanted to limit direct U.S. political leadership in the islands—as part of a larger shift to the United States' use of "soft power" in the non-self-governing territories—and to heed, at least nominally, the UN's original intent for the trust territories to transition to self-government. At the same time, the Marshall Islands' current political status, as well as the migration rights it enshrines for Marshallese citizens, are also the product of islanders' desires and demands for self-determination, which were met with U.S. pushback, trepidation, and, ultimately, some concessions to islanders. The tension between these competing desires is revealed in the original Compact negotiations and continues to animate discussions of the Compact today.

The chapter's third section examines how, under the original U.S.-RMI Compact of 1986, the RMI, along with the FSM (and, later, Palau), successfully negotiated U.S. immigration rights for their citizens, which the United States granted contingent on receiving exclusive U.S. military access to the Marshall Islands. This access was secured vis-à-vis the policy of "strategic denial" in the Marshall Islands, a policy in which the United States denies other powers military access to other countries. This linkage of militarism and migration, as an exercise of U.S. colonial and imperial projects abroad, lays the foundation for my argument that COFA status—the legal status or category of migrants living in the United States under the Compact's migration provisions—is a kind of imperial citizenship. Furthermore, I argue, the Compact's pairing of militarism and migration reveals the links between U.S. colonial and imperial projects abroad and the contingent provision of migration benefits for the "beneficiaries" of U.S. occupation.

The chapter's fourth section shows how, over time, both the Marshallese right to immigrate to the United States and Marshallese sovereignty became more deeply entwined with U.S. militarism. It reveals that key changes in the 2003 Amended Compact in the areas of migration and U.S. military access were directly informed by the larger geopolitical context of the Global War on Terror, showing both the linking of militarism and migration and the geographically multiscalar nature of these political deliberations. The result was that FAS citizens nearly lost COFA status, exposing the instability of COFA as a protected legal status for Marshall Islanders and other FAS citizens living in the United States. This legal instability or precarity, I argue, is a key feature of imperial citizenship.

By the early 2000s, the Marshall Islands were increasingly reliant on U.S. economic aid and on the option of visa-free migration to the United States, a dependence intentionally fostered by the United States (G. Johnson 1979). U.S. negotiators, thus, had vastly disproportionate power in influencing the outcomes of the Compact renegotiations in this latest round. As such, the Compact serves as a document that cements U.S. hegemony in the Pacific more broadly. U.S. global hegemony has been "attained not only through naked force or threats but also through favors and coercion" (S. Davis 2015, 2). Those favors and coercion, in the context of military access and migrant mobility, are examined here. Yet visa-free migration provisions were also a crucial linchpin of the Compact for Micronesian, Marshallese, and Palauan negotiators, an assertion of Micronesian peoples' right to determine the political conditions of their own mobility. That these provisions were put on the table during political-status negotiations—and that they remain in place for FAS citizens today—is a testament to the political vision, savviness, and tenacity of Micronesian negotiators and activists who prioritized them.

Driving this chapter are my two original contributions to study of the Compact, one methodological, one theoretical. First, methodologically, I bring together an array of documents, materials, and accounts not commonly placed alongside one another to understand the political genealogy of Freely Associated Statehood, the Compact that enshrines it, and the migration provision that it spurred and continues to shape. The material I draw upon, gathered through a multisited ethnographic and archival methodology, includes U.S., UN, and Micronesian policy memos and reports from the 1920s to 2020s;

published oral histories with Marshallese and other Micronesian leaders; and more than twenty interviews I conducted with Micronesian, Marshallese, and U.S. policymakers and political actors from Saipan to Washington, D.C.

Second, using these diverse methods and materials as a foundation, I advance a *dual* analysis of two legal formations—COFA status as imperial citizenship and Freely Associated Statehood as an imperial political status—that were constructed in tandem during Micronesia's decades-long political-status deliberations. This dual analysis allows me to show how the nexus of these two legal formations and their historical construction in the Pacific are central to understanding the geopolitical dimensions of contemporary COFA migration.

The League of Nations Mandate and the TTPI: Producing (Non)Sovereignty across Scales

Marshallese sovereignty and self-determination have been produced, contested, delimited, and defined at multiple geographic scales over more than a century. This process has been forged through extended colonial and imperial influence and extensive militarization, which delimited the future potential for Marshallese sovereignty vis-à-vis the Compact. In particular, the two postwar periods were critical historical moments for the international *redistribution*, if not necessarily the remapping, of colonized territories around the world, and also critical openings for newly (or not-yet) independent populations to rearticulate their visions for self-determination. After each world war, there emerged a new international system for the colonial management of territory and territories, first under the League of Nations Mandate system, then under the UN trust territory system. In this way, global wars played a central role in determining the sovereignty and political status of the Pacific Islands, as they did in colonized places across central Africa and the Middle East that were conscripted into long-term colonial status. War and militarism are thus at the very foundation of the political status and citizenship of colonized people and places, including—and sometimes even more so—*after* their formal decolonization.

Both the League of Nations Mandate system and the UN trust territory system combined an avowed commitment to decolonization—or to its anemic cousin, self-government—with legal structures that enabled the expansion of empires, through the extension of their military power that would protect their economic interests. As Simeon Man (2018) has argued, the expansion of U.S. economic and military interests in the twentieth century was linked, paradoxically, with a discursive commitment to liberal democracy, progress and modernity, and freedom. This same paradox—the twentieth-century growth of imperial war-making under the auspices of democracy and freedom—was explicitly scripted into the UN Charter, shaping the long (and ongoing) process of formal decolonization in the Pacific Islands. Three texts—the League of Nations Covenant, the UN trusteeship agreements, and the UN Charter—are key to understanding how *ongoing* U.S. colonialism and imperialism in the contemporary Pacific, and in the Marshall Islands in particular, was built into law and itself built on previous periods of colonization, including those overseen by international agencies for the ostensible purpose of formal decolonization. Here, I turn to these texts, the geographic ideas they weaponized, and the political histories that produced them.

Western influence in the Marshall Islands well preceded the twentieth century: the islands' first contact with European travelers was documented as early as the 1520s (Barker 2004). By the mid-nineteenth century, the islands were subjected to a rapid succession of colonial projects. The first U.S. American missionaries arrived in the 1820s, aided in their settlement by the American Board of Commissioners for Foreign Missions (Lal and Fortune 2000). In 1885, after a brief period of Spanish occupation, the Marshall Islands became a German protectorate, a territorial status that persisted until Japanese capture of the Marshall Islands during World War I.

After World War I, global imperial powers vied for control over the territories formerly occupied by the defeated powers. In 1919, they convened to sign the League of Nations Covenant, redistributing territories taken from Germany and the Ottoman Empire to the war's victors—principally, Britain, France, and Japan—through the Mandate system. The Covenant established sixteen territorial mandates altogether, including the South Pacific Mandate, which encompassed the contemporary Marshall Islands, Federated States of Micronesia, Palau, and the Northern Mariana Islands, and which was given to imperial Japan.[2] The Covenant justified this redistribution on the basis that the peoples of these territories were "[un]able to stand by themselves under the strenuous conditions of the modern world."[3] For this reason, these peoples and their lands would be "entrusted to advanced nations who by reason of their resources, their experience *or their geographical position* [could] best undertake this responsibility" (League of Nations Covenant, Article 22, 1919, emphasis added). In a sense, then, the Mandate system was the League of Nations' attempt to control the colonial governance of non-self-governing territories: the Mandate system classified these territories, redistributed them to new colonial powers, and then oversaw their governance by these powers, much as the UN trust territory system would do in the second half of the century.

Geography figured prominently in the Mandate system's classifications, explicitly shaping designations about territories' political status and their peoples' right to be free from colonization. Most significantly, the Covenant drew direct parallels between a peoples' degree of civilization and the environmental or geographic characteristics of their land, the latter of which were, in the case of the Pacific Islands, presented as indication of islanders' incapacity to self-govern. The most explicit discussion of geography appeared in this section of Article 22: "There are territories, such as South-West Africa and certain of the South Pacific Islands, which, *owing to the sparseness of their population, or their small size, or their remoteness from the centres of civilisation, or their geographical contiguity to the territory of the Mandatory*, and other circumstances, can be best administered under the laws of the Mandatory as integral portions of its territory, subject to the safeguards above mentioned in the interests of the Indigenous population." In this text appears a theme that would be reiterated, fine-tuned, and played out repeatedly over the following century: the Pacific Islands, due to their nature as *small, sparsely populated, and remote from the centers of civilization*, were best suited to be administered by the Mandatory (at that time, Japan; later, the United States). In other words, the Covenant presented the islands' small geographic size, distance from centers of power or "civilization," and sparse(ly distributed) population—all geographic concepts—as proof of Pacific Islanders' intrinsic need to be colonized.

This environmental deterministic logic—one in which environmental conditions or physical geography are seen as predisposing societies to certain sociocultural characteristics and political outcomes—was enshrined in the Mandate system, setting the tone for future international involvement in the Pacific. The Mandate system marked the beginning of a formalized international presence in the Pacific Islands, a presence marked by two global wars and ongoing militarization, driven by the territorial ambitions of both ascendant and waning empires, and punctuated by anticolonial movements for self-determination. Under this international system, the Japanese occupation (1918–1944) of the Marshall Islands and other Pacific territories in the mandate set the precedent for later U.S. occupation and militarization of the islands, as future UN dealings over the region would rely on the South Pacific Mandate's territorial designations (Hara 2006). In this way, one imperial project laid the groundwork for others down the road.

During World War II, the Marshall Islands, like many Pacific Islands, became the staging ground for military battles between the Allies and the Axis powers. While islands like Guåhan and Hawai'i had already been formally occupied by the United States, the Marshall Islands were first *imagined* as,

FIGURE 3. U.S. Coast Guardsmen and Army troops on Kwajalein Atoll after the capture of the Marshall Islands from Japanese forces during World War II. Original title: "O'er the Land of the Free— And the Marshall Islands." Courtesy of National Archives, NAID 205586140.

and then scripted into, the map of the "Pacific Theater" that set the territorial stage for imperial land grabs (Shigematsu and Camacho 2010). The Marshall Islanders had long endured "the impact of foreign traders, proselyting missionaries, colonial reformists, and the destruction and dislocation suffered" (Mason 1989, 22). However, the postwar period would usher in an era of intensified and enduring external control, this time at the hands of the United States.

The war's conclusion in 1945 signified a major shift in the territorial distribution of U.S. power in the Pacific. The war's end brought the League of Nations' dissolution in 1946, leaving open the question of what to do with the remaining League of Nations Mandates such as the South Pacific Mandate.[4] To address this question, the UN established the UN Trusteeship Council in 1945, the administrative body that would oversee the trust territories' governance by their respective "administering authorities."[5]

Despite a fear broadly expressed by many Western European colonial administrators that the UN would be "a key instigator of empire's undoing" (Pearson 2017, 526), the United States as an ascendant empire had relatively little to worry about in that regard. While the UN was seen as constricting waning European empires, the UN Charter in fact unfolded new possibilities for U.S. empire, whose territorial scope and political power were expanding at a global scale. The UN Charter both presaged and prescribed a form of self-determination for the Pacific Islands that would not hamstring U.S. military hegemony in the region. It accomplished this by articulating the paradoxical marriage of colonized peoples' "fundamental freedoms" and "self-determination" with an imperative for "international peace and security."

The United States exercised a significant degree of influence in the TTPI, an area that encompassed the contemporary FSM, RMI, Palau, and the CNMI, a total area roughly the size of the continental U.S with more than two thousand islands and a total population of about a hundred thousand people (figure 3). This influence resulted from its institutional configuration and the language of the UN charter, which identified the TTPI as a "strategic trust territory"—the only one of the original eleven trust territories with this designation. This designation meant that the United States reported not to the UN General Assembly but to the UN Security Council, where the United States had permanent veto power. As a result, the United States was able to establish military bases in the islands, oversee their administration, and otherwise pursue its military and geopolitical interests there relatively unfettered (Leibowitz 1976; Teaiwa 1994).

The TTPI formally entered the UN trusteeship system on July 18, 1947. The TTPI's legal and political code, laid out in the Code of the Trust Territory and enacted in 1952, granted "full powers of administration, legislation, and jurisdiction over the territory" to the United States (Leibowitz 1976, 71). Between 1947 and 1951, the Code of the Trust Territory and the TTPI's general administration were overseen from Guåhan by the U.S. Navy, by five consecutive military governors appointed by the U.S. federal government. After that period, the TTPI was headed by a high commissioner, who had "virtual autonomy" as granted by the U.S. president (Mason 1989, 5).

While the UN's ostensible aim was to lay out a plan for the self-determination of formerly colonized territories, the UN Charter itself split hairs over the difference between self-government and independence, making ambiguous the UN's true aims for colonized peoples. A brief glance at the 1945 UN Charter's Chapter 12, which outlines the International Trusteeship System—and which was based on a U.S.-drafted proposal (Pearson 2017)—provides insight into the some of the self-purported motivations of the system itself. Yet there are also some contradictions between the Charter's articles in terms of objectives, one of which was "to promote the political, economic, social, and educational advancement of the inhabitants of the trust territories, and their progressive development towards self-government or independence as may be appropriate to the particular circumstances of each territory and its peoples and the freely expressed wishes of the peoples concerned, and as may be provided by the terms of each trusteeship agreement" (UN Charter, Article 76, 1947). At face value, this language appears to support the independence and self-determination of territories and to prioritize the collective will of each territory's residents—an official justification the UN continues to uphold for the Trusteeship System's implementation. Currently, for example, the International Trusteeship System's main web page echoes the Charter's original sentiments, emphasizing the UN's benevolent motives for creating the trusteeship system and stressing the system's purported development goals: "the promotion of the political, economic and social advancement of the Territories and their development towards self-government and self-determination. It also encouraged respect for human rights and fundamental freedoms and recognition of the interdependence of peoples of the world" (UN Charter, 1947). As this text shows, the UN charter's seemingly benign language purports to uphold self-determination and local development. Nonetheless, this same language has often served to limit the sovereignty of colonized peoples (Ewalt and Mokuau 1995). Julian Aguon, CHamoru legal scholar,[6] reminds readers to pay close attention to the Charter's language: "Note that Article 73 references 'self-government' and not 'independence.' The ambiguous first term was used originally to avoid the unambiguous second term, which European colonial powers, especially Winston Churchill's U.K., rejected" (2010, 49). The language of "promot[ing] the ... advancement of the inhabitants ... and their progressive development toward self-government" also showcases clearly the logic of "tutelage," a common justification given by colonial powers for territorial control over colonies, on the basis that the territories' inhabitants were not yet ready to self-govern effectively and needed guidance in doing so (including, for example, in the Philippines and Puerto Rico; see Go 2008).

In the years following the Charter's passage, the UN would further specify the meanings of key terms—self-government and dependence—that both clarified and muddied the meanings of these political categories in practice. In 1951, the UN eventually defined self-government as evidenced by either political independence or fuller incorporation under its colonial administrator. In other words, these two ends of the political status spectrum are both, paradoxically, deemed to be indication of "self-government." Dependent territories, conversely, were defined as those which had "not yet attained a full measure of self-government," which returns full circle to the ambiguous definition of self-government given above. As Pearson (2017, 537) writes,

> According to the guidelines set out by the committee, there were two means for a dependent territory to achieve self-government. First, it could integrate itself (at the request of its people) more closely and on equal footing with the metropolitan government that had been responsible for its administration. Second, it could achieve political independence, which would in turn be recognised by the international community as an entity constitutionally separate from the former administering power.

But what would sovereignty look for the citizens of the TTPI, who, at the century's midpoint, had little idea that they were in for another four decades of trust territory rule? As one scholar at the Institute of Pacific Relations wrote at the time, "In form, the [former Japanese] Mandated Islands have been placed under the trusteeship system of the United Nations; *in substance, they remain under the sovereignty of the United States*" (Maki 1947, 176, emphasis added). In other words, *U.S. sovereignty* would be paramount in the TTPI, while U.S. efforts at cultivating *Micronesian self-government* would be the main focus of UN evaluation in the TTPI. In the same vein, the UN Charter did not predestine the TTPI for autonomous rule or independence. Instead, it and subsequent U.S. and UN legal documents left open the possibility of other political-status outcomes for the islands, some of which would entail an even closer political relationship with the United States than had existed under the TTPI (Mink 1970; Armstrong and Hills 1984).

If the precedent for "the internationalism of colonialism" in the Pacific Islands and elsewhere was set by the League of Nations Mandate system, the origin of the contemporary U.S.-Marshallese colonial relations is the TTPI, as it was the first formal geopolitical linkage between the United States and the Marshall Islands. In one sense, the TTPI was an extension of a long-standing pattern in the region, one of outside occupation, colonialism, and militarization. In another sense, however, the TTPI's implementation marked the onset of a new stage of U.S. military empire, what C. Wright Mills recognized as a "military definition of reality" (1956, 198).

The postwar period was a time of immense territorial and military expansion for the United States, joining the periods after 1898 and 2001 as the "three periods of global ambitions in U.S. history ... associated with the acquisition of significant numbers of new overseas military bases" (Lutz 2009, 11). Between 1938 and 1945—in just *seven years*—the U.S. overseas-base network expanded exponentially, from fourteen military bases outside its continental

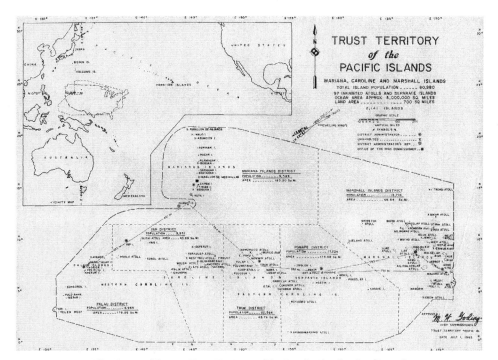

FIGURE 4. Official map of the UN Trust Territory of the Pacific Islands administered by the United States. The original TTPI included six districts spanning an area equivalent to the continental United States: Chuuk (Truk); Mariana Islands; Marshall Islands; Palau (Belau); Pohnpei (Ponape); and Yap. Courtesy of Library of Congress.

borders to thirty thousand military installations in about a hundred countries. Many of the most strategically important of these sites would be on islands in the Asia-Pacific region, marking the region's centrality in the shifting territoriality of global imperial power in the twentieth century.

Foreign military bases proliferate in growing empires (Lutz 2009). While an empire's rationale for expanding a base network is often presented as tactical or benevolent—for example, as facilitating the expansion of democratic ideals or the containment of aggressive adversaries—the purpose of expanding a military base network is, at its core, to expand an empire's territorial reach and influence. Empires inevitably and necessarily subsume, diminish, or constrict the sovereignty of the places they encompass. In this way, new military bases and installations expand empire not just by stretching the reach of the U.S. territorially but also by concurrently usurping the sovereignty of places hosting bases. Legally, this process of territorial and military expansion often takes place by treaty or bilateral agreement.

When empires negotiate treaties with their nonsovereign territories, those agreements have often been enacted, approved, and overseen by international bodies such as the UN, with their tacit or explicit approval of imperial military expansion. This was the case in the U.S.-administered TTPI, which incorporated the Marshall Islands. Militarism was baked into the very essence of the UN Charter's language on the trust territories, making explicit, for example, what it meant to "recogni[ze] the interdependence of peoples of the world."

> It shall be the duty of the administering authority to ensure that the trust territory shall play its part in the maintenance of international peace and security. To this end the administering authority may make use of volunteer forces, facilities, and assistance from the trust territory in carrying out the obligations towards the Security Council undertaken in this regard by the administering authority, as well as for local defence and the maintenance of law and order within the trust territory. (UN Charter, Chapter 12, Article 84, 1947)

This section of the Charter's text reveals how central the military imperatives were in the formulation of the trusteeship agreement. Furthermore, it clearly articulates that administering authorities could (and should) *make use of* territories under trusteeship for the "maintenance of international peace and security." This notion would become a central premise of the TTPI, and later, the U.S. Compacts of Free Association with the FAS. In effect, the Charter's language served as a carte blanche for administering authorities such as the United States to use the islands as their military laboratory.

The TTPI's strategic designation also enabled the militarization of the islands it encompassed. Militarization was evident not only in overt and spectacular manifestations, such as the nuclear testing and the building of a naval base and missile range site at Kwajalein, but also in how military strategies and priorities came to inform decisions and planning for everyday life on the islands. Over the following four decades (and into the twenty-first century), U.S. military interests would drive development in and governance of the islands, leading to a popular saying in the trust territory: "The islanders had the trust and the Americans had the territory" (Underwood 2017). The United States would be the last of the administering countries to relinquish its trust territory—nearly half a century after its creation—in 1994, with Palau's independence and the signing of the U.S.-Palau Compact of Free Association. As I discuss in the next section, the United States' lingering hold on colonial leadership would, by the early 1960s, become a point of anxiety for U.S. actors that would propel it toward negotiation and implementation of the Compact.

The United States would fully test the limits of that carte blanche during the Cold War, justifying increasing militarization of the islands by the threat of Soviet encroachment in the region.

U.S. military and colonial activities in the TTPI during this period ranged vastly from island to island and included nuclear testing, munitions storage, and aerial, sea, and land-based military training exercises (Shigematsu and Camacho 2010). In the Marshall Islands, however, the U.S. military was preparing to carry out one of the most massive and devastating nuclear testing campaigns in history, wasting no time putting to use the TTPI's and UN Charter's extensive provisions.[7] On July 23, 1947, five days after the TTPI's formal establishment, the U.S. Atomic Energy Commission announced the creation of the Pacific Proving Grounds, a number of sites across the Marshall Islands that would be used for nuclear testing (Buesseler 1997). Even before this formal announcement, however, the United States had engaged in military operations in the islands: a year earlier, on July 1, 1946, the United States had conducted the first atomic weapons testing in Bikini Atoll, which was also the first nuclear testing after the U.S. atomic bombing of Hiroshima and Nagasaki (Niedenthal 1997).[8] This test, nicknamed the Baker shot, rendered Bikini Atoll uninhabitable, leading afterward to the resettlement of all Bikinians to another atoll.

Fast on the heels of the Bikini tests came two major operations that would prove even more devastating to life on the Marshall Islands. In 1952, at Enewetak Atoll, the United States detonated the first hydrogen bomb device, nicknamed Ivy Mike, under Operation Ivy. Two years later, in 1954, the United States military launched Operation Castle and Castle Bravo, the latter popularly referred to as the Bravo shot—the first test of a dry-fuel thermonuclear hydrogen bomb (Barker 2004; Rhodes 2012). The degree of the test's explosive yield, according to conservative reports by the U.S. Defense Nuclear Agency, was "three times the most probable predicted value and twice the predicted upper limit" (Defense Nuclear Agency memo, cited in Simon 1997). The Bravo shot yielded an explosive blast equivalent to fifteen megatons of Trinitrotoluene (TNT), making it the most powerful nuclear device ever detonated.

Nuclear testing at this massive scale was, of course, made politically possible, even arguably *legal*, by the United States' colonial foothold in the region, enshrined by the TTPI (Barker 2004). Here, as before, U.S. actors justified this militarization through imperial geographical imaginaries of the Marshall Islands as remote and peripheral, all while using islands and islanders in ways which revealed them to be *central* to U.S. empire's expansion. The U.S. military's selection of Bikini Atoll for nuclear testing was explicitly premised on the idea of the islands' remoteness, as one U.S. military officer succinctly conveyed: "We just took out dozens of maps and started looking for remote sites. After checking the Atlantic, we moved to the west coast and just kept looking" (S. Davis 2005, 613; see also Mitchell-Eaton 2021). When asked about the search for a test site, he responded: "It looks like pretty far away is going to be the answer." In short, the United States portrayed the Marshall Islands as *geographically* distant to justify a terrifying kind of intimacy, as U.S. doctors and scientists confidently probed the affected lands, waters, and human and nonhuman bodies in the nuclear-fallout zone.

In the weeks and months that followed, the Bravo shot's preliminary radiological effects became clear: returning islanders, whom the U.S. military had relocated before the shot, started to experience symptoms including hair loss, nausea, and skin lesions, as did the crew of a nearby Japanese fishing boat, the *Daigo Fukuryu Maru*, or "Lucky Dragon No. 5." Contaminated fish populations were confirmed as far as the shores of East and Southeast Asia (Simon 1997). In other words, while the testing was conducted within the Marshall Islands' territory, the geographic spread of its effects was not contained to the contemporary RMI, or even to the broader TTPI.

Altogether, U.S. nuclear testing in the Marshall Islands included the detonation of at least sixty-seven nuclear bombs in the Marshall Islands' 750,000-square-mile territory (Barker 2004). Although the passage of the Partial Test Ban Treaty in 1963 put a halt to all U.S. nuclear testing in the Marshall Islands, the radiological effects on the local environment and local population was just beginning. As a result of more than a decade of almost-constant nuclear testing, residents of Bikini, Rongelap, Utrik, and Enewetak atolls were displaced and relocated to other Marshallese atolls (G. Johnson 1979), viewed by U.S. actors as removable because their islands were seen as interchangeable (S. Davis 2015). These relocations produced profound cultural and family dislocations and disruptions to Marshall Islanders' livelihoods (Hau'ofa 1994; Teaiwa 1994), another lasting effect of U.S. military presence in the islands that is still felt by many today (interviews, Honolulu, 2013, Springdale, 2014).

Negotiating Political Status: 1961–1986

Beginning in the 1960s and continuing through the 1980s, TTPI leaders and U.S. government held political-status negotiations to determine the political future of the islands and their political relationship with the United States. At the time, the TTPI included six districts: the Marshall Islands, the Marianas,

Palau (Belau), Pohnpei (Ponape), Chuuk (Truk), and Yap (the last four were eventually consolidated under the FSM). This process was stipulated by the trusteeship system: administering authorities such as the United States were expected to engage trust territory populations and their local leadership in a process of political discernment, during which peoples of the territories would participate in decision-making about their future political status. These discussions would determine the political status of the islands, and any political relationship to the United States, upon termination of the TTPI. These discussions were therefore of great interest to actors in both the islands and the United States.

U.S.-Micronesian political-status negotiations were officially set into motion by 1969, when delegates from the Congress of Micronesia, the region's legislative body, convened with U.S. representatives from the Department of the Interior, Department of Defense, and State Department in Washington, D.C. Delegates from the Micronesian Future Political Status Commission, established by the Congress of Micronesia, initially considered four political-status options for the region: 1) independence; 2) free association; 3) integration in some form with a sovereign nation, most likely the United States; and 4) remaining a trust territory (Leibowitz 1976). Each option would have a different long-term outcome for U.S. political positioning in the region, limiting or enabling, to varying degrees, the degree of political, economic, and military influence the United States could exert on the islands.

During the early 1960s, a period of heavy political contestation fraught with contingency and indeterminacy, islanders across Micronesia worked to envision and create a sustainable political status for their islands. As they did, they constantly looked outward to larger geographical scales, attentive both to decolonial movements across the Pacific and to the political statuses of other U.S. territories in Pacific, Caribbean, and North America (G. Petersen 2004). U.S. actors, for their part, despite painting the islands as isolated and remote, were in fact quite aware of—and concerned about—Pacific Islanders' global connectedness. The period of Micronesian political-status negotiations shows the fraught and nonlinear historical trajectory of decolonization, which in the Pacific "was not inevitable, nor was it unconditional" (Lal and Fortune 2000, 259). While neither decolonization *nor colonization* of Micronesia was inevitable, the terms of both were influenced by powerful U.S. interests that long conspired to perpetuate Pacific regional dependence on the United States. These interests are evident in archival documents such as the Solomon Report (described in more detail shortly), U.S. congressional hearing papers, and other

U.S. government documents from the 1950s and 1960s that address U.S. political and military objectives in the Pacific region. Overall, the terms and forms of Marshallese decolonization, even the plausibility of the islands *as fully sovereign*, shift depending on how we understand self-determination and its complicated link to formal political independence.

During the incipient days of the Cold War, the United States walked a delicate tightrope in terms of its national image, balancing an outward support of democratization, self-government, and opposition to colonial rule with the desire to contain Soviet expansion (and communism) through territorial expansion, military occupation, and proxy wars across Southeast Asia and Latin America. These global political tensions were made manifest in Micronesia as well, particularly in its leaders' political-status negotiations with the United States as a growing imperial power.

The 1960s opened with the Kennedy administration's interest in building Micronesian unity and strengthening a Micronesian political partnership with the United States, in part to weaken any potential Soviet influence in the region. Kennedy's declared desire for "a new and lasting friendship" with Micronesia, one that would tie the region to the United States "within our political framework," inaugurated a new era in U.S.-TTPI relations—an expanded Peace Corps presence, greater U.S.-TTPI administrative presence beyond Saipan, the TTPI district capital, and renewed attention to the question of Micronesia's future political status among U.S. politicians. These shifts signaled the paramount importance that U.S. administrators placed on the region as the United States attempted to expand its geopolitical influence in the second half of the century and to limit Soviet attempts to do the same.

The publication of the Solomon Report in 1963 was a key moment in U.S. Cold War–era relations with Micronesia, as it exposed U.S. state actors' underlying intentions in the region—to cultivate Micronesian dependence on the United States, thus perpetuating U.S. hegemony in, and military access to, the region—confirming what many Micronesians had already long suspected. The report's author, Anthony Solomon, was a senior consultant appointed by President Kennedy to head a Government Survey Mission in the TTPI, with the mandate to assess the island communities' economic, social, and political status (Mason 1989). Solomon conveyed his conclusions to the Kennedy administration in what later became known as the Solomon Report, which heavily emphasized the political advantages for U.S. empire in maintaining a close relationship with Micronesia, achievable by fostering the latter's economic dependence on the former. Its recommendations included intensifying U.S. economic support of the islands in the form of economic development. As Giff Johnson, long-time journalist in the Marshall Islands, writes,

> The Kennedy administration dramatically reversed past policies and in the early 1960's millions of dollars and hundreds of federal programs began pouring into the islands. Reacting to pressure from the U.N. and anti-colonial sentiment sweeping the world, Kennedy instituted these changes. But according to National Security Memorandum 145, the goal was to bring Micronesia into a "permanent relationship" with the U.S. by accelerating "development of the area to bring its political, economic and social standards into line with an eventual permanent association." Because of the Micronesians' overwhelming dependency on American aid, they have been forced to accept a status that falls far short of independence. (G. Johnson 1982, 43–44, cited in Diaz 2012)

The Solomon Report clearly laid out U.S. imperatives in linking development aid to the islands with the goal of ensuring ongoing U.S. political influence there. This strategy was used widely by the U.S. government during the Cold War to contain communism (Stur 2015). By delimiting the range of political-status options that would be economically feasible for the islands, the report framed the islands as inherently incapable of self-government and positioned U.S. political influence there as the only solution to this malady.

What is perhaps most striking about the Solomon Report is how plainly and directly it laid out U.S. intentions for maintaining political affiliation with Micronesia, and how much U.S. political actors were willing to do to secure a future U.S. presence in the islands. Central to the survey mission's stated goals was a concern over securing "a favorable outcome" in the plebiscite, a phrase repeated throughout the report. The report exposes, in excruciating detail, the United States' long political investment in keeping the Pacific region under U.S. control, even though this aim was at odds with the UN's stated objectives for the trust territories, with Micronesian sentiments on the ground, and in some cases, with U.S. press, humanitarian organizations, and other U.S.-based actors and interest groups.[9]

Second, the report made clear that U.S. development in, and aid to, the TTPI was tied to the advancement of U.S. political interests there. In the report, tools such as development, education, investment, and social programs were advocated as "soft" yet powerful tools of empire. Their provision by the United States was always self-interested, with an eye toward securing a favorable plebiscite vote, which was seen as the only viable way to convince the UN and international community (as well as the Micronesian "masses") that any political status outcome was the people's choice. Investing in social programs and infrastructural developments in the TTPI was seen as central to building a Micronesia that would see the United States as a benevolent friend and partner, a partner who cared about the well-being and future of the islands and who could be trusted in a long-term political "affiliation." In other words, U.S. investment projects were about building goodwill among the Micronesians and a good name for the United States for decades to come. Indeed, the possibility of a long-term political affiliation would depend on that goodwill and good name, and upon the promise of development.[10]

Finally, the Solomon Report demonstrated a keen awareness of international and domestic pressures, alluding to growing criticism of the TTPI within the UN, U.S. press, and "in certain ways, among the Micronesians." The report's authors were also acutely aware of the international significance of Micronesia's political-status deliberations in the context of a global trend toward decolonization. U.S. anxieties about dynamics at the international scale are evident in this passage, which conveys both the urgency and the delicacy of resolving the Micronesian political-status issue in favor of U.S. interests.

> There are, however, unique elements in *the delicate problem of Micronesia* in the attainment of our objectives that urgently require the agreement now with the president in the Congress as the guidelines for United States action over the next few years. First, *the United States will be moving counter to the anti-colonial movement that has just about completed sweeping the world* and will be breaching its own policy since World War I of not acquiring new territorial possessions if it is to make Micronesia a United States territory. (n.p., emphasis added)

This text indicates that U.S. state actors were closely watching independence movements in the Pacific and elsewhere. Here, the report also conveys, if implicitly, concerns that Micronesians might be aware of or influenced by, politics at a larger geographic scale, an observation that contradicts depictions of the islands as remote and detached. In other words, while the report painted islanders as "trapped in time" elsewhere, here it presented them as keenly attentive to contemporary global and regional political developments, much to the chagrin of their U.S. "custodians." The report's author also gestures to political pressures toward decolonization mounting at a global scale: "We cannot give the area up, yet time is running out for the United States in the sense that we may soon be the only nation left administering a trust territory. *The time could come, and shortly, when the pressures in the United Nations for a settlement of the status of Micronesia could become more than embarrassing*" (n.p., emphasis added). As the report later makes clear, Micronesia was not only seen as a problem for the political contradictions it exposed within the United States on the global stage. It was also characterized as a "deficit area," one whose population and natural resources would be costly to maintain due to the islands' underdevelopment.

> The 2100 islands of Micronesia are, and will remain in the now foreseeable future, *a deficit area to be subsidized by the United States*. . . . With a variety of racial mixtures, languages and cultures, essentially a series of individual island communities rather than a unified society, a lack of human and natural resources, tremendously difficult communications and transportation, the area has presented very serious administrative and developmental problems to the United States. . . . *The people remain largely illiterate and inadequately prepared to participate in political, commercial and other activities of more than a rudimentary character.* (s-1, emphasis added)

Yet, ultimately, the authors conclude that the problems and risks of managing Micronesia (and funding its development) are outweighed by the long-term benefits of maintaining a political affiliation there, one that would protect exclusive U.S. military and economic access. The report attempts to allay any U.S. concerns that retaining control over the Micronesian islands simply for their "strategic value" could become an expensive "folly," a drain on resources, imagining the future possibility of a tourist economy there: "In the still more distant future, although not now foreseeable, what looks like a 'Micronesian folly'—justifiable only for its strategic value—may very well develop into a viable economy based on American residents and tourists" (s-26). When the Solomon Report was eventually leaked and published in *The Young Micronesian*, island leaders and activists were infuriated ("The Solomon Report: America's ruthless blueprint," 1971; interviews, Saipan, 2013). Many felt that the Solomon Report unfairly painted the islands as incapable of autonomous rule and "was nothing less than a plan to manipulate Micronesians into a permanent relationship with the United States" (Howe and Kiste 1994, 231). Furthermore, as many island leaders and activists pointed out, the report set forth a U.S. policy in the region that was in direct violation of the UN charter.

Partly because of the Solomon Report, tensions were high in the mid- to late 1960s as U.S. and Micronesian political leaders entered into political-status negotiations. In 1964–1965, nearly a decade after the end of the nuclear testing program, island representatives formed the Congress of Micronesia, a political entity whose primary political objective was to examine the possibilities for self-government in Micronesia as a region according to the mandate set by the UN Charter twenty years earlier (Mason 1989). Trust territory administrators, it became increasingly clear, had no intention of leaving Micronesia's future political status to fate. In 1975, at the behest of a U.S.-based political action committee, administrators launched what would become the Education for Self-Government (ESG) program, (Mason 1989). This program, implemented in all six TTPI districts and funded by U.S. Congress, was designed to provide structured political education through workshops, public forums, and reading materials on Micronesia's future political-status options (P. T. Coleman 1977). Unsurprisingly, the ESG had many critics, among them Father Francis X. Hezel, a Jesuit priest who had gained wide support and trust from Micronesian communities due to his long career as an educator and activist in the region. In a 1976 essay titled "Micronesia's education for selfgovernment: Frolicking in the backyard?," Hezel wrote, "One does not tie a child to a clothesline in the backyard and then complain that he has never explored the other side of the street. Yet ESG is very much the child at the end of the clothesline, confined to the backyard by a solicitous mother who doesn't want her baby to stray into the dangerous road" (62). Hezel argued that despite the good intentions and committed efforts of many ESG staffers, the ESG mandate had been circumscribed by more powerful interests in the TTPI. His critique of the "tutelage"-oriented vision of ESG by U.S. political figures echoed the concerns of many in the islands, some of whom saw the ESG program as yet another attempt by the U.S. and TTPI leadership to assert heavy influence on the islands' future political status (interviews and fieldnotes, Saipan, 2013). These fears spoke to the heavy hand that the United States played in influencing political-status considerations. As anthropologist Glenn Petersen (2004) documents in an extensive set of interviews with FSM political actors (many of whom had passed by the time I began this book's research), many Micronesian leaders were skeptical of the U.S. interests and rejected repeated U.S. proposals for Micronesia to become a U.S. commonwealth.

> [Congress of Micronesia representative] Roman Tmetuchl predicted that in a Micronesia fully absorbed into the American polity Micronesians would be next in a long line of minorities, and would experience not only the dispossession of the Hawaiians and Indians but the marginalization of Blacks and Puerto Ricans. Micronesians would become citizens, he said, but they would be second class citizens.... Amata Kabua, who would go on to become the first president of the Marshall Islands, pointed to the experiences of the Hawaiians, Guamanians, Puerto Ricans, and Filipinos and marveled at the "agility" of the U.S. in applying the principles of self-determination.

As these quotes make clear, Micronesian leaders were keenly attentive to the experiences of both other U.S. territories and other racialized and colonized

FIGURE 5. The 1978 UN Visiting Mission arriving in Majuro, the capital of the Marshall Islands. The sign reads, "Please release us from the bondage of your trusteeship agreement." Courtesy of University of Hawaiʻi at Mānoa: Hamilton Pacific Trust Territory Archives, s-1862a.01.

peoples in the U.S. mainland, wary of a diminishment of their own rights of citizenship and self-determination. Such concerns added tension to the negotiations, already weighty due to the great significance both the U.S. and island sides placed on the future of the islands' political status.[11] These tensions led to increasing protests by Micronesians, including Marshallese, against an overbearing U.S. presence, as indicated in this photo of protesters in Majuro in 1979.

Despite well-founded concerns about U.S. intentions in the region, by 1979, official negotiations were underway throughout the TTPI to transition the islands to new forms of political status decided upon by island leaders (and, later, voters), in consultation with U.S. representatives (Mason 1989). Present at the TTPI political status-negotiations were representatives from the TTPI's Office of Micronesian Status Negotiations, Ambassador F. Haydn Williams, the U.S. president's personal representative for the political-status negotiations (1971–1976), head negotiators on each side, and their respective attorneys (interviews, Washington, D.C., 2014). According to one senior U.S. official, twenty-nine agencies were involved in the original Compact negotiations, primarily government agencies from the United States, the UN, and respective islands (interview, Washington, D.C., 2014). The UN mandate to negotiators was clear: reach agreement about the future political status of the TTPI, a political entity that had already been cleaved into several subdivisions.[12]

The negotiations were not without obstacle or controversy. In 1976, the CIA was discovered to have secretly bugged negotiating sessions in Washington, D.C., and Hawaiʻi, at the behest of Henry Kissinger (Woodward 1976). Discovery of this fact unsurprisingly heightened existing distrust of U.S. negotiators, and of the negotiating process itself, in the islands. Another issue was the Solomon Report, by this point infamous among islanders and anyone involved in island politics. Despite these accumulating concerns, it was clear that the United States intended to maintain a long-term presence in the Pacific region. Ambassador Williams, for his part, shared somewhat secretively in political-status talks at Hilo, Hawaiʻi, that the United States would not consider full Micronesian independence: "I cannot imagine . . . that my Government would agree to termination of the [TTPI] on terms which would in any way threaten stability in the area and which would in the opinion of the United States endanger international peace and security" (Friends of Micronesia 1973). Ambassador Williams's comment reveals the great significance the political-status negotiations held for the United States' ability to maintain its influence in the Pacific and, by extension, its influence on an international scale. Such considerations would continue to weigh on negotiations as they moved forward in the years that followed.

By October 1982, the FSM had moved to enter into free association with the United States. Yet many actors, in both the United States and the Pacific, still wondered whether freely associated statehood, or free association, would be a politically sustainable status. Francis Hezel (1976) wrote, "The Micronesian people's choice is rather simple over the long run: independence (or something akin to it) or American statehood. Anything short of either one of these statuses appears to be a rather unstable formula, as the recent political ferment in Guam clearly indicates. Free Association itself—that much discussed and little understood option—would almost certainly gravitate in time towards one or the other of these" (2). Hezel's position that free association, as a liminal political status between statehood and independent sovereignty, would be unsustainable in the long run was shared by many actors involved in Compact policy negotiations and U.S. policymaking in the territories (interviews, Washington, D.C., 2014). Associated statehood, nonetheless, was viewed by much of the UN leadership at the time as a viable decolonization option for small island territories and colonies (Broderick 1968; Igarashi 2002), in part because UN leaders may have been concerned about potential shifts in wider geopolitical dynamics if island territories gained independence (Aguon 2010).

FIGURE 6. Marshall Islanders vote in the 1983 plebiscite and referendum on the Compact of Free Association. Courtesy of University of Hawai'i at Mānoa: Hamilton Pacific Trust Territory Archives, 1862.06

These conflicting interpretations of the Compact highlight the different political imperatives held by negotiating parties, as well as the high stakes both sides placed on the islands' political status.

On September 7, 1983, the people of the Marshall Islands voted in a plebiscite on their political status, with 58 percent of voters voting in favor of the Compact of Free Association. Later that year, U.S. ambassador Fred M. Zeder II signed both the RMI and FSM Compacts for the United States (Reagan 1984). Three years later, in January 1986, U.S. Congress approved the Compact and enacted it into law.

Militarism and Migration in the 1986 Compact of Free Association

Having examined the historical events leading up to the Compact's enactment, I turn now to the document itself to examine its significance for Marshallese sovereignty, militarization, and migration. The 1986 Compacts, three altogether, defined the postcolonial relationship that each of the three remaining TTPI states—the Republic of the Marshall Islands (RMI), the Republic of Palau, and the Federated States of Micronesia (FSM)—would have with the United States. At the same time, the Compact linked formal Marshallese sovereignty to ongoing U.S. militarism and to Marshallese migration and citizenship rights in the United States. In doing so, it paradoxically delimited Marshallese sovereignty in practice and created a form of imperial citizenship for Marshall Islanders in the U.S. Analysis of the Compact exposes the deep links between immigration management and military strategy (Loyd et al. 2016), revealing both as central to broader imperial aims. Here, I pair a policy analysis of the Compact document with analysis of U.S., Marshallese, and other Micronesian political actors' *interpretations* of the Compact, garnered from interviews I conducted in Washington, D.C., Saipan, and Hawai'i and from oral histories collected by other scholars.

The Compact was the harbinger of a relatively novel type of political-legal arrangement and political status: that of Freely Associated Statehood.[13] It is an arrangement not easily characterized within dominant or traditional definitions of political statehood, sovereignty, self-determination, and colonialism, as it blurs separation between colonial powers and their former colonies after formal independence (Keitner and Reisman 2003). While the Compacts established the RMI, FSM, and Palau as states in free association with the United States, recognizing their sovereign political status (Lal and Fortune 2002), some legal scholars have argued that free association serves as a "political 'half-way house' to full independence," a "soft landing" from dependency (Hills 2004, n.p.). Yet for many Micronesian political actors, free association was far preferable to commonwealth status, as it protected a not insignificant degree of autonomy for FAS that included the right to enact a constitution, demand nuclear reparations, and assert land tenure claims (G. Petersen 2004). These varied interpretations of free association speak to the complexity of the Compact and the new political arrangement it established. In other words, the degree of "freedom" proffered through free association was, and continues to be, a matter of debate.

Yet the Compact was anything but a straightforward bilateral agreement between two sovereign states: it functioned more as an *imperial* agreement, as it extended, in a new political form, the long-standing U.S. political, economic, and military influence over the Marshall Islands, even after the RMI's formal political independence. The 1986 Compact of Free Association sutured the RMI to the United States in broad and profound ways, with provisions covering foreign affairs, economic development, health care, environmental protections, and federal services. It stipulated that the U.S. federal government would provide financial support through Compact Trust Funds to the RMI, initially for fifteen years. During that period, the U.S. military would have the right to operate armed forces in the islands, to request operating base space, and to exclude other countries' military forces from entering RMI territory (Underwood 2003). For the purposes of this book, two aspects of the Compact—its military provisions and its migration and citizenship provisions—are most germane. In the following two sections, I examine the Compact's military and migration provisions to show how the United States wielded its influence in the Compact in order to maintain imperial power, effectively delimiting Marshallese sovereignty.

MILITARY PROVISIONS AND STRATEGIC DENIAL

While the Compact's military dimension was not the sole factor driving its passage, a focus on military questions was pervasive in both the Compact (largely in its annex) and subsidiary agreements. The Compact's provisions for exclusive U.S. military access to the Marshall Islands enabled the perpetuation of U.S. empire, albeit through different political strategies than were used under the TTPI, which established *formal* U.S. political control (or "administration") over the Marshall Islands. While the Compact established the Marshall Islands as a formally independent nation, it simultaneously stipulated that the islands cede plenary power to the U.S., granting the United States full access to the land and sea within its 750,000 square miles of territory. FAS Compact signatories were expected to "sympathetically consider" any defense-related request made by the U.S. government, should it "require the use of areas within [the FAS]" in addition to those explicitly stipulated in the Compact. Such language clearly gestures to an ongoing obligation of the FAS to provide U.S. military access to their islands. As such, it exemplifies the kind of "soft-power" approach that characterizes contemporary imperial power, wielded here not as an absolute mandate but as a heavy-handed suggestion for compliance with U.S. imperatives.

The Compacts' military provisions were part of a larger military strategy to maintain U.S. access to the broader Pacific region through "strategic denial," a strategy characterized by two key elements: "the maintenance of friendly Western access to the region, and the denial of access to countries regarded as potentially hostile" (Herr 1986, 174). Pursuant to this strategy, a primary objective of U.S. Compact negotiators was to assure ongoing and exclusive military U.S. access to the Marshall Islands, and specifically to Kwajalein, which had been under a land-use agreement since October 19, 1982.[14] In effect, the Compact reserved millions of square miles of Pacific Ocean for American interests (Underwood 2003), producing the space as part of a larger Cold War geopolitical project to shore up exclusive U.S. military access around the globe (Farish 2010; Hara 2006).

U.S. political actors at the time clearly understood the Compact's potential impact on U.S. power in the region, where they were increasingly concerned about a shrinking U.S. geopolitical foothold. In the 1980s, for the first time in almost three decades, U.S. hegemony in the Pacific appeared to be in jeopardy. Such concerns appeared at the fore, for example, of the 1998 congressional testimony of Stanley O. Roth, then assistant secretary for East Asian and Pacific Affairs. Roth's testimony articulates the historical relevance of the RMI and other FAS to the U.S. military's designs on the broader Pacific.

> In the Cold War environment of the mid-1980s, the United States was keen to bolster its security posture in the Pacific. For much of the post–World War II period, the United States had had unrivaled influence in the Pacific. This position was challenged in the mid-80s as the Soviets undertook an aggressive campaign to increase their presence in the region, concluding a fishing agreement with Kiribati and opening diplomatic relations with Vanuatu. At the same time, consultations with the Filipinos had already begun to cast doubt on the future of U.S. bases at Subic, Clark and other facilities in the Philippines.

Compacts with the FAS, Roth and others surmised, could alleviate this problem in three ways. First, the principle of "strategic denial" elaborated in the Compacts guaranteed the U.S. exclusive military access to FAS countries and their surrounding waterways (GAO 2016). Second, the U.S. agreement with the RMI ensured continued access to the Kwajalein military facility, part of the Ronald Reagan Ballistic Missile Defense Test Site and a key test facility for U.S. missile defense operations (GAO 2002). Third, the U.S. agreement with Palau included the right to develop a military base should the United States need an alternative to the Philippines.[15] Combined, these three components of the Compact served to safeguard long-term U.S. military interests in the region.

Key imperial geographical imaginaries were once again instrumental in U.S. efforts to maintain, and justify, a Pacific foothold. Threaded through Roth's testimony are the geopolitical aims of the U.S. government as imagined, and thus *projected*, on to the Pacific. First, we see the geopolitical importance that the U.S. government, as articulated by this state actor, placed on U.S. military access to the Marshall Islands. His emphasis on military access echoes and reproduces Cold War cartographic logics (Farish 2010): territory is contested within a binary oppositional political sphere in which Pacific space—specifically, exclusive-access *base* space—must be defended against "aggressive" regional encroachment by the Soviets. Here, Marshall Islands, and Kwajalein specifically, are imagined as key points in the Pacific constellation of U.S. military bases (Kothari and Wilkinson 2010), yet another geographical imagination projected on to the region from afar.

Militarized geographical imaginaries also pervade the Compact's text, gesturing to U.S.-imagined uses of the islands.[16] The U.S. definition of the Marshall Islands as a geographic entity that includes "the outer limits of the territorial sea and the air space above such areas," in addition to land, indicates the expansive uses of space and territory imagined by the U.S. government and military at the time (Barnes and Farish 2006). These imagined uses, if implemented, would potentially impinge upon the Marshall Islands' ability to self-govern fully. In this way, by linking the Marshall Islands' economic and political development to the U.S. military interests in the Pacific region, the Compact imposed structural limitations on the islands' sovereignty, as it upheld provisions for heavy U.S. political influence and enabled the expansion of U.S. military empire there.

THE MIGRATION PROVISION

Among the central issues in Compact negotiations, especially for the island negotiators, were those of U.S. migration and citizenship for future citizens of the Freely Associated States, islands whose residents had held TTPI citizenship since 1947.[17] Negotiators on the island side were committed to incorporating provisions for Marshallese citizens to migrate to, and within, the U.S. territorial system (interviews, consular staff, Washington, D.C. 2014; Honolulu, Hawai'i 2013). As an FSM ambassador to the United States made clear, the Compact's immigration and military provisions were entangled from the beginning: "When [the Compact] was negotiated, [immigration] was quid pro quo with the security and defense [provisions]" (interview, 2019, D.C.). A senior U.S. government official characterized the two sides' priorities in this way: "My understanding is that migration was of the highest priority to the island negotiators while strategic denial was the primary objective for the U.S. negotiators. In general terms, the Compacts are typical Cold War agreements—the U.S. was seeking an agreement that would meet U.S. security interests (keep the Soviets/Chinese out) and it was willing to pay a high price. At the time, it was not expected that there would be a high rate of migration" (personal communication, 2014). Packed densely into this statement are a number of explanatory logics for the migration provision. As this U.S. official articulated (and as many other policy experts echoed in interviews), the migration provision, which was of utmost importance to the FAS negotiators, was generally seen by U.S. negotiators as having a low political and economic cost since U.S. negotiators anticipated a low rate of migration from the islands. Although the United

States had been "willing to pay a high price" to maintain exclusive military base rights and strategic denial in the Pacific region, the migration provision itself did not constitute such a high price. Its inclusion in the Compact, however, enabled the United States to push for its own primary objective: maintaining military access. Here, then, (Marshallese) migration was clearly linked to (U.S.) militarism, if not as a direct tit for tat, then as a contingent provision. Not surprisingly, Compact negotiations were influenced by these broader geopolitical objectives that worked across scales, in the same way that they were influenced by imperial maneuvers that preceded them.

It is important to note that Compact's migration provision did not *create* the Marshallese diaspora or Marshallese migration to the United States: migration streams within and across the TTPI, and from the RMI and FSM to other U.S. territories and states, were somewhat established before 1986. In particular, Marshallese students had long been migrating—sometimes temporarily, sometimes permanently—to other U.S. locations for higher education. Furthermore, internal migration within the Marshall Islands, from the outer islands to the TTPI-established district center of Majuro, had begun decades earlier, partly in response to the consolidation of U.S. federal funds, which pooled in the RMI capital of Majuro and in the U.S. military center of Kwajalein (Hezel 2013; Mason 1989). As the islands' economy shifted toward these centers, residents of more distant atolls began to move close to Majuro and Kwajalein to seek livelihoods. Forced migration and displacement within the islands, of course, had also occurred due to U.S. nuclear testing there, another aspect of Marshallese internal migration during the TTPI period. This internal migration is, thus, part of a long-standing connection between U.S. militarism and migration *within* the islands, one that preceded the Compact's passage.

Nevertheless, the Compact inaugurated a new phase of Marshallese *emigration*, accelerating it by creating a new legal pathway for Marshallese citizens to immigrate to the United States. The Compact established a liminal, exceptional, and precarious legal basis for Marshall Islanders' legal status in the United States, which I theorize as imperial citizenship. While I discuss COFA migrants' legal status in U.S. immigration law more fully in chapter 5, here I focus on how the Compact established this liminal legal status, setting up the conditions for Marshallese migration to places such as Springdale. According to Article 4 of the U.S.-RMI Compact, RMI citizens "may enter into, lawfully engage in occupations, and establish residence as a non-immigrant in the United States and its territories and possessions" (1986; U.S. Public Law 99–239).[18] This legal provision is far from a pathway to citizenship, though its misinterpretation as such is common, particularly in U.S. mainland communities receiving COFA migrants (interviews, RMI and FSM consular staff, Honolulu, 2013, Springdale, 2014, Washington, D.C., 2014). Section 141(a) does not provide any direct *or indirect* route to U.S. permanent residency, though it does not expressly prevent RMI and FSM citizens from acquiring U.S. permanent residency or citizenship (the latter generally comes by way of the former).[19]

Over the course of my fieldwork, I had several discussions, in both formal interviews and informal conversations and correspondences, with politicians, policymakers, and policy analysts from the U.S., RMI, FSM, CNMI, and Guåhan about the significance of the Compact's migration provision. Many of these discussions took place in Washington, D.C., where several of those involved with the original and the amended Compacts now live. Most were either retired or employed in other U.S. federal government agencies or Pacific embassies and, thus, still involved with government service. I spoke with these actors to garner their perspectives on the negotiation of the Compact's migration provision.

Consistently, interviewees conveyed that incorporation of the migration terms had been presumed from the beginning of negotiations (as they were demanded by island-side negotiators) and had not faced much pushback from U.S. negotiators, who perceived them as allowing the United States to make big gains in military access. According to a former U.S. ambassador to the RMI, the migration provision's inclusion in the Compact was "always on the table" during negotiations, and "it went without saying, almost" that a migration clause of some nature would be included in the final versions of the Compact with the FSM and RMI (interview, Washington, D.C., 2014). FAS negotiators and representatives interviewed conveyed similar recollections that the migration provision had always been assumed as a given by both sides. As the FSM ambassador explained, "There wasn't really any pushback [from the U.S. side]. The basic principle [of the migration provision] was a given" (interview, Washington, D.C., 2014). Including the migration provisions, it was felt, allowed U.S. negotiators to move forward with their own priorities.

Despite the obvious military interests of U.S. state actors during Compact negotiations, an "emigration as development" logic persisted in interviewees' historical narratives explaining the purpose of the migration provision. Such narratives reinforced a notion of the United States as a benevolent provider, rather than as an imperial power strong-arming its former colony. One U.S. government representative reflected on a common U.S. framing of the migration provision as a form of "uplift": "I do think that the background of this was that it was considered prodevelopment: you're giving people access to education, you're giving them access to jobs and training experiences, and then they can go home and help build their economies. So I think it was viewed as a helpful thing to be beneficial to [the island populations]" (interview, Washington, D.C., 2014). Relatedly, several interviewees brought up the notion of migration as a "safety valve" for the FAS islands, whose populations had limited economic and educational opportunities (due in part, of course, to several decades of U.S. colonization, military occupation, and nuclear testing, which wreaked havoc on the local environment and food systems and which are conspicuously absent in many U.S. state actors' reflections). This notion of the "safety valve" was linked in many U.S. actors' minds to the development logic, under which Marshall Islanders could leave the islands, study, and work in the United States, eventually returning to the islands with skills, capital, and other resources (interviews, Washington, D.C., August 2014). In fact, the "safety-valve" argument for legal immigration to the United States was clearly laid out at least as early as 1963, in the Solomon Report.

> Modern education, particularly secondary education, will create a demoralizing unemployment problem as graduates refuse to return to their primitive outlying lands and to the extent that they are not headed to continue on to college. It is essential that the safety valve of legally unlimited (and possible financially-aided) immigration to the United States be established. Fortunately, that would come to pass when the Micronesians are given United States national status, if not sooner. (s-26, emphasis added)

As I discuss in chapter 5, the supposed prodevelopment assistance to Marshall Islanders migrating to the United States would in reality be quite limited. Nevertheless, U.S. actors' assumptions at the time of Compact negotiations—that Marshallese emigrants would eventually return to the islands, rather than resettle permanently in the United States—give some indication as to why U.S. negotiators were not concerned about potential economic and political costs of granting visa-free migration.

Whatever the reasons for including the migration provision in the Compact, its inclusion did not appear to have troubled U.S. officials or negotiators at the time, and my research turned up little in the way of significant pushback to this provision. The significance of the migration provision would become more manifest in later years, however, as Marshall Islanders began to take advantage of it to leave the islands and resettle in the United States. As I discuss in chapter 4, emigration to new resettlement sites, first in the Pacific and then in places like Arkansas, would only increase in the decades that followed, and U.S. negotiators' predictions about Marshallese emigrants' return migration proved false.

Post-Compact Implementation and the 2003 Amended Compact: 1986–2003

Since the Compact's passage in 1986, and as a direct result of its terms, both U.S. militarism in the Marshall Islands and Marshallese emigration have become more pronounced. The Marshall Islands' economy has come to rely heavily on investments from private military contractors and U.S. government grants, some allocated as compensation for nuclear testing and the ongoing use of Kwajalein Atoll (GAO 2007). Simultaneously, Marshall Islanders have emigrated in significant numbers to the United States and its territories, in three main waves: one immediately following the Compact's enactment, one in 1997, and one in the early 2000s (GAO 2011).

A number of factors have precipitated these waves of emigration. First, an increase in payouts by the Nuclear Claims Tribunal for personal injuries related to U.S. nuclear testing in 2001 and 2002 led to a rapid migration to the United States by Marshallese payout beneficiaries, who now had the economic mobility to leave the islands. Second, certain Compact terms were set to expire in 2001, and many Marshall Islanders worried that the migration provisions would be retracted as well, leading large numbers to leave in the late 1990s (in the words of one U.S. Compact negotiator, the RMI started "bleeding Marshallese"; interview, Washington, D.C., 2014). Third, Marshallese emigration accelerated due to ongoing factors like high unemployment, economic instability, and a severely stunted education system (Graham 2006). For many, these factors made staying in the islands all but untenable. In other words, Marshallese emigration accelerated due to an active process of *under*development by the United States, rather than as a form of development provisioned by the United States, as U.S. actors had spun it previously.

In 1999, discussions around Compact renegotiation opened for initial consideration in advance of the Compact renegotiation slated to occur in 2001. In 2001, as renegotiations were still underway, a two-year extension was granted, during which time the Marshall Islands would experience a great deal of uncertainty over the renegotiations' outcome (Stege 2004). Finally, after extended negotiations with RMI government representatives and the U.S. Departments of the Interior and Defense, the U.S. Congress passed an Amended Compact of Free Association in 2003. The entire Compact was not meant to be subject to renegotiation at this point; negotiations addressed primarily the Title 2 funding provisions and a few additional provisions (Underwood 2003). Nevertheless, the possibility for amendment opened the door to renegotiation of key Compact terms, generating tensions on both sides about what might be gained or lost.

The renewed U.S. focus on the Compact's terms leading up to 2003 highlights the Marshall Islands' continued relevance to U.S. empire. In many ways, this amended agreement marks the beginning of a new era of U.S. territoriality in the Marshall Islands, one increasingly shaped by the cartography of what Keith L. Camacho (2012) has called "an empire of bases" or what David Vine (2012) describes as the "lily-pad strategy," borrowing from U.S. military vernacular.[20] Military access, though, was not the only sticking point for the renegotiated Compact in 2003. Its immigration and citizenship provisions also came under greater scrutiny from the U.S. side in the immediate aftermath of 9/11, as I discuss shortly.

Extreme economic, political, and military disparities between the negotiating parties colored negotiations over the 2003 Amended Compact. By the early 2000s, the RMI economy and labor market were overwhelmingly dependent on U.S. Compact funds, which in 2003 constituted 55 percent of the RMI's national government budget (Stege 2004). This dependency, fostered by earlier agreements, made the RMI much more vulnerable in ongoing negotiations. After twenty-five years of virtually unfettered migration to the United States, many Marshall Islanders were reluctant to jeopardize that provision, especially in the face of such strong economic reliance on the United States. In a 2014 interview in Washington, D.C., a U.S. actor intimately involved with the 2003 Compact Amendment gestured to these power disparities, referring to the relationship between the United States and FAS as "like the giant and the pea." (He was mixing metaphors and fairy tales, but it seemed an apt description nonetheless.) In his recollection, the 2003 process was less a negotiation and more a unilateral decision: "I spent much more time on the Hill than with Micronesians. We pretty much told them how it was going to be, more or less." This interviewee's comments again highlight the power disparities—or, at least, U.S. actors' perceptions of disparities—between the Compact's two negotiating parties, as well as the influence that the United States could exert on the Marshall Islands in setting Compact terms. Far from equal sovereign players in this bilateral agreement, in other words, the United States and the Marshall Islands continued to exhibit and reproduce long-standing colonial dynamics during negotiations.

The Amended Act of 2003 deepened military and economic ties between the United States and the RMI. In addition to extending the U.S. provision of economic assistance to the Marshall Islands through 2023, the Amended

Compact also authorized a "continue[d] defense relationship, including a new agreement providing U.S. military access to Kwajalein Atoll in the RMI through 2086" (GAO 2007). The renewed centrality of U.S. military access to the RMI was in some ways indicative of larger geopolitical dynamics underway in the early 2000s—namely, the intensification of U.S. military operations in the Pacific and worldwide under the so-called Global War on Terror (D. Gregory 2004; Amoore 2006; Camacho 2012). These geopolitical dynamics were manifested in debates around both the military and migration-related provisions in the 2003 Amended Compact.

The 2003 Compact renegotiation also revealed the instability of the migration provision, which came newly under threat after 9/11. During this time, there were widespread changes in, and debates over, U.S. immigration laws and their implementation in U.S. Pacific territories—such as Guåhan and the CNMI—and in places where U.S. immigration laws and policies differed from federal norms—such as the FAS. Here and elsewhere, immigration enforcement and militarization became even more intimately entwined under the "Global War on Terror" (M. Coleman 2012; Loyd et al. 2016). These dynamics informed negotiations for the 2003 Amended Compact as well. One government official, who had gotten "pulled back in" as chief negotiator on the U.S. side, emphasized the Compact's visa-free migration provisions were under threat during the Amended Compact negotiations. "After 9/11," he said, "I had to go to the assistant attorney general and make the case [for continuing the Compact migration provisions]. INS and DOJ were going around with hatchets" (interview, Washington, D.C., 2014).[21] As his comment makes clear, migration and citizenship provisions were no longer foregone conclusions for the Amended Compact on the U.S. side, as they had been in 1986: "It took a long time to formulate the citizenship and immigration provisions. When we finally got permission from INS, it was incredible!" (interview, Washington, D.C., 2014). In this instance, Marshallese immigration rights, rather than being a "foregone conclusion" or a low-stakes bargaining chip for the United States, presented a perceived threat to U.S. national security and U.S. empire's global hegemony. This debate over COFA migration as a national security risk exposes the inherent contradictions between the United States' emphasis on *fortifying U.S. borders* (which were heightened during the War on Terror) and its concurrent propensity to *transgress other nations' borders* and weaken their sovereignty, a common geopolitical strategy of empires. This historical instance of COFA status's possible revocation also exposes the instability of COFA status as a protected legal status for Marshall Islanders, Micronesians, and Palauans living in the United States. This legal instability or precarity is a key feature of imperial citizenship, as I discuss further in chapter 5.

The Amended Compact also made changes that would affect Marshallese immigration to the United States, including an added requirement that Marshall Islanders traveling to the United States hold a valid Marshallese passport. U.S. concerns about national security and border control in the Marshall Islands were heightened in the early 2000s due to the Marshall Islands' "passport debacle," in which senior members of the RMI government were discovered to have been selling passports, primarily to Chinese and Taiwanese nationals (Hezel 2006). These heightened concerns about immigration documentation and increased surveillance of U.S. border transit were simultaneously playing out in the U.S. mainland, as well as in other Pacific sites such as the CNMI, where the U.S. federal government increased its surveillance and militarization of U.S. borders (Camacho 2012). In all these ways, the global U.S. geopolitical project of the "War on Terror" made its way into the details of the Compact negotiations, revealing how geopolitical tensions and heightened militarization during this time colored immigration policy debates everywhere, even in regions not commonly thought of as central to the War on Terror.

Conclusion

The uneven power dynamics between Compact signatory parties, evident since the first negotiation phase starting in the 1970s, reveal the Compact to be more complicated than a simple bilateral agreement between sovereign states. Instead, each negotiation phase and the resulting agreements expose the contingent and unequal vantage positions held by the FAS in relation to the United States. The United States placed contingencies on FAS sovereignty by coupling U.S. development aid, military defense, and migration provisions with the U.S. exclusive military access to the FAS's islands and waters. U.S. development aid fostered the islands' economic and political dependence on the United States, making island leaders more amenable to (or less able to refuse) a sustained U.S. military presence.

However, as the prehistory of the Compact shows, Marshallese-U.S. political affiliation, through free association or another political status, was never a foregone conclusion for either the Micronesians or the United States. While it would be easy to look back at the last several decades of U.S. involvement in the Micronesian region and identify a continuity of U.S. presence there, it is just as crucial to look to the moments of contingency and possibility, possibilities that constantly unfolded in response to regional and global independence movements and larger trends toward decolonization, shifting U.S. imperial policies and military actions in the Pacific and elsewhere, as well as Micronesian desires for control of their own lands and governance.

As this chapter shows, this contingency is evident in two aspects or dimensions of the U.S. relationship with Micronesia and the Marshall Islands during the period between World War II and the signing of the first Compacts (1945–1979), aspects that are often neglected in grand histories of U.S. imperialism across the Pacific. First, there were strong Micronesian interests for independence or greater self-determination, evident not only in islanders' criticism and skepticism of the U.S. presence in the islands but also in the existence of groups that expressly opposed U.S. presence in the islands, including segments of the Congress of Micronesia, the Micronesian Independence Advocates (based in Hawaiʻi), and others. These actors asserted their demands for autonomy—demands such as landownership, exclusion of foreign business interests, and restrictions on U.S. military buildup—both in informal contexts and in formal political spheres, including in the outright rejection of a U.S. commonwealth option in the early 1970s. These actors were acutely aware of independence movements sweeping the Pacific in places such as Samoa, Nauru, and later, Papua New Guinea and fiercely critical of nuclear testing by both U.S. and France in the Pacific Islands.

Second, the political contingency of the four decades following World War II, produced by islanders' refusal to acquiesce to U.S. geopolitical visions for the Pacific, was acutely perceived by U.S. state and military actors, who clearly understood the precarity of the U.S. postwar presence in the region. Thus, despite constant U.S. attempts to frame the islands and islanders as inherently needing patronage and protection from larger, more modern and advanced nations, and to position islanders' nonsovereignty as inevitable and "natural," both historically and in the future, U.S. state actors were in fact very aware of, and concerned about, the possibility of losing the trust territory. This pressure came not only from the islanders but also from the UN, whose goal had always been to move the trust territories toward eventual independence. Increasingly, such pressure also came from U.S. civil society groups such as Peace Corps volunteers and the Friends of Micronesia, influential members of the U.S. press such as Bob Woodward, and U.S. political representatives such as Patsy Mink, who penned scathing accounts of U.S. administrative failures in the TTPI. In other words, while I underscore the United States' consistent use of geographical ideas of remoteness, smallness, and low population density to naturalize islanders' nonsovereignty, I emphasize that these actors deployed these concepts while clearly unconvinced of their absolute natures. The possibility of Micronesian independence disrupting U.S. aims in the Pacific was palpable to all involved in political-status debates and processes.

This contingency—a dance between the global momentum toward decolonization and the rapid U.S. imperial and military expansion at the height of the Cold War—is that which colored the protracted negotiations over the TTPI's future political status and what would eventually become the Compact of Free Association. It is with a keen eye to that contingency that this chapter has been written and with which this history should be read.

CHAPTER 3

"We Are Here Because You Were There"

War, Labor, Migration, and Empire in the Natural State

U.S. empire and its many incarnations—military occupations, resource transfers, diplomatic accords, citizenship and migration provisions, and more—play a central role in generating new migration streams, sometimes to unexpected places such as Springdale, Arkansas. In the sites where those migration streams land, new social relations are forged and different histories of empire come together in compelling ways (Hansen and Stepputat 2009; Mains et al. 2013; Yeoh 2003). In this chapter, I address the coproduction of migration, militarism, and empire in the context of Arkansas, through histories that reveal the state's longtime implication in the machinations of U.S. empire.

Migration between sites such as the Marshall Islands and Arkansas exposes these places as central to the workings of empire, rather than as "remote," a common framing of both Arkansas and the Marshall Islands in mainland U.S. discourses (Blevins 2002; S. Davis 2015). Portrayals of both sites as remote, peripheral, or isolated serve to uphold narratives of U.S. exceptionalism and progress (Kolchin 2009). Their actual embeddedness in empire, however, demonstrates an uncomfortable truth: the U.S. "colonial present" (D. Gregory 2004) is itself present, even in Arkansas, of all places. In that sense, new destinations of empire are places where the seemingly distant and disparate points of empire are drawn together, as migrants from former and current U.S. territories arrive, bringing with them, and bringing to the fore, different regional histories of empire.

As this chapter documents, Arkansas has *long* received migrant populations as a result of U.S. foreign military intervention. Subsequently, long-term Arkansans have developed both understandings of U.S. empire and ignorance about it through their encounters with and perceptions of these migrant populations. As such, Springdale is produced as a new destination of empire (NDE) not only by U.S. *imperialism* but also by intra-empire *migration*, migration streams that connect sites of the devastation wrought by U.S. military interventions and occupations abroad back to the U.S. mainland, in the process channeling their populations into prisons, work camps, factories, and sometimes—with varying kinds of reception—into local communities.

U.S. war-making and imperialism abroad have always played a heavy hand in the generation of new labor pools and immigrant populations in the mainland United States (Fujita-Rony 2003; Bender and Lipman 2015), leading to the common refrain of imperial migrants worldwide: "We are here because you were there." The contours of these human movements are shaped by militarism and war, which propelled the movement of people (as soldiers, workers, internees, and migrants), infrastructure, and capital into and out of the state during and since World War II. Indeed, as this chapter shows, the operationalization of Arkansas military bases for "migration management" and detention was part of a larger process being carried out in countless other U.S. military bases worldwide (Loyd et al. 2016; Mountz and Loyd 2014). Thus, in Arkansas, as in other sites of U.S. empire, migration has not just been *caused* by U.S. militarism but has also increasingly been *managed by the military* over the second half of the twentieth century.

A historical analysis of U.S. militarism, colonialism, and imperialism can reveal new logics of Asian and Pacific Islander migration to Arkansas, as well as Arkansan mobility to and within the Pacific. Such an analysis, however, requires that we understand U.S. war-making and land taking as more than push factors for potential migrants abroad. We must also understand these factors as being deeply entrenched in the U.S. mainland itself. To do so, we must simultaneously broaden our definition of U.S. war-making, conceptualizing the scale and scope of U.S. militarism as extending beyond formally declared war. I draw here on Rob Nixon's (2011) concept of slow violence and Ann Stoler's (2013) concept of ruination to show that migrant groups are often products of U.S. military and political intervention in "sending" countries, whether as refugees produced by U.S.-led wars (Loyd et al. 2016), economic migrants fleeing countries whose economies have been rendered unlivable by globalization and neoliberalism (Fernández-Kelly and Massey 2007), or "foreign combatants" and "national security threats" detained in U.S. prisons both onshore and offshore (Minca 2015; Nisa 2019). The presence of these migrant groups on U.S. territory offers a reminder—at times, an unwelcome one—of the global machinations of U.S. military imperialism.

To develop these ideas, I first detail the history of World War II as it molded the image some Arkansans held of themselves and of their country. Looking at the wartime formation of imperialist sentiment and economic development in Arkansas, I document how Arkansas was remade through federal wartime investments and how Arkansans used military boosterism to challenge geographical ideas about Arkansas as remote, provincial, and backward, fashioning themselves as central, worldly, and *mobile* agents of empire. I then turn to Springdale World War II veterans' narratives of the Pacific islands and their interpretations of the U.S. military's role in the Pacific, examining how narratives of U.S. empire have been sustained or reworked in these veterans' memories. Wartime offered an opportunity for Arkansan men to travel beyond Arkansas, often to the Pacific, through military service that would transform them into imperial actors—and *agents*—of empire. Through that service, Arkansan World War II veterans often experienced the Pacific and the effects of U.S. military imperialism there firsthand, bringing back to Arkansas detailed memories of those encounters. Their memories, stories, and the material archives they carry (in maps, notebooks, photographs, and other mementos) create lived connections between the Pacific and Arkansas that persist today. Moreover, Arkansan troops became part of the flow of wartime capital, infrastructure, and labor that crisscrossed—and, in so doing, *materialized*—the transpacific, from Arkansas to the Pacific and back again, in the mid-twentieth century.

Subsequently, I examine three recent periods in Arkansas's history to examine how the arrival (and, in some cases, detention) of "outsiders" has produced Arkansas as a destination of empire: 1) Japanese and Japanese American internees and German prisoners of war (POWs) during World War II; 2) Vietnamese and Indochinese refugees after the Vietnam War; and 3) Cuban *Marielitos* and Haitian refugees in the 1980s and 1990s. As this history shows, U.S. military interventions abroad have served as the genesis or trigger for the arrival of many refugee and migrant groups to Arkansas, where they received contrasting receptions from local, predominantly white Arkansan communities.

In the chapter's final section, I turn to contemporary reception of Marshall Islanders in Springdale, showing how Marshallese COFA migrants, rather being interpreted as a product of U.S. empire, get reworked into interpretations that frame them as either beneficiaries of U.S. reparations or refugees given U.S. sanctuary, two discourses bulwarked by U.S. exceptionalism. U.S. militarism and imperialism in the second half of the twentieth century shaped the U.S. exceptionalist discourses through which new arrivals themselves were framed, such as the rescue narrative for Vietnamese refugees of war or narratives about Japanese Americans as "foreign combatants." These discourses surfaced most frequently during and after periods of war, when refugee and internee arrivals peaked, but they also had long life spans, outliving the geopolitical conflicts that gave them form and meaning. The construction of these respective populations as refugees, prisoners of war, foreign combatants, or displaced persons were likewise shaped by wartime logics, framing certain groups, such as the Vietnamese (and, at times, the Marshallese), as deserving victims and others, such as the Haitians and Japanese, as threats or burdens to the nation. Critically, such notions are also products of U.S. *military* empire, as the effects of empire's brutality abroad create often equally brutal refashioning of sites "at home" in the U.S. mainland while obscuring empire's existence.

World War II and Arkansas

Just as World War II was a pivotal time in the Pacific Islands—insofar as it soldered U.S. imperial ambitions with the landscape and peoples of the Marshall Islands and beyond—the war also had profound effects on the political, social, and economic landscape of Arkansas and on its residents. In short, movement between these two regions, forged by war, coproduced them in significant ways: economically, militarily, geopolitically, and in some ways, ideologically, through the formation of geographical imaginaries. Both during the war and after, Arkansan World War II veterans formed a human connection to the Pacific and to the history and present of U.S. military imperialism there, both for themselves, through their own experiences, and for those in their local communities who learned about the Pacific through these veterans' presence there. This link in Springdale, and in small towns across the United States, served as a reminder that Springdale was not a remote, isolated small town untouched by empire. Instead, it had, and has, a historical legacy that implicates it in war and empire and that ties it historically to the Pacific.

Arkansans' (overwhelmingly, men's) mobility to and within the Pacific *as military personnel* carved an early channel of the emerging transpacific, a geography that connects "remote" and "removed" places like Arkansas and the Pacific Islands through the circulation of people, capital, infrastructure, and ideas about race and Otherness (Hoskins and Nguyen 2014; Yoneyama 2017). My analysis of militarized mobilities is informed here by the work of historian Simeon Man, who uses soldiering as "an optic through which the racial and imperial politics of the decolonizing Pacific were forged and became contested" (10). In a parallel vein, my focus on Arkansan veterans shows how they, along with their counterparts from across the United States, were made "worldly" through imperial war and, in the process, made worlds. That is to say, soldiers and other military servicemen helped *make* the transpacific through their movement across and within the Pacific, the militarized occupations they took part in, the violence they wrought, and the wartime racial logics and animus they received and repeated, fine-tuned, and brought home.

This chapter was born out of a desire to document the interwoven histories of Arkansas and the Pacific Islands, asking how interrelated processes shaping these two different regions within U.S. empire—militarism, imperialism, and racial capitalism—brought them closer together than they might initially appear, producing their geographies in distinct but relational ways. The more I delved into this topic during fieldwork, the more I found material that illuminated how militarism linked Arkansas and the Pacific Islands in the second half of the twentieth century. The following section grew out of such material: in it, I draw on interviews and news articles on World War II in the Pacific to analyze the war's impact on both Arkansas's economic development, labor, and immigration histories and on long-time Springdale residents' narratives and notions about the Pacific Islands.

WARTIME DEVELOPMENT, WARTIME POVERTY

While the rest of the United States was gearing up for World War II, Arkansas was still reeling from the effects of the Great Depression. The 1930s were economically devastating for the state, which had historically struggled compared with neighboring states and was especially hard hit by the economic collapse of the 1920s (Blair and Barth 2005). As a result, many poor Arkansans, unable to make a living, left the state in droves (J. N. Gregory 1991). The late 1930s and early 1940s also marked a shift in the state's economic makeup, from predominantly agricultural and based in small farms to mechanized agrobusiness and dominated by the poultry industry as well as trucking (M. Schwartz 2010). These economic changes, in addition to remaking geographies of labor and capital *within* Arkansas and establishing new industries and labor needs that would be filled by immigrants later in the century, also set the stage for out-migration from the state.

The out-migration of poor and working-class white Arkansans from the state—primarily to California—sparked debate about interstate migration in other parts of the United States (J. N. Gregory 1991).[1] In California, which received high numbers of Dust Bowl migrants, for example, "Arkies" often faced resistance to their arrival from both legislators and long-term residents. Despite this pushback, many Arkansans took their chances and fled in record numbers: between 1940 and 1943, nearly 10 percent of Arkansas's population left the state (Halevy 2014). As a result of Arkansas's relative poverty, local and state debates over the country's entrance into World War II were heavily influenced by the war's potential to bring federal investment and jobs into Arkansas (Bolton 2002). These debates made their way to Arkansas's public institutions, including the University of Arkansas: "J. William Fulbright,[2] . . . then the president of the University of Arkansas, warned that if America failed 'to give immediate assistance to England by sending our naval and military planes, and the British Empire is destroyed . . . the only hope for this nation is to consolidate the Western Hemisphere under our control'" (C. C. Smith 1986, 5). In this quote, Fulbright tied the future of the United States as a nation to its ability to leverage imperial and military control at a hemispheric and global scale. His thinking, evidenced here, is just one example of U.S. imperialistic and militaristic discourses at work in Arkansas. In other words, far from being remote from discussions of U.S. military and geopolitical hegemony, actors in Arkansas were directly encountering and engaging in such debates. Furthermore, U.S. military ambitions were already beginning to shape Arkansas and its people in material ways before to the United States' formal entrance into the war.

By some measures, Arkansas's economic development during World War II was astronomical. Altogether, more than $340 million in federal funds were spent on defense buildup and the establishment of military bases in Arkansas (Halevy 2014). In military-base and camp towns across the state, defense-related employment opportunities grew, and the arrival of new investors provided a cash injection into local economies for a time (B. F. Johnson 2014a; Bolton 2002). Another source of jobs was Arkansas's ordnance plants, which grew to provide work for as many as twenty-five thousand workers who produced war explosives, chemicals, and other defense technology. Arkansas communities, left impoverished and underemployed by the Great Depression, were particularly in need of these war-related jobs provided by federal funding. More than just recipients of federal aid, however, Arkansans were also central to the nation's ability to continue its involvement in the war: Arkansas came in twelfth overall in terms of war-bond money raised within the continental United States (Halevy 2014). As a state, thus, Arkansas generated significant economic and material contributions to the war effort, despite its meager means (Blair and Barth 2005).

The economic effects of World War II, however, were unevenly spread across Arkansas and its people. On the surface, some towns seemed to thrive on federal wartime investments, benefiting from a surge in employment opportunities and infrastructural development (Bolton 2002; C. C. Smith 1986), though the low wages of most wartime production jobs, along with near-exclusive funneling of federal wartime investments into military infrastructure, offset arguments that the war was exclusively, and sustainability, a boon to such towns. Other areas, however, were nearly emptied as residents abandoned their lands and farms, heading westward to California or elsewhere. And, of course, there was a war going on. Hundreds of thousands of Arkansans were on their way to serve in the military, with many of them headed to the Pacific.

ARKIES IN THE WAR EFFORT, HOME FIRES BURNING

Only a decade past the Dust Bowl exodus from Arkansas in the early 1940s, the nation was on the cusp of war. Compared with residents of other states, Arkansans did not enlist in the military in great proportions: as B. F. Johnson (2014b) notes, "Poor health and inadequate education meant fewer Arkansans were pressed into military service during World War II. About a 195,000 men served in the armed forces, although the *forty-three percent rejection rate* of the state's inductees was the second highest in the nation" (n.p., emphasis added). Despite their relatively high rejection rate from military service, Arkansans were drawn into the war effort in other ways. Many who had left the state during the previous decade, for example, sought employment in the defense industry in places such as California and Washington state (B. F. Johnson 2014a). Others worked in military ordnance plants: during the war, Arkansas became home to six ordnance plants that collectively employed up to twenty-five thousand workers at the peak of wartime production (Halevy 2014). In a variety of ways, then, Arkansans both in the state and elsewhere were bound up in the machinations of the war.

Back in Arkansas, the war colored the pages of local newspapers, as it did in small towns across the country. Nestled among clippings of World War II news articles and photographs, in a vertical file at the Shiloh Museum, I discovered a photocopy of a poem. The poem's author remains anonymous, signed simply, "Another Okie." Its words, however, encapsulate the link between "Arkies" and "Okies" and the larger projects (and geographies) of U.S. military empire, especially involvement in World War II.

ARKIES AND OKIES

Sure, we took California without losing a man,
We Arkies and Okies could still take Japan,
But while we'd fight the dad burned foe,
Who'd build the ships? We'd like to know.

If we swam the ocean put the Japs to flight,
We'd have to swim back and work all night,

> To supply ourselves and the allied nations,
> With sufficient arms and ammunitions.
>
> We Okies and Arkies are among the best,
> We knew how to work before taking the test.
> Our forces combined, we aid Uncle Sam,
> So squawk all you please, we've taken our stand.
>
> We're not ashamed of the old home state,
> In face, we are proud—we think it is great.
> And when this war's over and you Callies are safe,
> We'll gladly return to that wide open space.
>
> —"Another Okie" (Shiloh Museum, ca. 1944)

This poem conveys both the patriotic bravado of wartime boosterism and a wounded resilience to the rejection and belittlement that some Arkansans felt at the hands of their country. It also gestures to the sense of white supremacy as a driving logic of the U.S. national project, with reference to "put[ting] the Japs to flight." Anti-Japanese sentiment during and after World War II often manifested as explicit racism in popular poetry and music, and the use of the term "Japs" was a common racial epithet (Burkholder 2010). Defeating the wartime enemy, thus, was articulated in overtly racialized and Orientalist terms, framing the Japanese people as the military opponent. In other words, defeating Japan was not only a military but also a racial project, a framing with vast and damaging implications for Japanese and Japanese Americans in Arkansas during and after the war.

The poem also conveys that the U.S. potential to carry out military projects *abroad* was made possible by Arkie involvement in the war at *home* ("our forces combined, we aid Uncle Sam," the poem reminds readers). Military service here is a source of pride, something Arkansans could contribute to the national wartime effort without leaving the United States even in the face of scorn and mockery of Arkies for many decades. "Squawk all you like," the poem goads imagined readers, but you cannot deny that Arkansans were a vital part of the U.S. military endeavors abroad by working at home.

The disdain that Arkansans confronted regularly outside the state during the 1930s and 1940s was also voiced by the nation's political and economic leaders at the time (U.S. House of Representatives 1940; J. N. Gregory 2006) and alluded to in archival material such as the "Arkies and Okies" poem.[3] This disdain, C. C. Smith (1986) argues, was often articulated as a mockery of an Arkansas hillbilly trope, which, after the Arkies' exodus to California, had acquired particular potency and circulation: "Nationally, Arkansas were identified with 'watermelons, the unshaven Arkie, the moonshiner, slow trains, malnutrition, mental debility, hookworms, hogs, the big fat lie, shoelessness, illiteracy, windy politicians, and hillbillies with paddlefeet who could not pronounce correctly the name of their state'" (a 1954 source, cited in C. C. Smith 1986, 20). Mockery of Arkansan hillbillies often centered around stereotypes of Arkansans as poor, dirty, uneducated, and unsophisticated, but above all, white (Blevins 2002). In the face of these stereotypes, military service and other contributions to the U.S. war effort served as a source of pride to some Arkansans and a way to resist their diminishment in the national image. In this way, imperial warfare offered some working-class whites both physical mobility and class mobility through military service. However, as discussed earlier, nearly half those Arkansan "hillbillies" were rejected from conscription due to illiteracy and medical issues, both largely caused or exacerbated by their abandonment by the state, causing them to forfeit that "paltry dividend" of whiteness (Kelley 2017).

In addition to this work supporting the war from home, communities across Arkansas also sent their young men to war, often first to Texas, California, and even Alaska for basic training.[4] From there, many men went to the innumerable aircraft carriers, man-of-war ships, and base installations that by that point dotted the Pacific Ocean.

Back home in Arkansas, local newspapers lauded these young men's efforts and sacrifices, drumming up both moral and material support for their military service. The Shiloh Museum's World War II folder contained a number of newspaper clippings from local and regional newspapers at the time, their tone assertively proud and resolute. Local pride in Arkansans' wartime service was reflected in this 1940 article, for example, in a segment called "On the Homefront": "Calling all Patriots: We have the finest little city in Arkansas . . . this Rogers, Arkansas, and won't we all be proud when we can see the name 'Rogers, Arkansas' embossed on the side of a warplane, a weapon of vengeance and reprisal that will, we hope, take a heavy toll among the death-dealing war machines of our enemies." Here, small-town pride for "the finest little city in Arkansas" is linked to pride in military service for the nation, much like in the "Arkies and Okies" poem, and the text celebrates small-town Arkansans' oversized contribution to the nation. In these ways, this passage speaks to the war's role in bringing Arkansans into U.S. military projects and U.S. nationalism at a larger scale, while gesturing to the effect of this participation on local discourses around Arkansan identities.

We Are Here Because You Were There   81

FIGURE 7. Razorback hog "Arkansas Traveler" nose art on a World War II B-24 bomber. Courtesy of National Archives, NAID 204991547.

FIGURE 8. Nose art depicting the "Arkansas Traveler" on a World War II P-38 fighter aircraft. Courtesy of National Archives, NAID 204892288.

Arkansas also expressed its support for the war effort by making its mark on the machinery of warfare itself, including paintings on planes, bombers, and other military equipment. The images below reproduce the trope of the "Arkansas traveler," bringing this icon to the far-flung sites of U.S. war-making during World War II. In the photo on the left, the Arkansas Razorback, mascot for the University of Arkansas, hauls a wheelbarrow with ammunition toward Berlin, the hog's aggressive expression conveying the bellicose nature of its task. In the photo on the right, the side of the plane features an image of the "Arkansas hillbilly" or traveler, complete with "hobo sack," pipe, and bare feet (C. C. Smith 1986). The Arkansas traveler depicted here appears as an itinerant wanderer, in an image that was presumably carried to the far sites of U.S. war-making on the side of this plane. These images visually mirrored narratives in archives from Northwest Arkansas during the war, narratives that extolled the nationalistic, hardworking, and patriotic virtues of small-town Arkansans.

As in the "Arkies and Okies" poem, these images present Arkansans as contributing their efforts to U.S. military empire during the war, through symbols historically used to demean them. As it turned out, however, military service, while allowing Arkansans to tout their role in U.S. military endeavors at home and abroad, also offered some Arkansans firsthand experiences with the people and places of the Pacific.

REMEMBERING THE WAR, (RE)WRITING THE NARRATIVES

World War II serves as a historical linkage between Arkansas and the Pacific region as the pretext under which many Arkansans went to the Pacific. As such, the war also became the lens and filter through which many older Arkansans, including Springdale residents, learned about U.S. militarism in the Pacific and about Pacific migrant–"sending" countries like the Marshall Islands. In this section, I examine key geographical imaginaries about the Pacific, deeply rooted in militarism and U.S. imperial actions, as articulated by Arkansan World War II veterans in interviews and archival materials. These materials demonstrate the deeply militarized nature of early geographical linkages—both in human mobility and geographic ideas— between Arkansas and the Pacific. They also show how ideas of U.S. exceptionalism pervade veterans' understandings of the U.S. presence in the Pacific, a phenomenon that also colors Arkansans' reflections on Marshallese migration to Arkansas, as discussed later in the chapter.

In Springdale, I interviewed three World War II veterans, all men in their eighties and nineties who were born in Arkansas and had spent most of their adult lives in Springdale. In the two vignettes presented below, I examine their recollections of the Pacific Islands and interpretations of the U.S. military's role in the Pacific, tracing key material and affective links between Arkansas and the Pacific. As some of the only non-Marshallese people from Springdale who have spent time in the Pacific or in the Marshall Islands, World War II veterans form an important, embodied link between the two sites.

My first interview with a World War II veteran was with a man named John Spade. Our interview took place in his living room, where we had a long discussion of his military service in the Pacific Islands. As it turned out, the Marshall Islands was Mr. Spade's unit's second engagement, which he recalled this way: "Well, now Enewetak and Kwajalein, they were shot up pretty bad. Majuro, I don't think—best I remember, it didn't take much gunfire. But Kwajalein and Enewetak, there was quite a few land battles on that. And shelling from the naval and bombs from the air, just took all the palm trees off." After we discussed Mr. Spade's military experiences in the Pacific, I asked him a few questions about the Marshallese presence in Springdale. In his responses, Mr. Spade made sense of the Marshallese arrival to Springdale through his familiarity with U.S. military history in the islands, many of which he had visited: "Well, I don't know why [the Marshallese] are here now. I assume it's just because [the U.S. government] used one of those islands [Bikini Atoll]. And I know that that's the reason they came in. I don't know that they came to this area, specifically, but they came to the United States because it just . . . it just run 'em all off of those islands." In these comments, Mr. Spade drew a causal link between nuclear testing on Bikini Atoll and the exodus of Marshall Islanders to the United States. His interpretation of these factors is not entirely inaccurate—the U.S. military nuclear testing in the Marshall Islands did *precede* the Compact's negotiation, though the testing was not a central reason for its visa-free migration provision, as discussed in chapter 2. Nevertheless, Marshallese emigration has been prompted by the long-term effects of the nuclear testing, as well as by other economic, social, and environmental effects of the U.S. military presence there (Hezel 2013; GAO 2011). Thus, Mr. Spade was at least partially right.

Later in the interview, Mr. Spade again connected U.S. nuclear testing in the islands and the Compact's visa-free migration provision for Marshall Islanders

> **EME:** So, after the war, the Marshall Islands became part of the Trust Territory. And when the Trust Territory ended, [the Marshall Islands] negotiated an agreement with the U.S. that Marshall Islanders could immigrate to the U.S. without a visa. Which is very rare!
>
> **Mr. Spade:** Yeah, it is! But I guess that was their way of thanking them for getting to use their islands down there to test all those A-bombs.

While in some ways this claim echoed Mr. Spade's first comment, it also introduced the concept of the visa-free migration provision as retroactive compensation or reparations—a "thanking" of sorts—for nuclear testing. As I discuss later in the chapter, this link is significant, as it and the "reparations" logic it conveys provide an explanation for Marshallese migration to the United States that upholds U.S. benevolence and ability to right its own historical wrongs.

For Mr. Spade, World War II was also a time when he, like other Arkansans fighting abroad, developed racialized wartime ideas about Japanese people (as soldiers, as "sneaky" and devious, etc.): "I remember when we was there.... I didn't see it happen, but I just heard it. There was a ship anchored out there just off Saipan, and a Japanese climbed the anchor! Climbed the anchor chain and was trying to get on the ship! And the guard shot him, shot him right off the anchor chain [laughs]." As Mr. Spade mentioned during the interview, the war was the first time he encountered Japanese people, and, as this was in the context of war, they were seen as foreign combatants. Between Mr. Spade's military service in World War II and, subsequently, in the Korean War, he spent almost four years in the Asia-Pacific region as part of U.S. military engagements. Mr. Spade's military service in the Pacific Islands and subsequent return to Arkansas, thus, constituted a human connection between the two sites, a connection fundamentally shaped by U.S. imperialism and militarism abroad. Military service in the Pacific, and U.S. imperial-racial logics about Japanese people forged *through* war, also shaped Arkansan's racialized ideas about Japanese as threatening outsiders when Japanese Americans were interned in Arkansas, a point I return to later in the chapter.

The second World War II veteran I interviewed was Roger Thomas, another long-term Springdale resident. A self-trained archivist, Mr. Thomas came to our interview well prepared, carrying with him personal photos, notes, and annotated maps from his time in the Philippines. (In this sense, he was a dream interviewee!) Early in the interview, we talked about his prior unfamiliarity with the Philippines and the broader Pacific region, an unfamiliarity shared by most of his fellow servicemen:

> **EME:** What did you know about the Philippines?
> **Mr. Thomas:** I didn't know anything! Hadn't even heard about them [laughs].
> **EME:** Did you have any images in mind, from what people had told you?
> **Mr. Thomas:** Nope. None whatsoever.

Mr. Thomas received his printed orders to attend officer candidate school in New Jersey. From there, he was sent to a radio factory transmitter school in Long Island, where he received orders to go west. He was first stationed in a camp in Sacramento, California, then was put on a river steamer, the *Delta Queen*, headed for Oakland. From Oakland, he immediately boarded a ship going to the Pacific, a ride that would last thirty days.

> Mr. Thomas: Incidentally, on the boat was the traveling troupe for *Oklahoma* [the musical]. And they would rehearse on topside every night. So I got to hear *Oklahoma* for about thirty days [laughs]!
> EME: So you had a little bit of the Midwest with you, on the ship.
> Mr. Thomas: Yep.

Later, Mr. Thomas spoke about the troops' collective lack of geographic knowledge of the Pacific region prior to their service.

> EME: Did you have any further thoughts or conversation with your fellow servicemen about where you were going?
> Mr. Thomas: No. None whatever. Of course, we didn't know—no one knew, none of us knew where we were going.

Mr. Thomas's familiarity with the Philippines developed over the year or so that he spent in Manila in the military, creating a mental map of the Pacific indelibly linked with militarism. Among the personal archives he brought to the interview was a map titled, "City of Manila," printed by Air Forces Pacific, U.S. Army, in August 1945. In precise, carefully drawn lettering, Mr. Thomas had marked the spots relevant to his work sites, including "SMALL SHIPS RADIO," "OFFICE," and "QUARTERS." These details, and the various material artifacts that Mr. Thomas had kept, constituted a time capsule of his experiences in the Pacific during World War II, a miniature archive of U.S. military presence at the time. Like his memories of wartime service, such small items formed a material link between the wartime Pacific and Arkansas in the present.

Experiences such as those of Mr. Thomas and Mr. Spade about completing military service in the Pacific have been well documented in World War II oral history projects dedicated to veterans' memories of wartime. In Arkansas, archives such as the Arkansas Educational Television Network's World War II Oral History Project and the World War II Veterans History Project at the Fort Smith Historical Society compile the narratives and memories of Arkansan veterans, many of whom left Arkansas for the first time when they joined the military. One veteran, Charles Alley, for example, said, "It was the big battle in the Pacific against the Japanese. And we were in all the island-hopping, we called it, with that big fleet. And Saipan was one of our biggest battles and we killed 7,500 Japanese by count . . . that was the beginning of our jumping from island to island, on up to where we got to Japan" (Fort Smith Historical Society, ca. 2010). For Mr. Alley, who traveled to the Pacific (and out of the country) for the first time during World War II, military service gave him his first image of the region—an image, he later reflected, that stayed with him for several decades. Another veteran interviewed, Thurman Odell Jordan, reflected on hearing about Pearl Harbor while back home in Arkansas.

> On December 7th, 1941, our time, we came down off of Rich Mountain and the fire tower; and at our home, we had a battery-operated radio. The announcement of the Pearl Harbor attack had been going on. And so a lot of people in our community hadn't known a thing about Pearl Harbor. But we had a neighbor boy, Riley Hibbs, who was in the Navy and he'd been home on leave from Pearl Harbor and had told us about Hawai'i. So we at least knew where Pearl Harbor was located. (Fort Smith Historical Society, ca. 2010)

For Mr. Jordan and his neighbors in Rich Mountain, Arkansas, military service (in this case, of the "neighbor boy") made the geography of those Pacific sites familiar, visible, and knowable to a local population. Hawai'i, and by extension Pearl Harbor, came into legibility for them through the lens of war. For a third Arkansan veteran interviewed, R. C. Goodman, military service in the Pacific also presented local men with an exciting opportunity to see the world: "While we were [stationed in Tennessee], they told us we were going to the Philippines when we got back to Little Rock. Well, being a bunch of old country boys, that just thrilled us to no end, [to] get to go to the Philippines" (Fort Smith Historical Society, ca. 2010). Although Mr. Goodman ended up being sent to Alaska instead, his excitement at the possibility of seeing the Philippines stayed with him as he recalled the memory he shared with his peers, "a bunch of old country boys," as they awaited deployment to somewhere far beyond Arkansas.

These World War II veterans' memories and the discourses that shape them matter for two key reasons. First, they are representative of larger (U.S.) geographical imaginaries about the Pacific, which are forged through militarized mobilities. These early human links between Arkansas and the U.S.-occupied Pacific were what enabled Arkansans to have an understanding—if a limited one—of the Marshall Islands and broader Pacific. Second, these geographical imaginaries, brought to life in World War II vets' memories and stories, have long circulated in everyday life throughout small towns in Arkansas. They also contradict two notions: first, that war is exceptional and time bounded (not quotidian), and second, that the Pacific is impossibly distant (not intimately proximate or relatable). Rather, both militarism and the Pacific—always entwined in memory— appear in these veterans' conversations and anecdotes as they move through everyday life in their Arkansas hometowns. Moreover, men such as these interviewees are living their lives—though in rapidly dwindling numbers—in thousands of communities across the United States every day, sharing and reproducing these same militarized geographical imaginaries about the Pacific.

Narratives like the ones shared by these veterans conjure almost nostalgic wartime geographical imaginaries of the Pacific and were echoed in many Northwest Arkansas newspaper articles published at the time. Archived news articles titled "Local men served, sacrificed in World War II" and "Okinawa invasion recollection" recall the Pacific while celebrating local veterans' sacrifices and selfless servitude as particularly Arkansan qualities. In an article from a local paper titled "At Home and Abroad, War Touches Everyone," the author reviews a book compiling interviews with Arkansan World War II vets and published concurrently with the launch of an exhibition at the Shiloh Museum, "Over here and over there: Northwest Arkansas and WWII" (Harington 1995). The article's author, who grew up in Little Rock, reflected on World War II's enduring influence on local residents' memories.

> Of all our country's wars, it was the Second World War, whose conclusion 50 years ago is being observed lately in so many commemorations such as this book, which looms largest in terms of its excitement, of the way that all of us who lived through it were caught up in it, of the many opportunities it offered us to demonstrate our strength and cooperation and passion.... Like almost everyone else... I followed the daily progress of the armies as they moved across Europe and deeper into the Pacific, shown by maps and arrows that showed the excitement of victory. (Harington 1995)

This nostalgic look to the past, published as a commemoration of the wartime era, holds up World War II as an event that "looms large" in the memories of those who experienced it, even from Arkansas. Here, the Pacific appears as part of Arkansans' mental map, tied to the war and visualized in "maps and arrows that showed the excitement of victory." Such images may well have been the first representations of the Pacific that many Arkansans encountered during the time, as they were for this author, a nine-year-old boy at the war's end.

War also presented the promise of geographic (and, to some degree, social) mobility for Arkansans, an escape from the provincialism that had long been the albatross around their neck. Local news articles, in addition to celebrating local servicemen, extolled the war for what it offered young Arkansan servicemen: namely, a way out of Arkansas. One such article, titled "They are more travelled," describes the worldliness acquired by young soldiers: "The service man of today has a lot more savvy than we had 25 years ago. Before he starts to fight for his country he gets to know it by seeing a considerable chunk of it, and in the process sheds his prejudices and provincialism. That's Americanism at its best" (*Arkansas Times*, ca. 1944). This excerpt frames Arkansans' military service as an opportunity to shed provincialism, escape small-town life, and see the world. Military service, the text implies, offers the young "service man of today" savvy worldliness. Through military enlistment and military-enabled mobility, the serviceman comes to embody "Americanism at its best" by traveling far beyond the confines of home. During World War II, these narratives of war were among the only contexts in which the Pacific Islands appeared in local newspapers. For area residents who had not traveled there, such images and stories may well have been the only images of the Pacific region they encountered.[5]

Freedom Seekers, Internees, Enemy Combatants, and Refugees: U.S. Wars and Immigration

War not only remade Arkansas economically and infrastructurally, sending some Arkansans abroad for the first time. It also transplanted people from the far corners of the globe—spaces which had themselves been remade by U.S. military interventions and occupations—to camp towns, factories, and communities across Arkansas. In this way, U.S. wars abroad have been central motors in bringing "outsiders" to Arkansas since World War II. Since the 1940s, the state has witnessed the forced internment of Japanese and Japanese Americans and German prisoners of war (POWs) during World War II; the post–Vietnam War detention and resettlement of Vietnamese and Indochinese refugees in the 1970s; and the arrival and detention of Haitians and Cuban asylum-seekers during the 1980s. Each of these groups' arrivals in some way reproduced Arkansas as a destination of empire, just as their presence, met with varying degrees of racist vitriol and exclusion, carved new grooves into deeply sedimented geographies of white supremacy across the state.

WORLD WAR II: JAPANESE INTERNEES AND GERMAN POWS

On the heels of the Arkie out-migration to California during the 1920s and 1930s, a massive countermovement of people *into* Arkansas was taking place by the end of the 1930s and early 1940s: thousands of Japanese and Japanese Americans were being forcibly relocated from their home communities in California and other West Coast states to Arkansas. As many as sixteen thousand of these U.S. residents were sent to army camps functioning as Japanese internment camps in Arkansas between 1942 and 1945 (Halevy 2014): Camps Rohwer and Jerome (figure 9). At the same time German POWs were also being moved into the state, mainly to military installations.

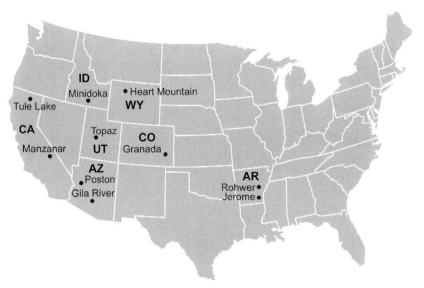

FIGURE 9. Ten "Relocation Centers" used by the War Relocation Authority for Japanese Americans during World War II. Map by the Syracuse University Cartographic Laboratory.

The arrival of Japanese Americans and Japanese and German POWs to Arkansas, and their contrasting reception by long-term residents, exposes the racialized nature of assimilation and integration of "foreigners" during wartime, as well as the Orientalist roots of U.S. depictions of wartime threats. An important distinction is that none of the Japanese Americans interned in Arkansas during World War II was documented as having any involvement with the Japanese government or other Axis powers during the war and that, further, many Japanese Americans registered to serve on the U.S. side to demonstrate loyalty (Lipman 2014). On the other hand, German and Italian POWs detained in Arkansas were enlisted soldiers captured during battle. Despite this fact, Germans and Italians often received better treatment by white Arkansans than did relocated Japanese Americans, the former frequently building close working and social relationships with local long-term residents (C. C. Smith 1986, 1994; Bowman 2016).[6]

I emphasize this point not to legitimate the legal or extrajudicial detainment of any group on the pretense of wartime necessity but to call attention to the racialized scrutiny of Japanese and Japanese American subjects—most of whom were U.S. citizens or permanent residents during the war—and to the questioning of their dedication to the nation and ability to fully assimilate to U.S. cultural citizenship (Berlant 2014). Many historians of U.S. racial formations have examined the production of Asian immigrants' "unassimilability" through the perpetuation of xenophobic stereotypes, racialized fearmongering during wartime, and legal constructions of Asians and Asian Americans as inherently and irresolvably alien to the United States (Cheng 2013). Such concepts shaped white Arkansans' reception of Japanese Americans interned in Arkansas during the war.

Soon after the arrival of Japanese internees in the early 1940s, Arkansas also became a temporary detention site for as many as twenty-three thousand German and Italian POWs in army camps around the state (Halevy 2014). These camps included Camp Robinson, Camp Dermott (previously named Jerome Relocation Center, where Japanese American internees were imprisoned), and Camp Chaffee, also known as Fort Chaffee (figure 10), a facility which would feature in subsequent refugee and migrant detainee stories later in the century. Bowman (2016, n.p., emphasis added) notes that Camp Dermott's "*remote locality* . . . made it the perfect site to house German officers," presumably a characteristic that also made it appealing to state officials detaining Japanese internees a few years earlier. Paradoxically, that is, geographical imaginaries of Arkansas *as* remote were used to justify actions that made Arkansas *less* remote, by bringing foreign populations there and by tying the state directly to U.S. imperial projects at larger scales.

Military infrastructures have long enabled the control and surveillance of migrant, asylee, and refugee populations, both materially and discursively. In the United States, wartime infrastructures have been used repeatedly over time to detain displaced peoples, and the military's infrastructural capacity to detain has been used to justify the incarceration of displaced and vulnerable migrant populations (Stoler 2013; Loyd et al. 2016; Lipman 2014). As such, military forts, camps, and bases, which are often repurposed as immigrant detention facilities, form another material link between militarism and migration. Arkansas's infrastructural capacity to detain people had also roots in U.S. militarism: most of the federal funds injected into the state were funneled directly into war-related infrastructural investments during the 1940s (Bolton 2002), making World War II pivotal in Arkansas's economic development and in its production as a site where imperial migrants could be detained, processed, made to work, and resettled. Infrastructural developments during the time included the ordnances and factories described earlier in the chapter and numerous army camps constructed or augmented during the war. The federal and state governments also made use of existing Civilian Conservation Corps, a New Deal public work relief program, to serve as barracks for POWs (Reiss 2005). Military and federal investments in the state thus enabled ongoing detention efforts, both during and after the war.

We Are Here Because You Were There   91

FIGURE 10. German POW camps in Arkansas used in World War II. Fort Chaffee, also known as Camp Chaffee, was later used as a relocation camp for Vietnamese refugees (1975–1976) and then for Cuban refugees (1980–1982). Camp Dermott was established as the Jerome Relocation Center for Japanese American incarceration (1942–1944). Map by the Syracuse University Cartographic Laboratory.

Wartime in Arkansas also brought to the surface entangled debates over military investments, labor, and racial integration, debates playing out statewide and at the national scale. These debates made clear that projects of militarization were deeply linked with processes of racial exclusion, which produced new geographies of white supremacy across the state. Perhaps nowhere are the politics of the time better embodied than in the figure of Governor Homer Martin Adkins, Arkansas's wartime governor (1941–1945). Governor Adkins, a World War I veteran and Ku Klux Klan member from Little Rock, embraced federal funding through military expenditures in the state, bringing over $300 million into Arkansas for defense plants and military installations. At the same time, he was more than ready to use states' rights claims to uphold his white supremacist vision for the state and for the Democratic Party as a party of white voters. Governor Adkins perceived these visions being threatened by rights claims made by African Americans and labor union federations such as the Congress of Industrial Organizations (CIO), which he decried as "leftist" and beholden to "foreign-isms" (Williams 2017, n.p.).

Channeling these same racial and xenophobic animosities, Adkins's opposition to hosting a Japanese American internment center was staunch and swift. He finally acquiesced to requests from the federal government, agreeing to hold internees at Camps Rohwer and Jerome on two conditions: first, that all internees would be supervised by white guards, and second, that all internees would be required to leave Arkansas at the end of the war. To ensure that internees, once released, would see little reason to stay, Governor Adkins also backed the Alien Land Act of 1943, prohibiting anyone of Japanese ancestry from owning property in Arkansas. The act was a direct appeasement to white constituents worried about Japanese Americans taking their jobs and their land, its language justifying the prohibition "on account of the standards of living of the Japanese people; a white person cannot profitably compete with the Japanese either in agriculture or business" (Senate Bill No. 11, Act 47, 1943). With a keen eye to civil rights claims being made at universities in Arkansas and beyond, Governor Adkins also opposed allowing Japanese and Japanese American students into Arkansas universities, wary that their admission would open the door to higher education's integration across the state. In other words, as the first internees began to arrive to Arkansas in October 1942, they entered a context that was being forged in new ways by white supremacy and concurrent struggles over labor, capital, land, and rights.

German POWs experienced a greater geographic dispersion and, generally, a warmer reception, across the state. While the majority of German POWS were kept in barracks in and around camp towns, others were sent to small towns to perform labor in agriculture and factories (Ward 2007). Archival research revealed that many German POWs were sent to Springdale to work in Welch Grape Juice plants, processing fruit products. News articles from the time reflect a cheery and warm receptive environment for German POWs, a dynamic that has been reported in other towns as well (Reiss 2005). One article, "Personnel changes at German war prison camp," describes the 120 German prisoners in the local Welch Grape Juice plant as amenably working "under contract with the government." The article makes even greater use of euphemism in the following paragraph: "The men all *volunteered* for the work here which was necessary because of shortage of male help at the Welch Plant which processes food for the government" (*Springdale News*, 1944, emphasis added).[7] Another article, "Labor problem aided by German war prisoners" (*Springdale News*, 1944), describes the Welch's grape juice camp in Springdale at a plant operational from 1923 to 1978. During the time when German POWs were employed at the plant, the article states, local women workers taking bathroom breaks were accompanied by armed guards, presumably to protect them from the Germans. Nevertheless, news coverage generally conveyed a conflict-free and amicable coexistence between German POWs and local residents.

Threaded through these archives are discourses that justify and even celebrate the use of German POW labor, presenting German POWs as nonthreatening and collegial. An article titled "Prison labor necessary says Welch head" (*Springdale News*, 1944), for example, describes how Kenneth Watkins, Superintendent of the Welch Grape Juice Company, explained the reasoning behind using German POWs to work the Springdale grape crops.

> At no time was there any trouble with the prisoners—these men were captured July 3 in Normandy and were working in Springdale July 21—they seemed to realize the war was over for them, their cause lost and glad to be here in America. They respected the rank of our officers in command and during their stay only 2 or 3 were sent back to camp and they begged to be allowed to come back to town to work. Without their help we could not have gotten the crop run. (*Springdale News*, 1944)

In Mr. Watkins's recounting, the experience of both the "officers in command" at the POW camps and the POWs themselves is overwhelmingly positive, almost glowing. Not only was there "[no] trouble with the prisoners," the company's superintendent lauded them for their respect, comportment, and contribution to the company's efforts.

In contrast to many German POWs' experiences in Arkansas, Japanese Americans' reception by local receiving communities was decidedly less sunny (C. C. Smith 1994; Anderson 1964). While Japanese and Japanese American internees were never detained in Arkansas's northwest corner, Springdale and nearby towns such as Rogers did receive a small number of Japanese American families during the 1940s and 1950s who came for a different purpose (and of their own volition): to work as chicken sexers in local poultry plants (interviews, Springdale, Ark., 2014).[8] This topic came up in a few interviews and conversations, two of which I excerpt below.

The first interview I discuss was conducted with a long-term Springdale resident named Lana Fischer, a Japanese American woman in her early 60s. Lana, a U.S. citizen by birth, moved to Springdale in 1959 with her parents and siblings when she was about eight years old. Lana's father had been trained as a chicken sexer in Japan and came to the Midwest by way of Stockton, California, at the behest of an American poultry company. Her mother had been in an internment camp in Poston, Arizona. In her interview, Lana described the contrast between her parents' experiences in the United States.

> **Lana:** The interesting thing about those times was that all the children in my mother's family were first-generation.[9] Well—I'm trying to think, are they? You know, I honestly don't remember. But I think that they had to be. I was thinking that my great-grandparents migrated over here. But in all of that internment, they lost their farm. Mother was probably not

quite a teenager, maybe twelve years old at that time. She and her brother, maybe the youngest brothers, were in camp, incarcerated in Poston, Arizona. I guess the oldest brothers that were old enough to fight in the war, fought in the war. So when they came home, they came home . . . *to camp*. On furlough, or whatever.

EME: Wow.

Lana: Yeah, is that not just crazy? Being citizens and natural-born. I mean, they were *born* in the United States. So, [it's] interesting. But all that to say that during the war time, when Mother's family was incarcerated, Daddy's chicken-sexing [work] was so important that at various in the Midwest, he actually had Secret Service to protect him, because of the chicken industry.

EME: So your father was never incarcerated?

Lana: No. And he says it's because they needed this work, it was the economics part of it. So, there were . . . you know, I can't remember . . . he tells the story of . . . [*pause*]. There was a lot of discrimination. So having the Secret Service was sometimes very comforting.

This dramatic juxtaposition of Lana's family's experience of wartime United States, as Japanese immigrants and Japanese American U.S. citizens, reveals a broader tension and paradox of U.S. militarism and empire: a dependence on wartime labor that is foreign or immigrant (or racialized as such), paired with the larger systematic exclusion of such populations "at home" (e.g., in wartime internment camps) and committing of atrocities against them abroad (e.g., the 1945 U.S. atomic bombing of Hiroshima and Nagasaki). Lana's family's experience of racist treatment, discussed below, speaks to anti-Japanese and anti-Asian racism both in Arkansas and at the national scale, which took on a particularly virulent form after Pearl Harbor and during World War II.

The topic of Japanese chicken sexers also came up in interviews with older white Springdale residents when I inquired about immigrant communities they remembered. In my fieldnotes, I reflect on a conversation with a Springdale resident: "Mr. Ottman, an elderly white long-term resident of Springdale, mentioned Japanese chicken sexers in our interview this morning, and I brought it up with [a local archivist] afterward. 'Yes, that's right—we might have something on it under the Poultry files. I guess they were being used because people thought they had small hands, so they were considered better for the job. And they got a reputation for being hard workers'" (Springdale, May 2014). In Mr. Ottman's interview, he expounded on the role of Japanese families in Springdale:

> Mr. Ottman: When the Japanese chicken sexers came here, they integrated into the community in a hurry, because they were interested in educating their children, and they were good citizens.
> EME: In what sense, good citizens?
> Mr. Ottman: Well, they participated in civic activities.
> EME: Like church groups? Or school?
> Mr. Ottman: Well, they were interested in the schools, primarily.
> EME: I'm curious about that question, about what makes someone a good citizen, and especially a newcomer group.
> Mr. Ottman: Well, first off, they have to realize the customs of the community. They have to obey the laws. And they have to be willing to contribute to the community.

Mr. Ottman's perception that Japanese families integrated quickly and relatively successfully speaks to a notion of Japanese Americans' "good citizenship" at the local scale of Springdale. However, such markers of Japanese families' "successful integration" in Springdale were not always accompanied by favorable treatment by white residents, as Lana reflected.

> I can remember one time, it was Mother's Day, and my mother had given us some money to run into the Piggly Wiggly, right there across from the school administration [building] on the corner of 71 and Huntsville. There used to be a Piggly Wiggly there. I remember going in there, and I was standing at the Golden Book rack, looking at books, and this little girl came up, and . . . apparently, I looked like a little China doll, that's what everyone would say. Because my hair was short and I had real black hair, that sometimes when you looked at it in the sun, it kind of looked blue. So I was always used to people coming and petting my hair [laughs]. But I do remember this girl—I was so small, and this girl came up and she was just enthralled by me. And I can remember her talking to me and petting my hair. But then her mother came and just jerked her away from me, saying something like "Don't touch her! She killed your uncle." (interview, Springdale, 2014)

Lana's story echoes the racism and xenophobia faced by many Japanese families in Arkansas, both during internment and after the war. These two histories—of Japanese American internees and German POWs—show how white supremacy and militarism unevenly shaped the terms of "outsiders'" reception by white Arkansans.

REFUGEES AT FORT CHAFFEE:
VIETNAMESE, HAITIANS, AND CUBANS AS IMPERIAL MIGRANTS

While the forced resettlement of Japanese internees and German POWs into Arkansas during World War II were among the first examples of imperial migration into the state—following, of course, the nineteenth-century arrival of white settlers, as I discuss in chapter 4—they were not the last. In the 1970s and 1980s, racialized tensions began to manifest in many of Arkansas's "base communities," or areas surrounding the camps detaining POWs and Japanese Americans during World War II. Such tensions were most notable around Fort Chaffee in Fort Smith, Arkansas. Operational as a military camp since the beginning of World War II (Radcliff 2016), Fort Chaffee became a destination of empire for foreign arrivals—refugees and other entrants—beginning in the mid-1970s, when over fifty thousand Vietnamese and Indochinese refugees from the Vietnam War were detained and processed there (Radcliff 2016).[10] This group, after being evacuated from Vietnam and transferred through (and often detained on) U.S. Pacific Island territories and base sites like Guåhan, Wake Island, and the Philippines, was finally sent to sites in the mainland United States, including Fort Chaffee. There, they continued the long and arduous process of waiting for U.S. bureaucratic paperwork to release them from the camp (Loyd et al. 2016; Lipman 2014; Nguyen 2012). This Vietnamese presence in Arkansas once again served as a reminder to local populations of U.S. military engagements abroad, as the human effects of those military interventions came home to roost.

Fort Chaffee, as a site used to detain multiple refugee groups during the mid- to late twentieth century, became, as Jana Lipman (2014, 81) writes, "a 'nerve center,' or perhaps, in more loaded language, 'a kind of Ellis Island.'" In this way, it served as a destination of empire, funneling the human products of the U.S.-led war in Vietnam into new sites in the U.S. mainland. Lipman's (2014) meticulous research on Fort Chaffee examines how media coverage in the state often circulated discourses that celebrated the U.S. military's role in the refugee crisis, lauding the military as a humanitarian force in refugee resettlement. Through detailed analysis of local Arkansan newspapers' coverage of the Vietnamese arrival at Fort Chaffee, she shows how media images featured young children and women aided by military officers and Arkansas politicians greeting refugees, thus presenting the United States as a benevolent protector to a local readership in Arkansas.

The rescue narrative concerning Vietnamese refugees positioned the

United States as a compassionate savior of the same refugee populations it had played a large part in creating. This narrative framed Vietnamese refugees as war survivors or victims rescued by the U.S. military, rather than victims *produced* by U.S. military interventions (Stur 2015; Lê Espiritu 2006). Such discourses, Lipman writes, "enabled [the United States] to rhetorically claim a 'win,' which had been so elusive in Vietnam" (2014, 62), an approach Yến Lê Espiritu refers to as "we-win-even-when-we-lose syndrome" (2006). This discursive spin on U.S. military humanitarianism and refugee reception would reappear in contemporary Arkansan framings of Marshallese COFA migrants, as I discuss later in the chapter.

My archival research at the University of Arkansas Special Collections turned up materials with similar framings of U.S. military benevolence in its assumed role as humanitarian refugee resettlement agency. One such article, "The Light at the End of the Tunnel," ran in the University of Arkansas campus paper, *The Grapevine* (Calhoun 1975), and featured a story about a local Vietnam veteran who decided to sponsor three adult Vietnamese refugees at Fort Chaffee and bring them to Fayetteville. The article opens with a sentence setting up a romantic image of a virtuous veteran assisting refugees in his home state: "Imagine yourself as a Vietnam veteran who, after watching the chaotic fall of South Vietnam and the near-debacle of refugee removal, decides to help ease the refugees' plight by offering sponsorship to some of them" (n.p.). The piece subsequently highlights the generous efforts of the veteran assisting the Vietnamese refugees in their relocation. This news feature is but one example of the ways in which the Vietnamese rescue narrative, closely related to narratives of U.S. exceptionalism, was articulated in local Arkansan media. In particular, this narrative helped to make U.S. military losses in Southeast Asia more politically palatable in their aftermath. It also reinforced discourses of U.S. exceptionalism by emphasizing the U.S. military as a positive influence abroad, a logic also present in U.S. actors' presentations of the Compact migration provision as a benevolent opportunity for the Marshall Islands to pursue "development through emigration," as discussed in chapter 2.

While a fairly small percentage of Vietnamese and Indochinese refugees ultimately resettled in Arkansas, their presence in the state in the mid- to late 1970s sparked the emergence of key discourses on imperial migration in Arkansas media, such as the rescue narrative described above. Vietnamese and other Indochinese refugees are, thus, part of the state's history of imperial migration, as the U.S. military was deeply entrenched, both politically and military, in the "sending" countries of Laos, Cambodia, Thailand, and Vietnam

(Guerrero 2017). These groups can therefore be considered imperial migrants, as their forced departure from their homelands, as well as their resettlement in the United States, were shaped by U.S. military imperialism in Southeast Asia.

In the decades following the Vietnamese and Indochinese arrival to Arkansas, two additional groups of migrants arrived at Fort Chaffee: Haitian and Cuban refugees. Both groups of refugees or asylum-seekers fled their island homes by the thousands, many heading for Florida to make claims for protection by the U.S. government (Fernández 2007). In 1980, an estimated hundred and twenty-five thousand Cuban refugees came to the United States during the Mariel boatlift. Over the course of six months, 19,048 Cuban refugees passed through Fort Chaffee, once again bringing the human effects of U.S. Cold War policies abroad to Arkansas, this time from the Caribbean, another archipelagic region where the United States had long wielded colonial and imperial power.

Cubans entering the United States during this period faced intense hostility and scrutiny from U.S. media. In contrast to media coverage of previous waves of Cuban émigrés, often framed as "anti-communist freedom-seekers" (Lipman 2014, 71), the Cuban *Marielitos* were demonized in the U.S. press as racialized criminals and homosexuals and, thus, threats to the nation (Loyd et al. 2016). Local media coverage of the refugees detained at Fort Chaffee at the time revealed a tense and conflicting set of messages about these imperial migrants, whose arrival to and detention in the United States raised questions about U.S. geopolitical involvement abroad in the Caribbean. A *New York Times* article titled "Pickets add to problems for refugees in Arkansas," for example, described the situation at Fort Chaffee after the first Cuban refugees arrived in 1980, conveying the tense and combative energy pervading the surrounding areas: "By tomorrow there will likely be 5,000 in the temporary encampment of freedom seekers, political prisoners, *and almost certainly, criminals.* By Wednesday the settlement at this Army post outside the town of Fort Smith is to have grown to 10,000 people; and by the following Sunday, to 20,000" (Stevens 1980, emphasis added). The article also called up Fort Chaffee's history of refugee and migrant detention, recalling the temporary holding of about fifty thousand Vietnamese refugees in 1975. As of 1980, Stevens noted, about two thousand six hundred Vietnamese people were still in Arkansas, constituting an ongoing reminder of the war and the refugee flows it generated. 'What are they going to do now—relocate us Americans?' Sign carried by a young unemployed mother from Fort Smith, who was protesting the detention of the Cubans near their town. 'I have compassion for the Cubans,' she said. 'I feel for them. But there's children here who need food, and men and women needing jobs, and Arkansas doesn't have them.' While she spoke, a cry of 'Send 'em home!' came from a passing car" (Stevens 1980). As this excerpt indicates, in the 1980s, resentment toward Cuban arrivals started to build in communities surrounding the base, sometimes articulated through concerns that refugees (in this case, Cubans) would resettle locally and take much-needed jobs (Maher 2016). Again, in this context, racialized foreign Others were framed as drains on a struggling local economy while, nationally, fearmongering reverberated over the *Marielitos'* arrival and their perceived criminality, often explicitly articulated as/through anti-Blackness.

Such reverberations would find an echo a decade later, when Haitians arrived at Fort Chaffee in the 1990s. Their presence again cemented Fort Chaffee, and Arkansas, as destinations of empire. As in earlier decades, Haitians' arrival was connected to U.S. military actions abroad. In 1990 and 1991, the Bush administration came under scrutiny for its treatment of Haitian asylum-seekers fleeing the dictatorial regime in Haiti of "Papa Doc" Duvalier and the Tonton Macoutes (Crossette 1991). In 1994, then-President Clinton, who lost his bid for governor of Arkansas over the so-called rioting of Cubans at Fort Chaffee, threatened Haiti with U.S. invasion, before pushing for UN sanctions and organizing a multinational invasion that forced the hand of the Haitian government. In these ways, Haitian exodus from the Caribbean was directly, if not exclusively, linked to U.S. military, economic, and political influence exerted on Haiti and other Caribbean nations (Renda 2001).

Haitians' arrival to Arkansas would also again inflame controversy, both locally and nationally, as Haitians became the target of local white anger, xenophobia, and anti-Black racism (Loyd et al. 2016; Paik 2016). In Arkansas, local resistance to Haitians' presence at Fort Chaffee appeared in news coverage as well as in constituent letters to the state's political leadership. At the Special Collections archive at the University of Arkansas, for example, the papers of Arkansas Senator Dale Bumpers contain letters such as this one from a Jonesboro, Arkansas man: "First, Please do not permit any more Haitian immigrants to land in this country, to stay in this country, to migrate to this country. Secondly, if at all possible—bring as many G.I.s home from Korea as is politically feasible. I was stationed there ('65–'66) for (397) days. We accomplished nothing but giving that country our money, our time, our energy. I understand we are 33,000 Americans strong there. We need to cut that [number] drastically" (Special Collections, University of Arkansas, 1991). This man's letter gestures to a connection, if a tenuous one, between the arrival of Haitians and the investments of U.S. military and troops abroad—a Haitian presence *here* precipitates concern for an American presence *there*. While he draws no direct link between the costs of U.S. military engagements abroad and the (implied) costs of hosting Haitian immigrants in the U.S. mainland, the author reveals both issues to be of importance to him by mentioning them together in his letter. Furthermore, his failure to connect the dots—the deployment of U.S. troops abroad and the arrival of Haitian refugees to the U.S.—constitutes a gap in knowledge about the interrelated workings of U.S. military empire, one that obscures the central role that U.S. military interventions abroad play in *creating* migrant and refugee streams to the United States.

Another more strongly worded appeal was sent to Senator Bumpers at his Washington, D.C., office from a constituent in Newport, Arkansas. Titled "Re: Haitians," it is steeped in xenophobic racism and white supremacy: "Dear Senator Bumpers, Is our goal for the United States to become a teeming mass of people like Pakistan? How stupid can we get? We do not want a single Haitian, shoot them if you have to but don't let them in. Sincerely, Joe Harris" (Special Collections, University of Arkansas, 1991). In this letter, the author operationalizes Orientalist notions of overpopulation elsewhere (the "teeming masses in Pakistan"), leveraging that logic in the service of nativist, anti-immigrant resistance to the arrival of Haitians. His letter reveals how new arrivals to the state were made sense of through larger discourses about the United States in relation to "elsewhere" and even speaks to the U.S. potential to remove or detain foreign entrants militarily, if necessary. His imperative to "shoot them if you have to" uncannily echoes the central role the U.S. military had played in migrant and refugee management in the decades since Vietnam War.

"You Lost Them at Imperial": Imperial Sense-Making and COFA Status

Only a decade after the Vietnamese arrival to the state, in the mid-1980s, Marshall Islanders began arriving to Springdale, Arkansas, in significant numbers. Yet despite their settlement there, by the 2010s even the public actors and local residents most familiar with the Marshallese community were still largely in the dark about the *imperial* nature of the U.S.-RMI relationship, unaware that the Marshall Islands had long been a U.S. colony and persisted in an arguably neocolonial legal relationship (FAS) with the United States. In this section, I examine what I call "imperial sense-making," moments when Northwest Arkansans attempted to make sense of a Marshallese presence in their area and of larger connections to U.S. military imperialism in the Pacific. Their explanations reveal the persistence of key narratives concerning the U.S. role in the world, narratives that occlude the U.S. global role as an imperial power.

Instead of seeing both past and present migrant streams into Arkansas as *produced* by U.S. imperialism, Arkansans I interviewed continued to return to the U.S. exceptionalist "rescue narrative" (Lê Espiritu 2006) that positions the United States as a provider for refugees and migrants. More specifically, long-term (mainly white) Arkansans commonly understood Marshall Islanders' visa-free migration provision in one of two ways: first, as *reparations* for nuclear testing (in other words, as retroactive compensation for the testing's effects), or second, as *refugees*, whom the United States relocated, resettled, or offered sanctuary. Both explanations upheld logics of U.S. exceptionalism, framing the United States as a democratic, just, and humanitarian country (logics that first appear for us in chapter 2, in Micronesia's political-status negotiations). Neither of these two explanations, however, fully grasped the colonial and imperial dimensions of U.S. global power, both past and present, over the RMI and other Pacific Islands. More simply, Springdale residents and other Arkansas generally failed to see Marshallese COFA migrants as *imperial migrants* or *imperial citizens* because they could not see the United States as an empire. While it is perhaps unsurprising that Arkansans *didn't* make this connection—typical liberal rhetoric frames the United States as an immigrant haven or refugee-receiving country, not an empire, and is pervasive across the continental United States—the fact that they didn't, and the *ways* in which they didn't, reveals the endurance of imperial geographic ideas that paradoxically obscure the United States' role as an empire. These discourses matter because they show how U.S. Americans often explain—or miss—the connections between empire, migration, and geography, connections that nonetheless shape place, mobility, and citizenship in profound and far-reaching ways.

The sense-making moments I analyze here include long-term Arkansans' speculations on COFA migrants' legal status, (mis)understandings about the United States' political relationship with the RMI, and ways of narrating the historical U.S. military presence in the RMI, including nuclear testing. My aim in conducting these interviews was not to seek an "accurate" description of facts, nor to shame interviewees for their "incorrect" responses, but, rather, to identify the frameworks and discourses Arkansans used to understand Marshallese migration and COFA status. In identifying these discourses, I theorize the political work that they do for empire—namely, to perpetuate it by occluding it.

For many interviewees, a Marshallese presence in Arkansas had heightened their knowledge of the U.S. nuclear testing in the islands, forging a geographical imaginary of the Marshall Islands as a place negatively affected by past U.S. military actions but not necessarily as one with a history of U.S. colonialism.

One public official mentioned that she "didn't know much" about the Marshall Islands before the Marshallese began arriving in Springdale, other than that "[it] was a testing area" (interview, Springdale, June 2014). Another Springdale public official said that Marshallese resettlement enabled her to connect the U.S. nuclear testing to the Marshall Islands: "Before I started in this position, I was pretty clueless of the Marshall Islands itself. I remember stories of the atomic testing, but I guess I just didn't ever really connect the two as being the same" (interview, Springdale, May 2014). Her realization that nuclear testing was carried out in the *particular* site of the Marshall Islands was only made possible through her encounter with Marshall Islanders in her hometown, making that "remote" geographic site familiar through Marshallese migrants' proximity.

Long-term residents who worked as public officials or social service providers, and whose work put them in contact with Marshall Islanders, were especially likely to be familiar with the Compact. Often, these interviewees linked the Compact's existence to U.S. nuclear testing in the Marshall Islands (much as World War II veterans did). One Springdale public official, for example, explained the Compact's genesis by saying, "Well, it was a . . . treaty may not be the right word, but it was a diplomatic solution that was reached by the two governments, based upon our nuclear [testing]" (interview, Springdale, 2014). For him, the Compact was an agreement born out of U.S. nuclear testing in the Marshall Islands, though his statement left unclear whether he interpreted its provisions as an exchange for testing or as reparations conveyed retroactively.

Another interviewee, Sue, a health care provider in Springdale, spoke to the Compact's longer history as she tried to make sense of Marshall Islanders' limited health benefits: "Well, fifteen years ago, many of the Marshallese had insurance cards. It was the Bikini Atoll card, and that went away with the provisions in the Compact. And I would think, because we bombed their islands repeatedly, with such strong bombs, that there really wouldn't be an expiration clause to that. Especially when you know how many times greater those bombs were than in Hiroshima." As these excerpts show, many Arkansans I met were intimately familiar with the nuclear testing and its lingering effects. Yet they generally did not make the connection between U.S. nuclear testing and U.S. colonial power in the Pacific; virtually no one referenced that the United States was able to conduct testing there precisely because the Marshall Islands was a U.S. colony at the time.

Instead, when respondents brought up nuclear testing came up in the context of Marshallese migration, as they often did, they generally connected the two phenomena using either a *refugee* logic or a *reparations* logic. The *reparations* logic, which assumes that visa-free migration was a form of reparations given to Marshall Islanders by the U.S. government, was articulated frequently by interviewees. As one state-level politician put it: "It's my understanding that it's very easy, or much easier, anyway, for the Marshallese to come and go to the U.S. because of arrangements we have with them. It's also my understanding that we did it as a way to make up for the fact that we bombed their islands like crazy back in the '40s and '50s" (interview, Little Rock, Ark., June 2014). A public health worker I interviewed shared a similar perception. When I asked her, "Why do you think that the Compact included the migration clause?" she responded, "Our way to make up for what we did, is what I think. Retribution." This speaker's choice of wording here, while likely a slip—she may have meant to say "restitution"—was unintentionally poignant: "retribution" has a double meaning, interpretable both as reward and punishment, "especially in the hereafter." Indeed, COFA status, with its attendant restrictions (see chapter 5), as well as the military costs yoked to it through the Compact's other provisions (see chapter 2), could easily be interpreted as both a punishment and a reward for the Marshall Islands' ongoing ties to U.S. empire.

The refugee logic also appeared in Arkansans' assumptions that the U.S. federal government had relocated Marshall Islanders to Springdale. One elderly World War II veteran I interviewed mused, "I have no idea *why the government brought them here*" (interview, Springdale, 2014, emphasis added), and another interviewee, an academic and policy expert, wondered aloud: "Am I correct? The Marshallese, because of their *relocation,* have insurance?" (interview, Little Rock, Ark., 2014, emphasis added). Their comments conveyed a perception that the United States had relocated Marshall Islanders to the United States, accepting them as refugees and providing benefits and visa-free residency as part of that offer. While this perception was common among interviewees, they virtually never drew a connection between Marshall Islanders and previous refugee groups in Arkansas, though the history of those refugee arrivals, documented earlier in the chapter, was widely known. That long-term residents did *not* connect these dots, despite readily available histories of mass immigrant or refugee arrival prompted by U.S. militarism, speaks again to the occlusion of U.S. empire.

While these two narratives used to make sense of Marshall Islanders' visa-free migration provision—Marshall Islanders as recipients of U.S. reparations and Marshall Islanders as refugees taken in by the United States—may appear very different, they rest upon a similar premise: both narratives frame the United States as a uniquely democratic, just, and benevolent nation, upholding notions of U.S. exceptionalism. Per the reparations logic, the United States has made good for its past transgressions (the nuclear testing), while in the refugee logic, the United States provides shelter and a new life for struggling denizens of other parts of the globe. The second logic in particular obscures the United States' role as an *imperial* power that created many of the conditions necessitating Marshallese emigration in the first place, and whose provision of visa-free migration served to uphold and safeguard U.S. military and imperial power in the Pacific for the foreseeable future. The internal contradictions of U.S. exceptionalism are on full display here, perhaps best summarized by former president Bill Clinton, that most famous of Arkansans, who once declared proudly, "There's nothing wrong with America that what's right with America can't fix."

When I discussed this paradox with a University of Arkansas law professor familiar with Marshallese COFA status, she outlined the ironies of this imperial migration phenomenon and its unintelligibility to mainland U.S. residents.

> "The Compact is like a gentleman's agreement," she says. "Well, what I mean by gentleman's agreement is this: we were like: 'We're sorry we bombed your islands.' But then, we end up getting way more out of it than they do. And they don't want to ask for anything, don't want to demand more; I don't know why." I offer that maybe COFA status feels too precarious for those holding it: perhaps Marshall Islanders are afraid of jeopardizing that "special status," or find it hard to ask for more when many other immigrant groups have fewer rights. That might be the case, she agrees. "That's one of the interesting things about this. I mean, I was recently at a conference in Puerto Rico, and I realized—we're an imperial country! We just don't think of ourselves that way. For example, when people talk about traveling on vacation to Puerto Rico, they'll say, 'It's such a nice country, it's a foreign country!' Well, no, it's not." We both laugh. She continues: "I think if you ask local residents something like that, they'll probably know about the history of the nuclear testing and WWII, and then say how nice it is what we're doing for them now. It's like, you lost them at imperial."

I include this conversation because it summarizes many of the contradictions often conveyed in imperial sense-making. As this section shows, such contradictions arise when local residents are presented with clear evidence of U.S. empire—namely, the presence of imperial migrants from the Marshall Islands—and yet, due to the occlusion of the U.S. imperial role in discourses around migration and the U.S. presence abroad, are unable to see that presence as evidence of empire. Instead, Marshall Islanders' presence in Arkansas—like Vietnamese refugees' presence before them—gets reworked into narratives that bulwark notions of U.S. exceptionalism.

Conclusion

In the 1970s and 1980s, as in the 1940s and 1950s, Arkansas witnessed the arrival of various migrant or refugee "beneficiaries" of U.S. foreign policy, imperial migrants whose presence in the state made the human effects of U.S. militarism abroad visible at home, through war. That link persisted even if it was not always, or often, articulated by long-term residents. These migrants' arrival to Arkansas brought national media discourses to the state, generating narratives that grappled with complex and tense political dynamics: namely, how to represent refugees that U.S. militarism had *produced* while representing the United States as benevolent in *providing* for these refugees through resettlement. These media discourses were only able to imperfectly uphold notions of U.S. exceptionalism, as they also revealed its instability. As the chapter's final section shows, such discourses persist to the present, framing the United States as a benevolent provider or honorable granter of reparations to the Marshallese, even while the human proof of U.S. militarism's most pernicious effects are present.

Finally, the migration or relocation of outsiders to Arkansas during wartime reveals how central the state has been in the wartime military management of foreign populations since World War II. Repeated arrivals of refugees, immigrants, internees, and POWs—arrivals which collectively number in the hundreds of thousands—counter notions of Arkansas as "remote" within the United States or separate from the geographies of U.S. empire. Studying this history reveals that Arkansas has been central to the military management of wartime outsiders and, thus, pivotal in the workings of U.S. empire. Such dynamics, however, are only visible through a historical analysis of U.S. militarism and its effects on human mobility both *into* and *out of* the state, both during and outside formal war. These dynamics reveal Arkansas's long history as a destination of empire.

CHAPTER 4

"Of All Places!"

*Springdale, Arkansas,
as a New Destination of Empire*

In the decades following the Compact's initial implementation, Marshall Islanders left in droves, their migration carving out new pathways and sites in the Marshallese diaspora. I now turn to a key site in this diaspora, Springdale, Arkansas, following Marshallese migration patterns from the Pacific to Northwest Arkansas. Marshall Islanders began arriving to Springdale in small numbers after the Compact's 1986 passage, and in recent years, the town's Marshallese population has swelled to nearly twelve thousand, a number that includes many second- and third-generation Marshallese Americans. Springdale, Arkansas, is now home to the single largest population of Marshallese living outside the Marshall Islands, having surpassed even Hawai'i's Marshallese population in size,[1] despite Hawai'i's geographic proximity to the Marshall Islands, earning the region the nickname the Ozark Atolls. Accompanying this community's growth are the establishment of several Marshallese-led organizations and a Marshallese Consulate, established in 2008, and over thirty Marshallese churches.

Alongside the Marshallese are Springdale's Latinx residents, primarily of Mexican and Central American descent, a population that also began to arrive in significant numbers in the 1980s. Marshall Islanders and Latinxs in Springdale increasingly share space in public schools; residential neighborhoods; worksites such as Tyson and George's plants, health care settings, and service jobs (including at Walmart stores); and, an expanding institutional web of immigrant-serving nonprofit organizations. Together, Marshallese and Latinx arrivals to Springdale since the 1980s—as well as the arrival of new (primarily white) residents from other regions—have boosted the city's population to nearly eight-five thousand as of the 2020 census, making it the fourth-largest city in Arkansas.

While Marshallese migration to the United States has long roots (Hezel 2013), Marshallese and Micronesian migration to the U.S. Midwest and South is a more recent phenomenon, having only materialized in sizable and proportionally significant communities within the past few decades. Nevertheless, that population shift has been meteoric. Collective Marshallese community knowledge locates the inception of Springdale's Marshallese population with the arrival of a Marshallese man, John Moody, who settled there as early as the late 1970s (before the Compact's passage) after attending college in Oklahoma. While it may be rare for immigrant communities to trace their arrival to one individual or family, word travels quickly and efficiently in the Marshallese diaspora: I was told this story by Micronesians and Marshall Islanders in Hawai'i, Guåhan, and Saipan in 2012 and 2013, before conducting fieldwork in Arkansas. That this story persists as a dominant narrative of Marshallese resettlement to Arkansas is testament to the close connections between Marshallese families in Springdale and beyond. Such stories circulate throughout the diaspora, carried by people on the move between sites or with extended family spread among different resettlement areas. These histories, and other social and economic factors discussed in this chapter, have made Springdale, "of all places," a logical and desirable destination for many Marshall Islanders since the mid-1980s.

If the first Marshallese migrants to the U.S. South and Midwest came for educational opportunities—as was the case for many other COFA migrant destinations previously (Hezel 2013)—the fast growth of Springdale's Marshallese population came as a result of the town's economic conditions, especially its (low-wage) employment opportunities and relatively low cost of living, as interviews with Marshallese community leaders and residents indicated. Those familiar with Northwest Arkansas's economic landscape will know it as a region shaped in recent decades by the poultry industry. Springdale is the headquarters of Tyson Foods, the world's largest meat producer, and has been officially dubbed "the Poultry capital of the world" (Ark. Senate Bill No. 949, 2013). As the world's largest producer of poultry, beef, and pork, Tyson has factories and farms throughout Northwest Arkansas and the rest of the U.S. Midwest and South (Leonard 2014). As the leading employer in Springdale and in many surrounding towns, Tyson employs an enormous number of area residents—particularly immigrants—and up to a hundred thousand Arkansans statewide) (Striffler 2009; Stuesse 2016). Indeed, many of Springdale's Marshallese residents initially came to work in Tyson plants, and newer arrivals often also seek these types of jobs. While many Marshallese residents of Spring-

FIGURE 11. *Local Industries* (mural study, Springdale, Arkansas Post Office), ca. 1940, oil on canvas, Smithsonian American Art Museum. Painting by Natalie Smith Henry. Courtesy of Smithsonian American Art Museum, 1962.8.54.

dale now hold white-collar positions, a large proportion of the Marshallese population initially filled manual labor posts, with some Tyson factories employing enough Marshallese workers to fill an entire work shift.

The concentration of immigrant employment in poultry in Northwest Arkansas mirrors regional and national trends of poultry farming and the "rural industrialization strategy" of many corporations (Kandel and Parrado 2021). As sociologist Steve Striffler (2007) writes: "In short, poultry did for the South what meatpacking has done for the Midwest. It not only brought foreign workers... into the heartland but it also made permanent settlement in the United States possible, attractive, and in some cases almost unavoidable for a growing number of migrants" (677). Increasingly, meat- and poultry-processing plants draw immigrant workers to the region, heavily influencing the reracialization of small towns and midsized cities such as Springdale (McConnell and Miraftab 2009). The presence of Tyson and other poultry companies as local employers is, thus, a key factor in explaining recent migration to Northwest Arkansas. However, other dynamics of migration to the area—such as the racial histories that produce shifting racial meanings of space and place—are just as important in understanding this site and its residents. In this chapter, I aim to flesh out some of those dynamics to explore their implications for Springdale and its residents.

To do so, this chapter brings together several complex histories to examine how Springdale, Arkansas, became a new immigrant destination (NID) for Marshall Islanders and, by extension, a new destination of empire (NDE). It takes as one of its key frameworks the notion of NIDs, defined most broadly as "places with little previous experience receiving immigrants" (Marrow 2013,

107). While NID scholarship is wide-ranging, addressing issues of immigrant integration and incorporation (Chambers and Williamson 2017; Winders 2012), economic and labor dynamics (Ribas 2016), shifting social and cultural identities, and sites of encounter (Ehrkamp and Nagel 2012), this chapter focuses primarily on NID racial histories and geographies, showing how longstanding, place-specific discourses about race in Springdale create the racialized conditions into which Marshallese immigrants arrive. At the same time, it situates Springdale within larger racialized processes of territorial dispossession, racial cleansing, and immigrant arrivals, all processes by which racial geographies are historically and presently constructed. Just as chapter 3 cast light on the invisibilized histories of empire across Arkansas, in other words, this chapter aims to cast light on invisibilized histories of white supremacy in Northwest Arkansas.

While the city of Springdale and its population have experienced these phenomena in particular ways, such phenomena are by no means unique to Springdale. Rather, they have occurred and continue to play out—albeit in varied ways—across the United States: settler-colonial expansion removed Indigenous populations from almost every corner of the contemporary United States through genocide, forced relocation, and containment (Wolfe 2006), and Black populations, whose enslaved and stolen labor built cities and towns across the United States, have also been forcibly removed, resettled, surveilled, and contained (Gilmore 2007; McKittrick and Woods 2007). These racialized spatial processes, geographies of what Cedric Robinson (1983) termed "racial capitalism," are foundational to U.S. empire. Springdale, of all places, is thus a site through which we can tell a key story about U.S. empire and human im/mobility under racial capitalism, because it was forged historically through the intersection of these power structures *and* because those power structures still shape racial and classed dynamics between Springdale residents today. The history of Springdale's racial geographies forms a necessary precursor to understanding it as a new destination of empire, revealing key details about the town's racial present and how it came to be.

To develop these ideas, I first explore Springdale's changing racial makeup in the context of the Northwest Arkansas region and its political economy. This context is key to situating Springdale's racial identity *regionally*, since Northwest Arkansas residents' perceptions of Springdale, both as an "immigrant town" and as a "racist town," exist in relation to other towns and cities in the region. This relationality also shows how Arkansas—and at a larger scale, the U.S. South—is often framed within larger geographical imaginaries as both racist and remote, through an assumed or explicit contrast with "everywhere else" in the United States (Winders 2005). Defining or depicting places as racist and remote or "backward," or conversely, nonracist and progressive, informs understandings of racialized life, both from within and outside sites such as Springdale. As such, places such as Springdale—and processes of white supremacy—are often understood as *exceptional* within, rather than exemplary of, the United States. It is this logic, I argue, that gives rise to non-Arkansans' incredulous reading of Arkansas, "of all places," as an unlikely destination for immigrants from the Marshall Islands, who themselves are read as exceptional in their new hometown. Yet Northwest Arkansas, in its formation and *trans*formation through racial capitalism, is neither exceptional within nor external to broader processes of empire playing out simultaneously at larger geographic scales.

Next, I delineate three historical processes by which Springdale's racial geography was (re)made before the arrival of Marshallese and Latinx immigrants: Indigenous displacement and dispossession, white settlement, and Black exclusion. These racial histories and the geographies they sedimented are foundational to understanding the racialization of Marshallese residents in Springdale and contemporary racial geographies of Northwest Arkansas. Drawing on U.S. ethnic studies scholarship on comparative racialization (Cacho 2012; Cheng 2013), I argue that the *particular* dimensions of Marshall Islanders' racialization in Springdale emerge from both *local* understandings about racism and racial identity in which different racial groups are constructed against one another and *larger* structures of racial capitalism, imperialism, globalization, and militarism. Springdale, therefore, serves as a site where both local and larger dynamics of racialization—both material and discursive or ideological—can be examined as part and parcel of U.S. empire.

Third, I outline Springdale's more recent transformation into an "immigrant town," most significantly through the arrival of Latinx immigrants from Mexico and Central America, who now make up over a third of Springdale's population, and, in smaller numbers, through Marshall Islanders' resettlement in Springdale. Here, I show how local white reception and racialization of different immigrant groups draws on longer and broader histories of racism and exclusion, deepening racialized understandings of "legal" vs. "illegal" immigrants and their respective places in Springdale. Finally, I close with two vignettes from Springdale and neighboring Fayetteville, involving the Rodeo of the Ozarks and a Marshallese softball game, to show how these events, juxtaposed, reveal contrasting place-based notions of identity and belonging in America.

Ultimately, as I argue in this chapter, *where* in the diaspora immigrants resettle matters for their experiences of race and place: immigrants to the United States come into particular regional economies, politics, and histories of white supremacy. These particular geographies inform immigrants' social location in their new destination, how they are categorized in racial terms, and what kind of social, economic, and political purchase they have in their new homes. As migrants move from former or current colonies to new sites in the U.S. mainland, they establish what I call new destinations of empire. In these sites, race matters profoundly. *How* it matters is complicated and place specific, shaped by intersections of race, class, and legal status (among other things), and always shifting yet ever present. This chapter offers an analysis of processes of racialized place-making in one site of empire, Springdale while listening for how such racialization reverberates at larger scales of empire.

Throughout this chapter, I argue that the state, capital, and white residents and settlers made the region through the racialized control of human mobility. Racialized control of mobility occurs through five processes examined here and elsewhere in the book: *active removal and relocation*, as experienced by both Indigenous peoples like the Caddo, Quapaw, and Osage(and the Indigenous Bikinians of the Marshall Islands, examined in chapter 2)[2]; *displacement* through nuclear testing, militarization, and environmental devastation; *containment and internment*, for example, Japanese internment (which I examine in chapter 3) and Native reservations (which only appear in this chapter as a looming specter to the West); *spatial exclusion*, as experienced by Black domestic workers in sundown towns such as Springdale; and finally, *labor migration* of working-class immigrant workers from elsewhere in U.S. empire, such as Marshallese, Mexican, and Central American immigrants, many solicited directly by employers like Tyson and drawn into U.S. empire in slightly different, but no less meaningful, ways.

A study of racialized mobility also accounts for the processes that produce and enable (white) settler mobility and capital accumulation. Whiteness and capital are moved into regions in diverse ways: state and nonstate actors, for example, solicit white people to the area not only as *workers* but also as *settlers* and residents, draw in Black workers for their labor power while preventing them from residing locally, and lure businesses from beyond the region with promises of "lily-white" workers and "all-American stock" (Perkins 2014). Each of these processes of racialized mobility and immobility generates movement across multiple geographic scales: across towns, regions, national borders, and empires. Attention to these flows and their stoppages shows how new destinations of empire are constituted, shedding light on both place-particular and broader processes of empire.

Springdale in Geographical Imaginaries of Racism: White Town, Immigrant Town, Racist Town?

In Arkansas and beyond, discourses about whether, or why, Springdale is a desirable immigrant destination—or even a *likely* one ("Springdale, of all places!")—tend to turn on two concepts, each with its own set of geographical imaginaries. The first concept centers on Springdale (and Arkansas) as ostensibly "racist" places, and the second centers on understandings of Springdale (and Arkansas) as "remote" and provincial places. This chapter section takes on both concepts—racism and remoteness—and their imagined geographies in tandem to show how both operate in long-term, primarily white Arkansans' sense-making of Springdale as an NID.

Historical geographies of Northwest Arkansas have long painted the region as remote, difficult to access, and isolated from the rest of the state. Geographer Patrick Hagge (2009) has analyzed how such accounts have typically attributed the region's purported isolation and remoteness to the region's *physical* geography: first, the presence of the Ozark and Ouachita mountains as "natural barriers" to outward expansion; second, the state's southeastward-flowing rivers, which made westward movement difficult for commerce and white settlement during the nineteenth and early twentieth centuries; and third—this last factor beginning to unveil the political and social nature of "physical" geographic barriers—that "the Indian Territory (now Oklahoma) to the west served as a political roadblock to westward expansion or commercial growth" (4). As Hagge writes, Northwest Arkansas's emergence as a thriving hub of commerce was seen as improbable at best:

> Faced with such fundamental barriers to growth, *any prognosticator in the mid-twentieth century would write off northwest Arkansas as rural and remote.* Surely northwest Arkansas, a region in the foothills of the Ozark Mountains, would remain the land of yeoman farmers, unconnected to the commercial markets in port cities along the Mississippi River, disassociated from its own centrally located state capital, Little Rock. *The northwest would continue as a marginal land, overlooked and isolated among the American Mid-South.* And yet, such predictions would have been erroneous. (4, emphasis added).

This text gestures to a long history of Northwest Arkansas being perceived as inaccessible or undesirable due to its provinciality and remoteness. Yet the re-

FIGURE 12. Northwest Arkansas, which includes four of the state's ten largest cities. Map by the Syracuse University Cartographic Laboratory.

gion's explosive economic and population growth in recent years tells a different story. For many Arkansas residents and visitors, the Northwest Arkansas region now serves as a hub of cultural production, an economic engine for the state, and a dense population center that is markedly different from the rest of the state. Tourist websites tout Northwest Arkansas as a top tourist destination and "one of the fastest growing and most dynamic regions in America" (Explore Northwest Arkansas [2015]). As I discuss in this section, the dynamics between the region's four main cities—Bentonville, Rogers, Springdale, and Fayetteville—and their dramatically varied economic and demographic landscapes shape the region's broader context as a destination for new arrivals.

While in Arkansas in 2014, I made frequent drives to the Northwest Arkansas Regional Airport, located curiously and inconspicuously in the middle of the countryside, several miles from any major town. During these drives, I reflected on the landscape and speculated about the experiences of other new arrivals driving these roads away from the airport, perhaps finding themselves in Arkansas for the first time. In my fieldnotes, I wrote: "On the drive between the airport and I-49, the landscape is filled with rural pastures and grazing livestock, small abandoned and decrepit houses, and curving fences running parallel to the winding road. Once I-49 appears, the view becomes littered with hotels and signs for more hotels. I wonder, Is everyone here a visitor?" At the time, this observation—that Northwest Arkansas would have so many visitors from outside, and thus, a need for so many hotels—struck me as ironic, since Springdale originally seemed to me like a place where "old-timers" were the vast majority. This was no doubt a naive outsider's perception; I soon realized that due to the influence of Walmart's headquarters in Bentonville, people traveled to the region in droves for business purposes (Moreton 2006). The tension between the two dynamics I was witnessing—the (perceived) historical insularity of small towns *in* Northwest Arkansas and the region's booming population growth from people's movement *into* Northwest Arkansas—has shaped this part of Arkansas over the past forty years in important ways.

Particularly noteworthy in this tension are the drastic historical differences between how each city's population has been established. Just to the south of Springdale is Fayetteville, a city of about ninety-five thousand that houses the University of Arkansas and draws students and faculty from across Arkansas, the surrounding states, and beyond. Rogers, a slightly smaller city of seventy thousand, is similar to Springdale in its economic and demographic makeup and, as a result, is often held up for comparison. Like Springdale, Rogers has seen massive growth in its immigrant populations in recent decades, though predominantly Latinx, with few Marshallese residents until very recently (U.S. Census Bureau 2020). Finally, furthest to the north, and about a 35-minute drive north from Fayetteville, is Bentonville. Half a century ago, Bentonville was barely a dot on the map, as interviews with long-time residents revealed. Now, however, the city is a regional center for wealth as the headquarters of Walmart, home to the Walton family, and, more recently, home to the elite representatives of Walmart's corporate partners, such as Procter & Gamble.

Across the Northwest Arkansas region, two distinct but interrelated processes of population growth and economic expansion have played out over the past forty years: as racialized working-class immigrant workers arrived in large numbers, transforming the towns of Springdale and Rogers, white retirees and other economically mobile, white-collar students and workers (as well as capital) flowed into Fayetteville, a university town, and Bentonville, a "twenty-first century company town" (Farmer 2021) blanketed by the looming presence of Walmart and the Walton Family Foundation. As I explore later in this chapter, both the warmly welcomed arrival of white workers and capital and the conditional inclusion of racialized workers are place-making phenomena with long histories in this region. In Springdale, these processes created a heavy reliance on immigrant labor (and *appeal* to new immigrant residents), engendering a massive demographic transition and, as a result, shifting and sometimes conflicting notions of Springdale as a "white town," "immigrant town," and "racist town." As such, both processes have foundationally shaped the region's economic growth and its racial and class geographies.

Just as flows of labor and capital into and within Northwest Arkansas have produced materially uneven geographies of class and race there, discourses around these intraregional differences often frame the four cities as diametrically opposed, in ways that belie their coproduction. In local narratives, Springdale finds a foil in each of the surrounding towns and cities. In informal conversations and interviews where I asked about racial dynamics in the region, for example, long-term residents frequently brought up Springdale's "small townness," comparing it to the university city of Fayetteville or the up-and-coming corporate hub of Bentonville. One interviewee originally from Springdale discussed it in this way:

> EME: I've noticed that people often talk about Springdale as an immigrant town now.
> Julie: Yes, definitely.
> EME: But in a way, Fayetteville has a lot more people from outside of Arkansas. Tell me a little bit about the comparison that people [draw between the two towns].
> Julie: I think there has always been a stigma—like, Springdale has been the farming hub, I think. I don't know that it was ever necessarily smaller than Rogers, and Bentonville was just sort of a non-entity until the Walmart thing. But I think there's always been an inferiority complex for Springdale people that has to do with the comparison to Fayetteville. That Fayetteville's more "up-town," that's where the smart people are, that's where the university is, that kind of thing. (interview, Springdale, May 2014)

Like this interviewee, many others drew comparisons between Springdale and surrounding towns like Fayetteville and Bentonville, cities mobilized in conversation to highlight Springdale's provinciality. At times, I solicited these comparisons (e.g., asking "How would you describe Springdale compared to other towns in the area?"), but just as frequently, people made these juxtapositions on their own.

For long-term residents, Springdale's small size and racial homogeneity—that is, until the immigration boom starting in the 1980s—also helped explain its historic stereotype as a "racist town." As one white Springdale city official reflected, "You have to understand, we probably have to go back thirty years to say that this region—this entire part of the state—was very, very white. Anything outside the city of Fayetteville, and that was because there was a university there."

For some interviewees, Springdale's racism was *due* to the historic lack of "minorities" or racialized populations, while for others, the absence of racial diversity until the 1980s was counterevidence to claims that the town was racist (i.e., there were no people present to be racist *toward*). As one interviewee described it, "It's very difficult to say that, you know, these cities in Northwest Arkansas had a racial problem—there weren't any minorities to have any feelings of animosity about" (interview, Springdale, June 2014). Another white interviewee arrived at the topic of race in Springdale after a long reflection on outsider stereotypes about Arkansas. Ruminating on the lack of racial difference in the area when she was growing up, she concluded, "Mostly there was no talk about [race], because there was no *need* to talk about it" (interview, Springdale, May 2014). These comments convey a shared perception among long-term white residents that overt racism, or "racial problems," could occur only when white people in the town were confronted by residents of color, who could then ostensibly be targets of racism. Such perceptions, of course, disregard or diminish the effects of larger discourses about race, racism, and racial difference, discourses that circulate even in sites that lack significant racial diversity.

Arkansas historian Guy Lancaster countered this logic that racism required the physical presence of a population targeted by it.[3]

> If that were true—"Oh, we just weren't exposed to those people, then once they came in, how were we supposed to react?"—then you'd have racist French in World War I France, rather than Black GIs realizing, "I can walk down the street to Paris and hang out with a French woman and no one's going to lynch me." . . . That's a fallacious argument. It's not just that they weren't familiar or that Black people weren't around. They were still imbibing broader American racist culture. (personal communication, Little Rock, Ark., July 2014)

Lancaster's comments—referring to the improved treatment some African American soldiers experienced while stationed abroad in World War I, compared with their experiences of Jim Crow–era racial violence in the United States—gesture to the shifting meanings of race, and effects of racism, as people move between sites, especially during wartime. They also speak, however, to the ways in which racial references from the past are called upon to make sense of the racial complexities of the present. As Lancaster implies, the absence of racialized people from a place no more relieves that place of its racism than the presence of racialized difference guarantees it.

MAKING RACISM REMOTE

Conversations about why Springdale, "of all places," had become an "immigrant town"—and whether it was a receptive place for immigrants and Black, Indigenous, and People of Color (BIPOC) more broadly—were steeped in local and regional imagined geographies of race and racism. If long-term residents struggled to make sense of the town's shifting racial identity in the present, it was a result not only of the town's history of exclusion and dispossession—which, to some degree, most neighboring towns share—but also of the significance and signifiers the town has obtained through locals', immigrants', and visitors' comparisons between Springdale and other towns in the region. This phenomenon played out in Northwest Arkansas at nested and overlapping geographical scales, upholding the good name of perceived "progressive" or "nonracist" spaces in one place by downgrading others. Making racism "remote," in other words, was a key tool for forging geographies of white supremacy (see Ybarra 2021, on the entwined spatial politics of "relative remoteness" and white supremacy).

Such formulations about "racist" vs. "progressive" places surfaced regularly in my fieldwork in Arkansas. In interviews and conversations with long-term residents, I sometimes explicitly asked them to talk about race. For example, I might mention that I was studying the racial history of the area and its effect on immigrant reception, following up with a question about how interviewees would characterize Springdale's (or Northwest Arkansas's) racial dynamics. In some cases, I pushed further, inquiring about the perceived racism of a place with which they identified. For example, if an interviewee offered that Springdale was known in the area as being unwelcoming to People of Color, I would ask them to elaborate. In many of these instances, people would admit to the presence of such tensions historically, then offer an example of another site whose racism was, by comparison, much more pernicious. If the discussion was on racism in Arkansas, one might place the blame for "the worst of it" on Southeast Arkansas (the only area in the state with a significant Black population) or on Harrison, a town in Boone County, where the Knights of the Ku Klux Klan have established their headquarters (Dentice 2015).

Frequently, interviewees and field contacts spatially distanced themselves from racism and "racist places"—for example, claiming that Arkansas was not the "Deep South" and that Northwest Arkansas was not representative of Arkansas as a whole—to shift or redirect conversations about racism when I brought them up, if not to absolve Springdale of its racism altogether. Northwest Arkansas was often described as relatively progressive compared with the rest of the state, save Little Rock. "Once you leave Northwest Arkansas, you enter Arkansas proper," I was regularly told, and more than one person compared Fayetteville to Austin, Texas, an anomalous bastion of progressive politics in a red state. Even Arkansas itself, despite a checkered history of racial exclusion and violence, was often described as not truly part of the "Deep

South," due to political differences between Arkansas and neighboring states (Blair and Barth 2005). Such comments, in other words, pushed racism outward and elsewhere.

Pursue conversations about racism a bit further in Northwest Arkansas, and one is likely to hear about Harrison. Even those who have never been to Arkansas may have read something about the town of Harrison, Arkansas, as its association with the KKK has been well documented in recent years (Byng 2013; (PBS 2014). Harrison, a town of just over thirteen thousand, has a long history of hosting KKK members, including Thomas Robb, the national director of the Knights of the Ku Klux Klan. Robb, who lives just outside Harrison, has described immigration as "white genocide being committed against our people" (Bella 2014, n.p.). Harrison's tumultuous history of racialized violence traces back to the Harrison "Race Riots" of 1905 and 1909, in which white mobs attacked Black residents, burned Black churches, and drove out all Black residents (Lancaster 2014a). In 2013, Harrison attracted national scrutiny, this time for a billboard that declared: "Anti-Racist is a Code Word for Anti-White." In response to this event, residents created the Harrison Community Task Force on Race Relations.[4] Actions like this, and the topic of Harrison's racism, surfaced regularly as a reference point when I asked interviewees about racism in the region, particularly in interviews and conversations with immigrants' rights and antiracist activists. While Harrison was not invoked as an explicit denial of Springdale's racist history and present, it was sometimes offered as an example of more egregious racism in the region, deflecting conversations about racism in Springdale to other sites like Harrison.

The distancing or displacing of local racism by white residents is by no means unique to Arkansas, but it was manifested in particularly geographic terms that compelled me to give it further attention. During fieldwork, I began to notice an interesting scalar effect in the way that local (mainly white) residents talked about racism and place. In both informal conversations and interviews, area residents often deployed a discursive tactic that displaced "racism" from the site in question to a distant—or, if not geographically *distant*, then smaller or more geographically *isolated*—site to which racism could be pinned. For example, two Northwest Arkansas residents reflected in conversation that "Springdale's got its problems, but Harrison is *really* bad. In Harrison, though, it's not that the whole town is racist: really, the KKK are mostly out on the Zinc," the Zinc being a zip code on the outskirts of Harrison itself. In other words, long-term white residents I interviewed were constantly moving racism farther outward, to ever more "remote" and "provincial" locations.

This imagined geography of racism at local and regional scales—a geographical imaginary in which racism occurs in more remote or backward places—also reverberates at the larger scale of the nation, vis-à-vis the phenomenon known as "southern exceptionalism." Southern exceptionalism has been understood as the framing of the U.S. South as inherently different or separate from the rest of the nation (Winders 2005) or, put differently, "the belief that the South has 'possessed a separate and unique identity... which appeared to be out of the mainstream of American experience' (Billington 1978, cited in McPherson 2004, 1). Southern exceptionalism has long been leveraged by those outside the U.S. South to "contain" the nation's racism geographically, serving *discursively* to exonerate the rest of the nation from its troubling racial past and present. The formulation of southern exceptionalism described above thus speaks back to a long history of the South—or parts of it—being positioned as the nation's regional and internal Other.

OUT, LOOKING IN: ARKANSAS AS BACKWARD (AND WHITE)

Arkansas is "a state almost fabulous," the German American author H. L. Mencken once observed. "(Who, indeed, has ever been in it? I know New Yorkers who have been in Cochin China, Kafristan, Paraguay, Somaliland and West Virginia, but not one who has ever penetrated the miasmatic jungles of Arkansas)" (cited in Friedlander 1979). Mencken, a known eugenicist writing out of Baltimore, penned the comment in a 1921 article titled "The South begins to mutter." The article in its entirety was a scathing critique of southern cultural "backwardness." Although it dedicated very few lines to Arkansas specifically, those brief lines spurred an immediate and bristling response from Arkansans, as they dredged up long-standing resentment at stereotypes of cultural backwardness in Arkansas and the Ozark region more broadly. In response to Mencken's attack, local Arkansan newspapers published angry editorials, challenging his unflattering depiction of the state (Friedlander 1979).

This passage points to another element of Arkansas's positioning vis-à-vis not only the nation but the South itself: its image as "backward." Arkansas has long struggled with an external perception—coming from mainstream U.S. media and, often, from academia—as backward, if not fully Deep South (Perkins 2014). Arkansas historians have written extensively on this "image problem," which they describe as either a pervasively negative image (of Arkansas as "backward," populated by hillbillies, etc.) or a lack of knowledge about Arkansas at all (in a sense, a *nonimage* image problem) (Blevins 2002, 2009).[5] Arkansans I met during fieldwork expressed frustration with these representations of their state. Indeed, Arkansas's "inferiority complex," as one interviewee termed it, was a frequent topic in interviews, news articles, op-eds, community meetings, and historical archives.

These two image problems also materialized through and alongside another pair of conflicting images: Arkansas as welcoming and Arkansas as racist, two images that would reappear with immigrants' arrival to Springdale in the 1990s. A 1990s promotional brochure for a local museum, for example, celebrated Benton County's cultural diversity ("By 1995, Rogers School District had 26 native-language backgrounds, including Spanish, Vietnamese, Korean, Laotian, German, and Urdu"), while conceded that "in Northwest Arkansas, warm personal relationships existed side by side with racism and nativism" (Rogers Historical Museum brochure, ca. 1995). Like this brochure, local news articles and op-eds from the early 1990s to the present frequently highlighted the progressive nature of some Ozarkians, while grappling with the coexistence of deep, racialized rifts that marked the area's history and present (Morris 2014). These materials speak to the provisional, tense, and conflicting dynamics of immigrant reception in a context tinged—and, in many ways, forged—by nativism and xenophobia.

These conflicting sentiments also emerge in response to an uneasy tension between outsider perceptions of Arkansans as white *racists* and as white *hillbillies* who are provincial, backward, and underdeveloped (Parker 2011). As Harkins (2003) writes, "Uniquely positioned as a white 'other,' a construction both within and beyond the confines of American 'whiteness,' the hillbilly has also been at the heart of struggles over American racial identity and hierarchy" (4). The hillbilly figure and stereotype are central in notions of—and resistance to—Arkansan inferiority circulating within and beyond the state.

The Arkansas hillbilly stereotype gained wide currency in popular media references throughout the nineteenth and twentieth centuries. Popular nineteenth-century folk tunes like "The Arkansas Traveler" and "The Ozarks Are Calling," for example, perpetuated images of the white Arkansan as "living in squalor." Despite the negative portrayal of Arkansans in these caricatures, their whiteness—a key feature of the hillbilly stereotype—was also often understood by public figures and government agencies as a redeeming characteristic throughout the twentieth century (Lancaster 2015). Educational reformers in the early twentieth century leveraged discourses about Ozark hillbilly whiteness to advocate for rural Ozarkians' inherent potential for uplift (implicitly contrasted with poor Black people, who were seen by these reformers as unredeemable). Despite being geographically isolated, poor, and uneducated, reformers argued, mountain hillbillies were of "pure-blooded" and "lily-white" stock (Perkins 2014, 201) and, thus, capable of achieving great social progress. These discourses also had material effects, as their promise of local "lily-white' labor "stock" drew capital investment to the region.

These perspectives link class, race, and region in revealing ways. The well-known figure of the Arkansas traveler, for example, draws together these contradictions: originating as a folk tune by the same name in the mid-nineteenth century, the Arkansas traveler almost always appears as a lanky white male who is barefoot, wears a straw hat, and holds a piece of grass in his mouth. The stereotype he embodies solidified Arkansas's "rural or 'hillbilly' reputation," one of "shiftlessness, indolence and improvidence" (Blevins 2002, 2009) and one of which many of my interviewees were keenly aware. While the figure is clearly portrayed as poor, rural, and unsophisticated, his depiction as a white male, a caricature of the "quintessential Arkie," can also leave others to conclude (erroneously) that Arkansans are racially and economically monolithic.

For one long-term white Springdale resident I interviewed, the hillbilly or "redneck" stereotype explicitly targeted Springdale, rather than neighboring towns like Fayetteville.

> EME: If you were trying to explain Springdale to someone—let's say, someone from New York who's never been here before—what would you tell them?
>
> Mr. Holland: For one, I'd say we are friendly. We are more down-to-earth people. I don't know whether you call them rednecks or what, but we border on being a little bit toward a redneck country.
>
> EME: What makes someplace a redneck country?
>
> Mr. Holland: I guess you can say not being real high-falutin' or something. They don't mind sitting on the ground, or driving an old car. They are not society-minded, I guess you would say. We never did have a very big society-minded company here. It's almost something rural in Springdale, more so than Fayetteville, [where people might] look down on people because of their education.

For this resident, Springdale was characterized in contrast to its neighboring town of Fayetteville by being "down to earth," simple, not "high-falutin'" or "society-minded." Although he uses the term "redneck" rather than "hillbilly" to encapsulate this idea, his comments allude to many of the characteristics associated with the figure of the hillbilly, such as being simple or unsophisticated, while also conveying a humble sense of pride in the "down-to-earthness" of Springdale residents.

The image of the hillbilly, an arguably southern trope, also figures centrally in geographical imaginaries of the U.S. South and geographic and sociocultural borders. Elsewhere in the country, deliberations over whether a place is southern often turn on considerations of how racist or "hillbilly" the place is perceived to be, factors which many northerners attached to "southernness" itself (Mason 2005; Blevins 2002, 2009). Southern author Flannery O'Connor famously spoke to this tendency in a 1960 lecture, remarking that "anything that comes out of the South is going to be called grotesque by the northern reader, unless it is grotesque, in which case it is going to be called realistic" (cited in Martin 1994, 45). The tendency O'Connor described pervaded my discussions with non-southerners about this research and has been well documented by U.S. South scholars (Greeson 1999; Winders 2005). Such discourses around Arkansas whiteness, "hillbillyness," remoteness, and racism profoundly shape the meanings of race in Springdale but do not work alone. It is to some of the other processes shaping these racial meanings that I now turn.

Making and Narrating an "All-White Town": Historicizing Racial Geographies in Springdale

Like all places, Springdale's contemporary racial dynamics and geographies rest on a particular set of historical conditions, shifts in political economy and labor, and territorial occupations. Racial formations and geographies of the nineteenth and twentieth centuries laid the groundwork for Springdale's "racial present," the context into which new immigrants would arrive and make claims for rights. These processes situate Springdale within larger processes of territorial dispossession, racial cleansing, solicitation of racialized labor, and immigrant exclusion, all processes central to U.S. empire. If, indeed, "we live in racial history" (Omi and Winant 2014, 316), then that history is crucial for understanding contemporary dynamics of empire in new destinations such as Springdale.

In this section, I analyze what I term "racial geographies" in Northwest Arkansas by drawing on several well-established and interrelated theories of race, space, and place, each identified briefly below. In some places, I use these terms individually, while in others, I use the broader term "racial geographies" to refer to the processes and phenomena they collectively identify. Racial geographies are geographically and temporally contingent, emerging differently in different sites, even in adjacent towns such as Springdale, Fayetteville, Rogers, and Bentonville. Nevertheless, processes of racialization in these towns are also informed by racial structures and discourses working at larger scales—regionally, nationally, and transnationally (Singh 2017).[6]

Central to my understanding of racial geographies are geographies of white supremacy, a geographic framework that attends to "the ongoing significance of white supremacy and the white racial identities produced through a taken-for-granted logic of settler colonialism" (Bonds and Inwood 2016, 178) This approach emphasizes the linkages between white *identity*, white supremacy, and settler colonialism and their intertwined roles in producing space, particularly in settler-colonial countries such as the United States. As geographer Laura Pulido writes, "white racial domination necessitates racial exclusions that can only be made possible through the 'taking or appropriation . . . of land, wages, life, liberty, community, and social status'" (cited in Bonds and Inwood 2016, 4). In other words, the racialization of space and spatialization of race are at once structural, material, social, and ideological processes (Eaves2020; Daigle and Ramírez 2019; McKittrick 2011).

By mapping out a history of Springdale's racial shifts, as well as the sociopolitical and economic structures that have undergirded them and given them meaning, I aim to "make visible 'the materiality of racial exclusion'" (Bledsoe, Eaves, and Williams 2017). In this section, I do so by historicizing the geographies of white supremacy that have materialized at the local scale in Springdale, but also those have also emerged at larger scales, to examine their coproduction. My approach is informed by recent geographic scholarship on white supremacy and racial capitalism (Gilmore 2022; Pulido 2017) which not only attend to local place-making but also frame the broader, mutually constituted *structures* of white supremacy, settler colonialism, and racial capitalism that produce space at national, transnational, and diasporic scales.

Just as concepts of "racist places" are historically produced, so, too, is the concept of whiteness, produced over time and in the present through white supremacy (Harris 1993). Efforts to frame white supremacy as a historic relic or a phenomenon occurring on the margins of society—or, for example, on the geographic margins of a town, city, or region—result in "caricatures" of white supremacy as extreme or extremist, obscuring its ongoing role in shaping space (Pulido 2018; Bonds and Inwood 2016). Racial categories must therefore be analyzed as they emerge over time through larger political, economic, and social processes (Haney-López 1994). The racial logics Springdale residents use to organize their perceptions about, and interactions with, people they see as different from (or similar to) themselves are grounded in historical, social, and political structures and narratives that work across scales.

Finally, this section examines the coproduction of discourses about "race" and the material process that shape those discourses. Omi and Winant (1994) refer to these dynamics as racial formations, which they define as historical, socially constructed, and changing structures of race and racialization (see also Haney-López 1994). Springdale was constructed as a white settler town, and later, as an "immigrant town," through various interrelated material processes of white supremacy. Local discourses erase some of these processes (i.e., settler colonialism) while anxiously and constantly revisiting others (i.e., anti-Black violence). Over time, racialized practices and discourses shift to accommodate new racial formations at larger geographical scales. This chapter attends to these discourses while emphasizing their relevance to material constructions of *white supremacy* over the social constructions of *whiteness*.

These racial logics are not only discursive: they also have material effects, and they have a geography. As Ruth Wilson Gilmore (2022, 109) emphasizes in her analysis of the entwined material and ideological dimensions of racism, "To describe is also to produce." An examination of the historical acts that produce a "white town" such as Springdale reveals white supremacy as something that must be actively and continuously produced. Again, a "white town" is produced not only *discursively*, through naturalizing narratives of whiteness that both obscure and enable white control of space through settler colonialism (Bonds and Inwood 2016), but also *materially*, through physical acts of policing and (re)producing "white space" by expelling, dispossessing, or excluding racialized people and groups.

In his writing on racial cleansing in Arkansas, Guy Lancaster (2014b) calls for a historical analysis of Arkansas's white supremacist geographies—in his words, "the creation of all-white space through violent means" (3)—by using a lens of racial cleansing, rather than by focusing exclusively on "sundown towns," which systematically excluded Black people from residing there and appeared throughout the country (Lancaster 2014a, 2014b; Loewen 2005). Below, I follow Lancaster's call to attend to various historical processes of racial cleansing in Northwest Arkansas, especially Indigenous dispossession through settler colonialism, the terrorizing, expulsion, and exclusion of Black populations, and the active solicitation of white workers and capital from other regions. While not all of these processes were carried out through overt, physical violence against racialized populations, they all served to (re)produce white supremacy materially and spatially.

SETTLER COLONIALISM AND INDIGENEITY ON THE TRAIL OF TEARS

The possibility of Springdale as a "white town" was first created through the state-led and extralegal dispossession, removal, and genocide of Indigenous peoples vis-à-vis a process of settler colonialism that continues to present. Settler colonialism is fundamental to the formation of white supremacist geographies in Northwest Arkansas. Understanding this history situates whiteness in a historically "white town" as ongoing settler colonialism, rather than as a simple or "natural" fact of a demographically monolithic community into which immigrants of color (and other racialized people) arrive. Anything but "natural," Indigenous removal from Northwest Arkansas and the surrounding regions, carried out over the course of more than 400 years (Sabo 2014; Deloria 2010), created the *material* conditions for white settlers from the northeastern United States to move into the region and settle it. This material and physically violent process of removal has always been accompanied by *discursive* modes of erasure: regional and national discourses about indigeneity in Arkansas and the Ozarks have long romanticized "Indianness" while relegating Indigenous dispossession and genocide to the distant past (Wolfe 2006; A. Smith 2015). Such discourses, in obscuring the active process of white settler colonialism and in placing indigeneity at a far remove from contemporary Springdale and Northwest Arkansas, serve to naturalize whiteness and white/settler claims to space and place in the region.

Springdale's Indigenous history matters for the story of Marshallese migration to Springdale because the erasure of Indigenous genocide and dispossession is part of the larger erasure of U.S. imperialism and colonialism that this book works to combat. Examination of Indigenous displacement and genocide reveals the long-standing presence of U.S. empire in this region, as it links old imperial mobilities—the murderously tethered mobility of white settlers and Indigenous people(s)—to newer ones. European settlement of Arkansas formed part of a broader project of imperial settlement of the New World, which drew Arkansas into circuits of global power. Although settler-colonial geographies are often conceptualized as *separate* from U.S. imperial expansion—due in part to the pervasive ideology of Manifest Destiny that "naturalizes" settler expansion across North America—they reveal the enduring links between empire and mobility, race and space in places such as Arkansas.

The dispossession of Indigenous land and the removal of Indigenous populations originally residing in what became called the Indian Territories date as far back as the mid-sixteenth century, when Spanish colonizers in Hernando de Soto's army forcefully occupied what is now known as Arkansas, brutally displacing and killing many Indigenous residents (Bolton 1993). This dispossession was enacted over the following four centuries, dramatically reducing—through genocide and removal—the region's Indigenous population. By the nineteenth century, Quapaw, Caddo, Tunica, and Osage were the largest Indigenous groups in the area, the latter of which was most heavily concentrated around the Missouri River and Ozark region in contemporary Northwest Arkansas. Osage Indians from present-day Missouri resided seasonally in what is now Northwest Arkansas, but were forcibly removed from there and pushed into present-day Kansas by 1825 (Whayne 2002).

From 1805 to 1812, the French established permanent colonial settlements in part of the Louisiana Territory, an organized incorporated territory from the original Louisiana Purchase from the French. Once the area became Missouri Territory in 1812, the U.S. government, in a push to settle west of the Mississippi River, removed Cherokee, Chickasaw, Choctaw, Creek (Muscogee), and Seminole Indians from their homes in the present-day Southeast United States., pushing them westward (H. A. Peterson 2010). These populations were eventually forced into what is now western Arkansas, then into present-day Oklahoma and Kansas. Over a period of decades, this vast project of Indigenous removal relocated virtually all of present-day Arkansas's Indigenous populations.

The 1820s and 1830s were particularly devastating for the region's Indigenous peoples. The Cherokee Treaty of 1828 gave white settlers permission to claim land in Northwest Arkansas, leading to an influx of settlers from the eastern United States (Bolton 1993), pairing spatial processes of racialized displacement and (re)settlement that were aided by military and paramilitary forces. During this time, it is believed that of the approximately thirteen thousand Indigenous people forcibly (re)moved through the Trail of Tears, many passed through Northwest Arkansas while heading west on what would become known as the Northern Route (H. A. Peterson 2010).[7]

These processes laid the groundwork for Springdale's creation as a "white" town "settled" by "pioneers" throughout the 1830s (McLoughlin 2014). After the early establishment of an inn by a nearby spring, the area became a rest stop for other white settlers passing through to Indian Territory, which lay beyond the area to the west. The town of Shiloh, as it was then named, continued to be settled over the next forty years. The town survived the Civil War, despite the burning of several buildings, and was renamed Springdale in 1872, then incorporated in 1878. Since then, Springdale's white population has grown steadily, though slowly at times. The town's Native population, by contrast, is now exceedingly small, with recent census estimates setting it at less than 1 percent of the city's total population.

At present, there are no federally recognized Indian tribes in the state of Arkansas,[8] as most Indigenous peoples were forcibly relocated or fled by necessity to reservations in neighboring Oklahoma (Elkins 2014). This, of course, does not mean that Arkansas is without an Indigenous population—the 2020 U.S. census showed Arkansas's Native American population at close to thirty thousand—but, simply, that the U.S. federal government does not formally recognize established Indian tribes within the state. Nevertheless, the presence of indigeneity materializes in Arkansas in a handful of ways and sites. For example, highway signs in the area created by the National Park Service mark the "Auto Tour Route," identifying a road route that approximates the layout of the Trail of Tears (National Park Service 2016). Even the name of the state, Arkansas, is derived from Indigenous languages: it is a French pronunciation of "*akakaze*," a Sioux word meaning "South Wind People" (Whayne 2002).

Northwest Arkansas is also home to the Museum of Native American History, or MONAH, whose website, at the time of my fieldwork in 2014, invited museum guests to "take a 14,000 year journey through America's past" (MONAH, 2014). I visited the museum once during fieldwork in 2014, spending a couple of hours wandering between exhibits. At the time, virtually the entire museum collection was composed of "relics that date from over 14,000 years old to *historic* times," such as arrowheads, headpieces and other attire (promotional brochure, MONAH, 2016, emphasis added). There was barely a mention, however, of *contemporary* Indigenous life or more recent Indigenous history, and museum visitors could easily conclude that Indians were, indeed, a thing of the past. Even the museum's website positioned Arkansas's Indigenous populations as no longer in existence, reflecting wistfully, "Whether the first Americans originally entered the continent by land or by sea, evidence of their existence on the continent is found in the tools, weapons, and ornaments they left behind." Such evidence, like the populations whose historical presence it is meant to document, is thus anchored firmly in the distant past.[9]

Presentations like this one offer a reading of indigeneity as ancient history but rarely speak fully to the contemporary experiences of Indigenous people in the region or to the contemporary consequences of their historic removal. Thus, in Northwest Arkansas, the Trail of Tears' legacy remains in examples like the Auto Tour Route and even in the state's name itself. As in many places in the continental United States, however, this legacy does not translate into a local awareness of or conversation about contemporary *living* Indigenous people(s) or the lingering effects of their absenting.

With some digging in the archives, I found traces of the embodied violence of Indigenous removal, dispossession, and genocide. In my fieldnotes, I wrote: "Research today on the Trail of Tears. The archivist has gotten me a journal from a white settler missionary who accompanied the Cherokee and Creek on the trail. His journal entries read like an obituary section, dedicated to those lost to dysentery, exhaustion, and 'bloody flux.'" Reverberating through this white missionary's journal were themes of Indigenous peoples' grief, death, and loss through dispossession, family separation, and sickness, all caused by the violence of U.S. empire. Archival materials like these documented empire's physical, emotional, and spiritual costs for the region's Indigenous populations. However, these materials and the histories they documented were only accessible through intentional, and persistent, searching.

Furthermore, references to this violent history of displacement and resettlement rarely came up in conversations with long-term residents about Springdale's racial past and how it came to be an "all-white town,"[10] (though other processes, such as Black people's removal through Springdale's sundown town policies, were referenced often). Instead, many long-term Springdale residents talked about their familial heritage of pioneers, ancestors who had "lived off the land" and "built something where there had been nothing." These kinds of comments reinforced the notion that white pioneers were the first to populate the area, effectively erasing the historic (and ongoing) presence, and the active displacement, of Indigenous populations.

In Springdale, these narratives of what I am calling "settler romanticism" are intertwined with racialized notions of who belongs to a place—and *to whom* that place belongs—as well as the romanticization of white settler types since then (Blevins 2002). Stories of such settler or pioneer types appear in newspaper articles and written and oral histories about Ozarkian cultural life and history. One piece printed in the *Springdale News*, titled "Ozark pioneers survived adventures livelier than movie," describes a "German immigrant family, hostile Indians, plundering troops of the Civil War, murder, robbery, [and] incredible hardships" (Hughes 1988). In popular narratives like this, Indians either are absent altogether or appear as "hostile" aggressors to hard-working, well-meaning white settlers (who, in this case, are also recent immigrants to the United States). Long-term residents' historical narratives often exclude key aspects of how Springdale came to be, constituting an erasure of white settler colonialism in narratives of Arkansas's settlement. Such narratives often focus not on the colonization of an already-peopled land but on the myth of white settlers as building where "nothing" had been. The "present absence" of Northwest Arkansas's Indigenous population is thus significant for the construction of whiteness in the area, as narratives of the absence (or historical distancing) of Native presence in the region allow the arrival of white settlers to be the origin story for the region's development.

Indigenous removal as an imperial spatial strategy is intimately related to empire's production of mobility of colonial subjects for labor purposes, including through the destruction of their homelands. As Lorenzo Veracini (2013) has written, romanticized settler and pioneer narratives are often divorced from histories of colonization in settler societies such as the United States, a dynamic I observed during fieldwork in Northwest Arkansas as well. One elderly long-term Northwest Arkansas resident, for example, told me his ancestors were "practically the first people in this area," and others shared nostalgic stories following a museum presentation about how white settler families from the Ozarks had "built something out of nothing" (fieldnotes, Springdale, March 2014). This framing of settler presence marginalizes and invisibilizes Indigenous existence, resistance, and the histories of occupation and dispossession that made white space possible in the United States (Simpson 2016; Rowe and Tuck 2017). Policing and enforcement of whiteness attempted to cement Springdale's racial composition and identity for much of the twentieth century. I write *"attempted* to" because the material and discursive work it takes to produce, legitimize, and naturalize a white space under settler colonialism is never done; white supremacist and settler geographies must constantly be made and remade.

"OLD-TIMEY" SPRINGDALE:
SETTLER ROMANTICISM AND WORKING-CLASS WHITENESS

While Springdale's population is now officially more than 50 percent BIPOC (U.S Census Bureau 2020),[11] its multidecade identity as a "white town" is reflected in the town's institutions, many of which—including the chamber of commerce, the school board, the city council, and even the mayor's regular prayer breakfast—are still almost exclusively white. Whiteness is also written into the memory of many lifelong residents, who describe the town as historically without racial diversity. To reckon with Springdale as a new immigrant destination, therefore, is to reckon with more than a century of active "whitening" there through settler violence.

Narratives promoting Springdale as a white town can be traced through archival documents almost to the town's inception. One promotional piece on Springdale, published in a local paper at the turn of the twentieth century, lauded the town's appeal as an all-white town with all-American workers:

> Water is a pure freestone, unsurpassed in quality. The scenery is delightful; landscapes that delight the eye of the artist abound. And the people? *Straight American. Not an African; not an Asiatic; not even a Jew.* I make no suggestion as to whether these conditions are fortunate or unfortunate. But to give the lie to the assertion so often recklessly made that "It is a dead town where one does not find a Jew:" any traveling man who makes this territory will say that Springdale buys the most goods of the best quality of any town of its size

or near its size in that trade territory. For proof of the truth of this assertion, ask any jobbing house in St. Louis, Springfield, or Forth [sic] Smith. Yes, *if straight-bred unhyphenated American stock is wanted, it is nearly 100% pure in the Springdale District.* (Bouton ca. 1910, emphasis added)

In this text, the author offers "Straight Americanness" as a selling factor for would-be new residents and for potential developers and employers. The text never *explicitly* claims that Springdale is an all-white town; indeed, the term "white" does not appear at all. Nevertheless, the text, in lauding the town's population as "Straight American . . . [n]ot an African; not an Asiatic; not even a Jew," explicitly equates Americanness with the absence of People of Color, and by implication, with whiteness. That whiteness appears only by inference, and is conveyed as yet another of the town's "delightful" qualities, along with idyllic scenery and pure water supply, highlights its naturalization as Springdale's defining trait, pairing it discursively with—even presenting it implicitly *as part of*—the area's natural bounty.

Bouton also expounds on how Springdale's demographic makeup might prove beneficial for desirous capitalists, particularly those seeking new labor markets for manufacturing and other large-scale economic ventures. In doing so, Bouton's text reflects broader narratives of New South boosterism throughout the region in this era, which envisioned a regional economic recovery after Reconstruction that was premised, either implicitly or explicitly, upon white supremacy (Moneyhon 1996). The promise of (white) regional recovery within New South discourses also relied upon a powerful antiunionism that positioned white laborers as less troublesome than workers of color and immigrants (Tait 2005). These racist and antilabor discourses, while not always explicit in booster materials circulated in Arkansas, nonetheless appear in ways that readers at the time would have understood.

The implied whiteness of Springdale's labor force—alluded to but rarely named in booster materials—was also conveyed in advertisements, such as a 1947 ad in the *Fayetteville City Directory* that read: "Ice Cream Manufacturers: Ward's Ice Cream. *Made in All White Plant.* 121 N. Block Ave." (Fayetteville City Directory 1947, emphasis added). Again, here, whiteness is conveyed as a positive attribute of the local labor force and as hygienic. Statements about Springdale's "self-respecting," "straight-bred," and "unhyphenated" labor in advertisements and city promotional materials like these reflect active attempts to attract investors interested in a white labor force to Springdale in the early twentieth century. These details offer additional insight into how Springdale was actively made into and marketed as a "white town."

Similar themes appear in an article titled "Know your home town," published in a local Springdale paper in the early twentieth century. In it, the author echoed Bouton's sentiments about Springdale's "pure" "American" population, framing that population even more explicitly as white.

> The growth and success of any area depends entirely on people. We are fortunate to live in an area that is dominated by the purest strain of Anglo Saxon blood to be found any where in the U.S.A. Our population is all white, native Americans, energetic, industrious, thrifty and endowed with a loyal community spirit. They are banded together in numerous civic organizations and are willing to work for what they want.... *You just can't beat our kind of people. Aren't you glad you live here?* (Deaver ca. 1910, emphasis added)

Whiteness here is discussed as beneficial for the local economy, particularly for potential employers but also for current residents "glad" to live there. In this text, the author drew an equivalence between whiteness, that "purest strain of Anglo Saxon blood," and an industrious, hardworking nature, people "willing to work for what they want," implicitly situating this promising workforce in contrast to stereotypes of the lazy Black "slacker" or the militant urban/ethnic labor organizer (Roediger 1999). In Springdale, this article promised, the population's industrious, all-American whiteness was what enabled the town to grow and succeed. As such, it serves as yet another example of how Springdale was constructed as a white town, both materially and discursively.

Partly as a result of such racially inflected boosterism, in-migration into Arkansas during the late nineteenth and early twentieth centuries was undertaken primarily, though not exclusively, by poor and working-class whites from other states (Perkins 2014). By 1930, more than a quarter of Arkansas's population had been born outside the state (Metzler ca. 1940, 7). After a period of net out-migration from the state in the 1940s and 1950s, largely due to the Dust Bowl and shifting labor opportunities, in-migration to Arkansas picked up again, especially in the Northwest region. By the late 1970s, there had been a marked shift in population movement at the state level: more people were migrating into the state than leaving it. Now, though, a large proportion of new arrivals were immigrants, coming either directly from their countries of origin or from states on the West Coast or the southern border, such as Texas. Such patterns, again, were most pronounced in Northwest Arkansas, in places such as Springdale and Rogers. Thus, by the late 1970s, there was a net population gain in Arkansas of foreign-born residents, setting the state on a trend that would continue for the next several decades.

These demographic data, paired with the stories that emerged occasionally during fieldwork, suggest that Springdale and its environs received "outsiders" before the 1980s, contrary to narratives that the "wave" of immigrant arrivals began at that time. When prompted about this matter, most people were able to recall at least one story of a family or population from outside Northwest Arkansas or the Ozarks. Nonetheless, there remained a persistent narrative about Springdale that everyone knew one another before the immigration boom in the 1980s and 1990s. One older long-term white resident described Springdale's population changes in this way: "When I came to Springdale [as a teenager in 1958], they were bragging about reaching an eight thousand population, and now we're at seventy-two thousand, so it's changed a lot. You used to be able to leave your front door open and go all day to work and never lock your door. It was very rural thinking, very rural trust.... The way country farmers used to trust each other: I'll bale your hay, you feed my horse, on a handshake. Springdale was very much that way when I got here. And it's changed; it's had to change." Such perceptions about Springdale's historic "small townness" speak to long-term residents' more recent experiences of a disrupted sense of place and collective belonging. These interviewees rarely articulated that collective belonging explicitly in terms of whiteness or racial homogeneity, even when I asked directly about how the town's population racial makeup had changed. This avoidance to phrase Springdale's population shifts in terms of race was shared by many long-term white residents, especially older ones. In contrast, when I asked long-term white residents to talk about the town's racial *past*, they frequently turned to a discussion of Springdale's historic anti-Black racism, a (re)framing that tended to normalize Blackness as racial difference and anti-Black racism as prototypical racism. In this way, contemporary racism in Springdale was masked by a deflection to historic racism there.

SUNDOWN TOWN: ANTI-BLACKNESS AS "REAL" RACISM

Whiteness in Springdale, originally constructed through settler colonialism in the nineteenth and twentieth centuries, was also shored up through the implementation of "sundown" policies that all but eradicated Springdale's Black population. Some of these policies were formal; others were informal but no less systematically enforced (interviews and fieldnotes, Springdale, 2014). Despite the absence of an actual Black population residing in Springdale for most of the twentieth century, the idea of Blackness and the specter of anti-Black racism loomed large (Hallett 2012), weaving their ways through interviews and conversations with long-term white residents. Blackness has been a present absence, or an "absent referent," in Springdale, as it has been in predominantly white communities throughout the United States (Gates 1983). In Springdale and Northwest Arkansas, Blackness—or more specifically, anti-Blackness—operates centrally in producing racialized space, ideas, and material relations, even as the region's Black population continues to be very small.

Blackness continues to permeate many long-term residents' reflections on the nature of race and racism, despite the virtual absence of a Black population in Springdale. This was evident from my first visit to the Shiloh Museum of Ozark History. When I mentioned that I was interested in studying the town's racial history, a museum staffer took me to the archives storage in the basement to see the old "White Waiting Room" door from the Springdale's railroad station.[12] This artifact made no mention of Blackness or reference to a "Colored Waiting Room," though such signage was common in the U.S. South during the Jim Crow era and likely existed in Springdale. Rather, it brought up associations of Blackness and racial difference by implicit exclusion. Nevertheless, in Springdale, it is almost impossible to talk about race or racism, and therefore impossible to talk about whiteness, without referencing Blackness, either explicitly or implicitly. Historically, Springdale's framing as an all-white town often meant implicitly or explicitly painting it as not "tainted" by Blackness (e.g., in the booster materials previously discussed that celebrated Springdale as a town with "not an African; not an Asiatic, not even a Jew" (Bouton ca. 1910)). Another promotional pamphlet distributed at the turn of the twentieth century in Northwest Arkansas lauded Springdale this way: "We don't have saloons, negroes, mosquitos, malaria, chills, bandy houses or other vices of this nature" (January 22, 1904, Shiloh Museum). Texts like these reveal early attempts in Springdale's (re)settlement to actively build and market a town without a resident Black population, through its informal establishment as a sundown town.

The term "sundown towns" refers to the thousands of towns across the United States that excluded Black people from residing there during the late nineteenth and early twentieth centuries, forming an important part of contemporary racial geographies in the mainland United States (Lancaster 2014b; Loewen 2005). These towns gained this moniker from the signs that often marked their city limits, carrying messages that ominously warned Black people to leave by sundown. "Sundown towns" were prevalent across the United States, despite a common perception that they were a historical anomaly or only existed in the Deep South. Eileen Díaz McConnell and Faranak Miraftab (2009) estimate the number of sundown towns at "nearly 1,000 small towns, larger communities, and suburbs across the country" (605), and James W. Loewen (2005) attests to the spread of sundown towns in Arkansas and Missouri, documenting the presence of sundown signs across the Ozarks by the 1920s. Partly due to sundown towns' signs and policies, and also due to the Great Migration, a process of Black flight out of the U.S. South, the Ozarks' Black population dwindled to half its pre–Civil War total by 1930 (Loewen 2014). Thus, Springdale, as one of many possible sundown towns in the region, was not unique in its exclusion of Black residents or intimidation of potential new Black visitors and residents. Nevertheless, this history formed and continues to form a central component of Springdale's racial geography and a touchstone in residents' ruminations about race there.

Black exclusion and anti-Black racism—typified and codified through "sundown town" practices—are also a key part of the racial geography of many "immigrant towns" across the U.S. South and Midwest. As Lancaster (2010) and Loewen (2005) note, sundown towns were more common in highland regions of the U.S. South, including the Northwest Arkansas region of the Ozark and Ouachita mountains, and less so in the "Deep South" lowlands, which had built economies historically based on cotton and enslaved Black labor. As many such towns—former sundown towns—became organized around meatpacking, drawing more immigrant workers in the 1980s and 1990s, new racialized geographies of labor and exclusion layered atop older ones. NID scholars McConnell and Miraftab (2009) examine racial dynamics in a midwestern town that had recently become home to a sizable Mexican population and that, like Springdale, owed its historical whiteness in part to sundown town policies. In this way, they highlight the "value of situating contemporary migration within a historical context marked by the centrality of race" (607). Following their call, I locate Springdale's contemporary racial dynamics in a longer racial history (and geography) that includes the enactment of sundown policies and strategies.

Due to the paucity of formal documentation or research about sundown towns, many local discussions about Springdale's sundown town status revolved around the sign that, according to local lore, had been posted at the entry to town, one that read, "N——, don't let the sun go down on you in Springdale." This sign came up in numerous conversations about Springdale's history of racism—particularly when I asked long-term residents to describe race relations or racial dynamics in their town. I could find no photo documentation of the sign itself, despite concerted and ongoing efforts of many local historians and archivists. Nevertheless, many long-term white residents recalled seeing the sign at the town's border, some dating its presence up to the 1970s. One interviewee who had attended high school in Springdale recalled taking a picture to submit to the yearbook committee in the late 1970s, but a review of local yearbooks from these years turned up nothing. Despite this lack of "official" evidence—or perhaps as a result of it—the history of Springdale's racism and sundown town status was a vexing and consuming topic for many long-term white residents, given how frequently it was brought up (mostly unsolicited by me) when long-term residents talked about the town's racial history.

In one interview, a white woman born in Springdale and residing nearby reflected on Springdale's image as a "racist town," the lore of the sign, and the informal enforcement of Springdale's "sundown town" policy.

> **EME:** Something that I've noticed is that consistently, it's Springdale that people are saying is a "racist town," historically, compared to other neighboring towns.
>
> **Julie:** That's always been the lore. Which is funny, because there were no Black people who lived in Rogers, either; there never were.
>
> **EME:** Where do you think that [image of Springdale] comes from?
>
> **Julie:** Well, you know, there's always been that story about there being a sign at the city limits, saying, you know . . . but I think nobody's actually been able to prove that that was there.
>
> **EME:** But that story persists.
>
> **Julie:** It does. And I'll tell you another story about this house we used to live in. . . . So this used to be [U.S. senator for Arkansas] J.W. Fulbright's summer home. And in the basement, there was a bedroom and a bathroom, and there was this buzzer system that was rigged through the house. And the story that we were told was that Fulbright had the buzzer system put in because he had a couple of Black maids, and that when he had a party on the weekend, in the evening, the rule was that Black people were supposed to be out of town by dusk. So he would have them stay down in the basement, sort of hidden, and buzz them up when he needed them, so it wouldn't be known that they were actually here. Now, when I think about it now, I think, "Oh my God, that cannot actually be true."
>
> **EME:** Did you get the sense that was an enforced thing, that someone in the city would be watching and enforcing this thing?
>
> **Julie:** Yeah, yeah. I mean, I have no idea, because . . . I never saw a Black person here, *ever*, [until very recently]. . . . But I couldn't tell you that I was aware of an enforcement. I mean, as far as I knew, no one ever tested it.

In this conversation, Julie's uncertainty about the sign's existence is paired with her recollection of other practices, such as the rumored secretive employment of Black domestic workers, which might have reinforced local and regional perceptions of Springdale as a sundown town or at least a town where Black people were made to feel unwelcome. Whether such practices of Black exclusion and expulsion were formally enforced in Springdale, local white awareness of their implementation may have been sufficient to effect Black flight from, and avoidance of, the town. As such, Springdale's whiteness was constructed and reinforced through the paired expulsion and exclusion of Black residents and would-be residents.

While Springdale's sundown sign is the most infamous and oft-cited example of Springdale's racialized past, archival materials help document many more examples of this past. For example, in addition to the already-mentioned "White Waiting Room" door from the Springdale train depot, the Shiloh Museum archives contained an early twentieth-century article about a Black man discovered "skulking in the woods," who had been apprehended after "attempting to assault a white girl." The article's author concluded that "[if] this negro is insane he ought to be placed in the asylum. If sane he ought to be hung or placed in the penitentiary. Such brutes should not be allowed to run at large" (Shiloh Museum, ca. 1903). Together, historical details such as those presented above piece together a partial picture of the practices of racial exclusion and violence that reinforced Springdale's sundown town status shortly thereafter, practices by no means limited to Springdale.

For many long-term white residents, the memory of Springdale's *historical* enmity to Black people lingered into the present, translating into an understanding of their town as a place that was still hostile to Black people. My fieldnotes from Springdale, for example, recount this conversation with a local historian and area resident: "We shift into a conversation about race. Cynthia said, 'The other day, I saw a Black man crossing the street in Springdale. And I was just so surprised! I mean, I know there's a Black population here, but imagine, just that growing up near Springdale, you never ever saw them. I mean, I grew up in Fayetteville, and it was like, "Don't ever go there" [to Springdale, as a Black person]!'" (Springdale, March 2014). In Cynthia's mind, Springdale had long been a place inhospitable to Black people ("Don't ever go there!"), and her surprise at seeing a Black man in town dredged up this response. Perhaps as a result of this lore's potency, many long-term residents with whom I spoke articulated anti-Black racism as the "real" or "worst" racism. Often, this sentiment was conveyed in the context of immigrant incorporation and local reception, as (primarily white) people expressed that racism was not so bad for immigrants as they imagined it would be for Black people.[13] In interviews and conversations, long-term white residents postulated that immigrants to Springdale would probably fare worse or face worse treatment if they were Black, despite the fact that, as many residents were quick to point out, only recently have a few Black families chosen to settle in the area. A closer look at the language of long-term white residents, however, shows that these interviewees were not necessarily comparing Marshallese or Latinx *people* with Black *people*. Instead, they compared *anti-immigrant* sentiments—or xenophobia—with *anti-Black* racism, concluding that anti-immigrant bias is not so virulent or racist as anti-Black racism. In other words, many white residents hesitated to categorize race-based prejudice against immigrants *as* racism.

This perspective was not exclusive to white residents. In one interview, a Japanese American woman who was a long-term Springdale resident opined that her family's treatment by long-term white residents would have been worse if they had been Black rather than Asian. As she explained, "[Springdale residents] were so very welcoming, they really were! I think . . . if our skin color was different, I think it would be something really different." This resident juxtaposed her family's treatment with what she believed a family whose skin color was different would have faced. As her statement implies, different (and perhaps darker) skin color would be an indicator of more meaningful racial difference in Springdale and, thus, more violent racial exclusion. After my fieldwork, I had two separate conversations with Black Arkansan colleagues who now lived in the U.S. Northeast, both of whom commented on Springdale's historic anti-Blackness. As one colleague said, "growing up in Little Rock, my family always said not to go there."

In Springdale, as in so many other sites of immigrant reception, Blackness served, at least discursively, as the ultimate racial bane, the bottom of the racial hierarchy (McClain et al. 2006). At the same time, anti-Black racism was often situated as "the worst," the most extreme, or even the *only* kind of racism. The logics that underpin these tendencies, while forged beyond Springdale, gain much of their potency through their historic link to the town's sundown status and through frequent reiterations of this history in (particularly, but not exclusively) white residents' narrations of Springdale's race relations.

In summary, the history of Springdale's racial geographies brings to bear a necessary context on the town's racial present. First, this history exposes the particular ways in which Springdale's whiteness was historically constructed, or made "all-white by design" (Loewen 2005), through the forcible relocation of the Ozarks' Indigenous peoples and subsequently through white settler colonialism in the area. Narratives of Springdale's whiteness gloss over a violent history of Indigenous dispossession, relocation, and genocide, allowing Springdale to be understood as a historically all-white place.

Finally, both the town's demographic composition and many of its residents' understandings of the town's racism emerge from Springdale's historic status as a sundown town. That history is present in the minds of many long-term residents, as well as the residents of surrounding towns. In conclusion, then, a focus on the racialized history of Springdale's construction as an all-white town, before the influx of immigrant groups from the 1980s on, reveals how Springdale *became* all-white: through Indigenous exclusions forgotten and erased over time and through Black exclusions told and retold to the point that they became the sole reason for Springdale's whiteness. These material and discursive productions of Springdale as a white town created the racial landscape and racial geographical imaginaries into which immigrants arrived in the 1980s.

Becoming an "Immigrant Town": Latinx and Marshallese Arrival

Starting in the 1980s, Springdale's immigrant population grew rapidly and exponentially, changing the racial composition of the town in fundamental ways. Shortly after the Compact's passage in 1986, Marshallese migrants began arriving to Springdale, close on the heels of the first wave of Latinx immigrants who came primarily from Central America and Mexico. As the local paper reported, between the 1990 and 2000 census, the foreign-born population in Benton and Washington counties—Northwest Arkansas's two most populous counties—increased from 3,065 to 21,562, a growth rate of 603 percent (*Arkansas Democrat-Gazette*, ca. 1995).[14] By 2014, Springdale had the region's fastest growth rate, adding an average of four people *every day* to its population (Springdale Chamber of Commerce 2014). Together, Marshall Islanders and Latinxs (both immigrant and U.S.-born) now officially constitute more than 45 percent of Springdale's population (U.S. Census Bureau 2020). Latinx and Marshallese resettlement in the town has thus transformed Springdale, both demographically and in the eyes of many long-term residents, from a "white town" into an immigrant town. These demographic changes posed direct and unavoidable challenges to preexisting notions of Springdale as a white town and an "all-American" town (two framings often conflated) and to the United States as all-white, all-English-speaking, and all-American.

In many ways, Springdale fits the description of sites examined in the NID literature (Massey 2008; Smith and Furuseth 2006), which defines a new immigrant destination by the historical absence of large-scale immigration (Marrow 2011). Much of this scholarship attends to the ways in which arriving im-

FIGURE 13. The Apollo on Emma Theater in Springdale, Arkansas, built in 1949. Photograph by Carol M. Highsmith, 2020. Courtesy of Library of Congress, LC-DIG-highsm-64775.

migrant groups, particularly Latinxs, disrupt preexisting racial dynamics in places of resettlement. Latinx immigrants arriving to sites in the U.S. South frequently encounter a historical Black-white color line, a binary racial structure in which Latinxs of many ethnic and racial backgrounds are not immediately classifiable (Marrow 2009). Often, in NIDs, there exists a shared narrative about how communities came to be populated by white people. Contending with that whiteness and its place-specific genealogies is thus germane to the examination of new destinations.

Immigrants' movement into Springdale during the 1980s and 1990s was a result of processes playing out at various geographical scales, regionally, nationally, and transnationally. The migration geographies that now include Springdale stretch into transnational connections from Latin America to the Pacific. Immigrants arriving to the United States from Mexico and Central America during the 1980s and 1990s were themselves imperial migrants of a sort, as U.S. empire—wielded regionally and hemispherically through uneven power dynamics in the North American Free Trade Agreement, military and paramilitary influence on governance and elections, and militarization of the U.S.-Mexico border (Nevins 2002)—created many of the economic and political conditions that necessitated emigration from the region and made the United States a *necessary*, if not necessarily more desirable, destination.

Resettlement patterns visible in Springdale also map onto larger shifts in immigrant resettlement across the U.S. mainland. First, while some migrants were arriving directly from Central America and Mexico in the 1990s, many other immigrants were moving to Arkansas from California, in response to rising housing costs, increasing competition within the labor market, and, not least of all, new and proposed state-level policies antagonistic to immigrants, most infamously California's Proposition 187. Such resettlement trends also reflect how migration patterns have stretched beyond traditional immigrant gateway cities on the West and East Coasts to reach new sites in the Midwest and South, such as Nashville and Atlanta, and states such as Georgia, North Carolina, and Missouri. As a result of Latinx arrivals between 1990 and 2000, Arkansas's immigration population grew 196 percent, the country's fourth-fastest growth rate (Capps et al. 2007). This shift in the geographies of immigration has created opportunities for new ways of understanding immigrant incorporation by focusing on how the effects on labor and economic structures (Striffler 2009; Kandel and Parrado 2005), public institutions such as schools and churches (Odem 2004), and racial frameworks and formations (Winders 2005) might compare with or be different from what is seen in traditional immigrant gateways.

What makes Springdale different from other U.S. NIDs is that it is also a Pacific Islander new destination, a phenomenon less frequently studied in NID scholarship. The growth of Pacific Islander communities is also occurring elsewhere in the South, establishing new destinations from places like Enid, Oklahoma, to Copperas Cove, Texas, that have yet to receive sustained attention. While the U.S. Northwest is home to the largest *percentage* of Native Hawai'ian and Pacific Islanders in the continental United States, the South has seen the fastest *growth* of these populations in the past two decades (Hoeffel et al. 2012). In 2010, Washington County, where Springdale is located, was one of only six counties in the continental United States whose Pacific Islander population exceeded 5 percent of the total population. Such exponential growth of Pacific Islander communities in the South warrants further study within the NID literature, raising key questions about the entanglement of migration and empire.

The arrival of large numbers of immigrants to small cities such as Springdale is arguably more noticeable for long-term residents than it is in larger urban centers, as new immigrants' proportional impact on local demographics may be greater and more visible to nonimmigrant residents on a day-to-day basis than in larger cities (Nelson and Hiemstra 2008). Large cities also tend to see different residential patterns of immigrants than do small towns, with immigrant residents residing in a few neighborhoods that long-term residents might never pass through. Conversely, in smaller towns and cities such as Springdale, there are more *shared* sites of encounter where older and newer residents are likely to meet.

As Marshallese and Latinx immigrants resettled in Springdale in the late 1980s, both groups came to a town that largely saw itself as white and struggled to understand what it meant when immigrants began to appear in those shared sites of encounter—classrooms, grocery stores, health centers, and workplaces (interviews, Springdale, 2014; J. A. Schwartz 2015). The dramatic and rapid change in Springdale's population met with varied reactions from long-term residents and local media coverage, a process documented in other "chicken towns" (Smith and Winders 2008). During this era, as before, whiteness was policed through racial categorization and the policing of "out of placeness," through forms of outright exclusion and conditional inclusion. Local white reception of immigrants during Springdale's "immigrant boom" of the 1980s and 1990s thus serves as an example of how geographies of white supremacy can become (re)sedimented during a demographic shift, even as those shifts remake local racial geographies in meaningful ways.

Coverage of the region's demographic changes, particularly through immigration, dominated local news media coverage in the 1990s. One local writer summed up sentiments in this way: "If long-time Northwest Arkansas residents think the population influx and accompanying economic growth of the past decade have been mind-boggling . . . well, hang on, we're in for an even wilder ride" (*Arkansas Democrat-Gazette* 1993), while another described Springdale's population "explosion," writing that "in Northwest Arkansas, some people think the wheels are coming off the wagon" (Steward 1995). These types of articles, which increased in frequency in the 1990s, demonstrate the growing attention to immigrant arrival, resettlement, and integration in Northwest Arkansas during this period.

This process was not confined to Arkansas; it played out at larger scales as well. As immigrants came to numerous new destinations across the United States in the 1990s, initial media coverage was often characterized by panic and fearmongering about the surging influx of undocumented or so-called illegal immigrants, a phenomenon also described in chapter 3. Such negative coverage often converged with (and likely exacerbated) nonimmigrants' support for more restrictive immigration policies, such as increased deportations and the expansion of a U.S.-Mexico border wall. Even news coverage that was less vitriolic utilized the term "illegal" for undocumented immigrants, as was common in U.S. media until the mid-2010s (Guskin 2013). Many articles on

Latinx immigrants in Northwest Arkansas, even those expressing support for immigrants' rights, featured headlines such as "Illegal Immigrant Steps Out: Guzman Tired of 'Living in the Shadows,' Takes Part in Forum" (Hernandez 2011). Another article featured a list of immigration-status terms, the first of which was "illegal alien," defined as "a person who has no valid immigration document that allows him to live or work in the United States" (*Arkansas Democrat-Gazette* ca. 1992). By reproducing terms such as "illegal alien"—which, notably, was an official legal categorization at the time (and until at least 2016; see Library of Congress 2016)—such media representations circulated discourses of immigrants as either "illegal" or, by contrast, "legal."

This binary discursive framing of immigrants is one Michael Jones-Correa and Els de Graauw (2013) refer to the "illegality trap," a "single-minded focus on undocumented immigration in the contemporary immigration debate, and the inability to shift this focus" (186). The illegality trap that characterized national news coverage on immigration also appeared in local media, obscuring the particular legal status of Marshallese immigrants in Springdale. In news articles on Marshall Islanders, for example, local journalists struggled to find a vocabulary with which to describe their status in Arkansas or "pathway to citizenship." This is because Marshallese immigrants, as "lawfully present" "habitual residents" or "nonimmigrants" under the Compact agreements are not easily legible within a "legal"/"illegal" binary and thus are hard to place in, or describe through, dominant discourses on immigration such as the illegality trap. I return to this concept in chapter 5 to show how this trap also renders Marshall Islanders with COFA status unintelligible to public officials and political actors.

During the 1990s and 2000s, however, some local news coverage of Springdale's immigrants also focused on the region's "melting pot" and the new doors and pathways opening for immigrants and their second-generation children. One article, for example, featured a Laotian immigrant in Springdale who taught Laotian to immigrant children at a local Catholic Church (D. Robinson 1993). Another piece, titled "Long ride to work," championed the economic contributions and personal sacrifices of Latinx immigrants locally, declaring that "unskilled Hispanic workers are essential to the Northwest Arkansas boom" (Walter 2003, 12). Such coverage showed processes of local and regional sense-making about immigrants' new presence in the community and about their role in the region's changing social, cultural, and economic landscape.

This period, though, was not without tensions. Existing alongside this trend toward incorporation and assimilation was visible resistance to immigration in Springdale and neighboring towns, as many immigrants' rights advocates mentioned in interviews. This resistance was evident in increased policing, particularly through the adoption of 287(g), a federal measure issued in 1996(and later strengthened in 2009) in which local police could opt to create a formal partnership with the DHS and ICE through memoranda of agreements between the two agencies (Ridgley 2008; Wong 2012).[15] This policy was implemented in Springdale and nearby Rogers in 2007. The trend to implement 287(g) and other immigrant criminalization measures also played out at the regional and national scales (M. Coleman 2012; Walker and Leitner 2011), reshaping relationships between local police and immigrant communities across the country. These changing relationships affected relationships between community organizations and immigrants' rights activists locally, in some cases prompting changes in their organizing strategies, as I discuss in chapter 5.

When I asked long-term white residents how recent population shifts had changed Springdale, their feelings ranged from acceptance and enthusiasm to ambivalence and frustration. One long-term resident, an elderly white woman, told me, [Immigration] has changed the way neighbors communicate or don't. It's changed the way people trust other people. It's changed the way business is done. It irritates me to go to the bank and have it say, 'Do you want your information in Spanish or English?' This is America. It's English." This speaker's concern, in other words, was not only that Springdale had been disrupted from its white, English-speaking, "American" identity: she also jumped scales—from the local to the national scale—to express her distress that a similar process (immigration) was challenging national identity across "America." As her interview and other materials analyzed here show, Springdale's reception of immigrants has been more complicated and uneven than outright xenophobic, a dynamic also explored in other NIDs (Marrow 2011). Yet it is clear that even now, nearly four decades after the initial arrival of new immigrant groups, notions of Springdale as a historically "white town," and of a white, English-speaking America, persist. I now turn to two contemporary vignettes of life Northwest Arkansas to examine what their contrast reveals about belonging, race, and "Americanness" at the *national* scale, and how such dynamics are shaped by racial histories and geographies at the *local* scale.

Race, Nation, and Belonging: Two Acts

On the Fourth of July, 2014, I attended two social events in and around Springdale that together point to the social separation of Marshallese, Latinx, and white residents in the area as well as the very distinct understandings of nation, belonging, and identity present there. The first event was a Fourth of July Rodeo of the Ozarks, an event hosted annually in Springdale. The second was a Marshallese softball game, the opening game for the Namdrik Joor league (Namdrik Joor is the Marshallese Memorial Day). In many ways, the contrast between the Rodeo of the Ozarks and the Namdrik Joor event, held on the same day only a few miles apart, is great. Yet these parallel events both offer insights into the experiences of an NDE: first, experiences of the town as historically white, with virtually no immigrant presence; and second, experiences of the town as a node in a broader diasporic network. Moreover, these events evoke different notions of community: one, deeply grounded in a local history while celebrating a U.S. national history; and the other, diasporic, given meaning not (only) by the particular site of Northwest Arkansas but also by the convergence of Marshall Islanders from across diasporic sites gathering to celebrate a shared cultural event.

RODEO OF THE OZARKS

The afternoon of July 4, 2014, I drove with my partner to Springdale for the annual Rodeo of the Ozarks. This event, which Springdale has hosted since 1944, regularly draws hundreds of people from across Northwest Arkansas. My fieldnotes from that day examined the racial and nationalistic overtones of this event.

> Several hundred people here, mostly white and some Latinx, many people in "cowboy" attire. Once we are seated in the bleachers, the national anthem plays. Everyone in the stadium stands, removes their hats, puts their hand over their heart. In a bizarre spectacle, the specter of Ronald Reagan appears on the video jumbotron. In the video, he gives a speech lauding American freedom and those working to build the American dream, recognizing the high price paid by the military bring freedom to the rest of the world. The crowd is silent and attentive.
>
> Once the video ends, the announcer offers a short introduction, reminding the crowd: "People in Saudi Arabia can't enjoy freedom. In the United States, we have freedom." People clap and cheer. "Where are my people [in the crowd] from India?" No answer. "I was told there would be a group here from India. Maybe they don't speak English." He repeats this joke a couple of times, and each time it feels more uncomfortable. "How about from China? From England? Australia?" There's one East Asian family sitting a few rows ahead of us, a mom and dad with two or three small children. Otherwise, there were

none that we could see, aside from my partner, who is Korean. Not a single (discernible to me) Marshallese person there.

At this rodeo, Springdale's largest annual event, narratives of U.S. patriotism were interwoven with a clear articulation of local belonging and Americanness as whiteness. Foreign tourists—or those *assumed* to be foreign by the announcer because of their race or ethnicity—were called attention to, even though—or perhaps because—the crowd in attendance was overwhelmingly white. Whiteness and Americanness were thus simultaneously naturalized in this space through the announcer's narration. The overwhelming absence of Latinx and Marshallese attendees, populations who collectively compose nearly 50 percent of Springdale's population, also spoke to the racial and ethnic separation of social spaces in Springdale, further enabling the construction of the space as white and American.

Equally important, the lauding of U.S. military intervention abroad, through the honoring of Reagan's military appeals and the comment about Saudi Arabia, directly tied the local celebration of this rodeo, through U.S. patriotism, to U.S. militarism. In this way, the event linked a place-specific cultural event, the Rodeo of the Ozarks, to larger discourses about U.S. national, military, and imperial projects such as the Iraq wars and U.S. military presence in the Middle East.

Just as the rodeo event was trumpeted through militaristic and nationalistic tones on that day, its own historical origins rest in war, having been founded in 1944 at the height of World War II. As the event's official website describes the rodeo's founding: "People were working hard and around the clock. Entertainment and relief from the unrelenting headlines were much needed.... Hosting a rodeo was a perfect outlet to get rid of the stresses during hard times. Springdale was always a patriotic town and on the fourth, the city park was always gaily decorated. The town band played, there were old fiddler's contests, potato races, pie-eating contests, and fun was had by all." Here, local patriotism and wartime sacrifice are braided together with local cultural markers like "fiddler's contests," both in local memory and in ongoing retellings of the rodeo's place-based significance.

As Laura Barraclough (2018, 2019) has written, rodeos in the United States have long showcased hypermasculinist performances of Americanness and national pride, and are often imbued with settler-colonial ideologies of the frontier and settler fantasies of dominating nature. Despite rodeo's deep historical roots in Mexican, Mexican American, and Spanish cultures (where it is often referred to as *charro*) and its wide adoption by Indigenous and Black cowboys across the U.S. South and West, mainstream understandings of rodeo as a "White, masculine, and heterosexual American event" (Ford 2020, 15–16) continue to pervade popular (white) consciousness across broad swaths of the United States. In other words, just as Springdale's racial identity has been constructed discursively and materially through key absences (historically, Indigenous and Black, and here, Latinx and Marshallese), notions of Americanness, grounded in militarism and military service as well as whiteness, are manifest in this rodeo as an annual public event.

NAMDRIK JOOR DAY: MARSHALLESE SOFTBALL TOURNAMENT

Earlier that same day, I attended the *Namdrik Joor* softball games at a public park outside central Fayetteville, about eight miles from the Rodeo of the Ozarks site in Springdale. My fieldnotes describe the event in detail:

> There are around two hundred Marshallese people at the park when I get there. Some people are just arriving, while others are settled into their bleachers. I am there for almost an hour before Jeannette, a white professor and advocate who works with the Marshallese communities, comes, so I have some time to watch the games. Lots of young families with small kids—running everywhere!—and not a single non-Marshallese person that I can tell, aside from myself. Everyone's speaking Marshallese to each other with occasional words of encouragement shouted out in English ("One more! Good job!").
>
> The park has four baseball diamonds altogether, so I sit by the men's game for a while and then walk around. I spot John and then Marleen, two Marshallese community advocates, separately, but see them from afar and decide not to call them over (I don't know if they would remember me, and I also don't want to draw attention to myself). I suddenly feel very conspicuous—I notice people watching me as I walk through the space. This is the first entirely Marshallese event I've been at since I've been here, and I feel like a voyeur. I consider taking pictures of the event—I take one on my cell phone—but then feel that it's inappropriate and put my phone away.
>
> Jeannette finally arrives and tells me she's sorry for being late. She tells me that she had run into Dexter, an older Marshallese man, whom she knew had moved out to Washington state and thought he was coming back after three months, but it turns out he's there for good. It reminds me of a comment that a Springdale-based Marshallese police officer made to me yesterday, that many Marshallese people are moving to Washington state because the benefits are better (medical? housing? He also mentioned food stamps—perhaps there are others).

After chatting with Jeanette for a few more minutes, I head to the refreshments stand to buy a bottle of water. I'm waiting in line next to a young woman in a chartreuse t-shirt that says "Spokane." I make small talk: "Really hot out today, huh?" "Yeah," she says, "and I'm from Spokane, so I'm not used to this heat and humidity at all. It makes my curly hair go crazy." She's in her mid-twenties, I would guess, speaks English fluently and with a discernible American accent (I'd heard her talking to the little girls and asking after their father, seeming to know them). I laugh and say I'm from New York, so I can sympathize; I'm not used to the heat either. She asks if I knew about this event before, or if I was just driving by and decided to check it out. I think she must be wondering how I, one of two or three white people at this event, ended up here. I pause for a minute—how to explain my presence?—and tell her that I'm meeting a friend, Jeannette. "What about you?" I say. "Well, I'm from Spokane," she repeats, "so I came from there." Oh, I respond, realizing she came all the way for this. She says that she had a wedding to come for, too, so she stretched out her trip, and decided to fly here, but that many of her teammates drove, a trip that took two days. There were about twenty of them altogether, she says. "It's a long drive. But the prize money is good!," she laughs.

Shortly thereafter, I find Jeannette sitting with her friend Mercy, a Marshallese or Marshallese American woman in her mid-thirties. She's on the board of a Marshallese-serving organization, and she and her family moved to Springdale in December from Springfield, Missouri, where she says she lived all her life. It's not far, maybe an hour's drive. I ask how she likes it here so far. She hems and haws, finally says, "It's all right." In Springfield, there were maybe a hundred Marshallese people, she says. Her husband's family is here, so he wanted to move back. She says that she doesn't really have a lot of close friends here. "I mean, there's a lot . . . a lot of us here," she said, "but I'm not close with them the way I was back home." In passing, Jeannette comments that a team has come from California as well and that she's hoping to meet some of them while they're in Arkansas.

My notes from this event offer a glimpse into the diasporic encounters taking place in a new destination of empire such as Springdale (and, by extension, in neighboring Fayetteville), bringing together Marshall Islanders and Marshallese Americans from resettlement sites across the United States. Event-goers such as Mercy and the young woman at the snack bar shared reflections on other places they had lived, comparing them with Springdale and discussing the connections between these sites. Others, like Dexter, had lived in Springdale for many years but had relocated to another city or state, seeking better public benefits or proximity to family. Conversations at the Namdrik Joor games spoke to the heightened mobility of people moving between sites in the Marshallese diaspora, as well as the connectedness between them. This human movement and flux, and the connections they forged between diasporic sites, are part and parcel of new destinations of empire, as they bring broader transnational histories and contemporary lived experiences to sites of resettlement.

The scenes described above paint two divergent pictures of life in Northwest Arkansas: in the former, the rodeo embodied a performance of Americanness *as whiteness*, despite the handful of Latinxs in attendance, and of "freedom," along with the heavy-handed symbolism of the American flag, national anthem, and President Reagan.[16] In the latter, Marshallese residents of Springdale were joined by Marshallese groups from across the diaspora to celebrate a major annual event, one that barely appeared on the radar of long-term white residents. These conflicting performances and imaginings of the nation-state and of local identity are evidence of what Ali Behdad (1997) describes as "the insurmountable difference between America as an immigrant heaven and America as a 'pure' nation" (158). The two events analyzed here each reflect a part of this equation: on Namdrik Joor, we see a glimpse of the United States as an "immigrant heaven," whereas the Rodeo of the Ozarks event produces the United States as a "pure" nation. While these two events did not necessarily pose an "insurmountable difference" in their constitution, they clearly present divergent experiences and understandings of collective social life in Springdale. As such, they offer a glimpse into the conflicting performances and narrations of place and nation that appear in a new destination of empire.

Conclusion

The two vignettes just analyzed are examples of the ways in which racialized experiences of belonging play out in Springdale, often in proximity but in very different ways. I close the chapter with them because they speak to the broader themes it addressed; namely, the construction of Springdale's racial geographies through economic and political transformation, the town's changing face through recent immigration, and the social dynamics that have materialized through these changes. If, indeed, race and racialization pervade all of our collective social life (Hall 1980), then these events must also be understood as racialized expressions of place, space, and contested belonging.

Such questions of nationhood, identity, and belonging are also called up in the conversations Springdale residents have about race, racism, and racial identity. Whether lamenting Springdale's history of Black expulsion, implicitly calling up whiteness through settler romanticism, or ruminating on the effects of becoming an immigrant town, long-term white residents are thinking and talking about Springdale's racial formations in a multitude of ways. In sites with changing racial dynamics, notions of belonging have often been grounded in racist notions of who is (un)assimilable into Americanness and whiteness. Narratives of Springdale's historic static whiteness continue to inform local discourses about the town until immigrant arrival in the 1980s. Whether portraying immigrants as demographic disruptions to a historically white town or juxtaposing immigrants' experience of racism against the experiences of Black Arkansans, long-term residents make sense of the presence of new immigrant groups with an eye to the past, using frameworks and language particular to the history of the town and region (Winders 2013). Beyond dynamics of local reception, this chapter shows how a "white town" is produced (both materially and discursively) and how old imperial mobilities come to bear on geographies of newer imperial mobilities and migrations, such as those of Marshall Islanders. Such histories are crucial for understanding Springdale's contemporary racial geography.

CHAPTER 5

"No Such Thing as an Illegal Marshallese"

COFA Status as Imperial Citizenship

With the passage of the original Compact of Free Association (COFA) in 1986, the U.S. government created a new legal status for Freely Associated States (FAS) residents living in diaspora: COFA status. There is nothing exactly like COFA status in contemporary U.S. immigration law. Established by bilateral agreement between the United States and the Marshall Islands, the Compact's migration provision grants the option to live, work, and attend school in the United States without a visa to hundreds of thousands of people. COFA migration thus constitutes an anomaly in U.S. immigration law, though, as this chapter will argue, COFA status shares many characteristics with other provisional legal statuses historically granted to the United States' imperial subjects (Ngai 2004; Perez 2008; Lee and Pratt 2012). Categorically "in-between," the COFA migrant embodies a "taxonomic liminality" (Baldoz 2011, 74), neither fully and formally part of the U.S. nation-state and its citizenry nor fully outside it.

COFA status also generates some compelling, and vexing, *geographical* questions: Is COFA visa-free migration an *international* agreement, as part of the Compact of Free Association? Is it a *colonial* policy, elaborated between the United States and its former territories within the anomalous geopolitical arrangement of Freely Associated Statehood? Is it a U.S. *immigration* policy, one enacted the federal level, then interpreted and enforced at state and local levels? In other words, what kind of policy is the COFA migration policy, what kind of legal status is COFA status, and what is the geography of this phenomenon?

These questions are not easily resolved. As I show in this chapter, COFA migration policy—and, thus, COFA status—is complex for two reasons that have to do with its geography. First, COFA status is geographically *multiscalar*, which is to say that it intersects multiple realms of law and policy, from bilateral international agreements to U.S. immigration law to state policies to municipal ordinances. Since COFA migration policy exists on the margins—it pertains to places at the legal and geographic margins of U.S. empire and to populations at the margins of U.S. citizenship—it gets fleshed out at the interstices of different legal jurisdictions. Second, as a policy that mainly affects people living in a diaspora—Marshall Islanders, Micronesians, and Palauans living in the U.S.—COFA migration policy is a policy "on the move." As COFA status "travels" to new sites with COFA migrants, it constantly traverses different areas of law and policy and gets interpreted and implemented in incredibly uneven ways on the ground. These two geographical dimensions of COFA status—its multiscalar and mobile nature, both of which result from its *imperial* nature—exacerbate COFA migrant status's liminality and, thus, the marginality, illegibility, and exclusion that COFA migrants often face in diaspora.

As I argue, COFA status's precarious and partial nature constitutes a form of imperial citizenship. I define imperial citizenship as a legal status held by subjects of nonsovereign or semisovereign territories that is determined and enforced by the imperial power. Imperial citizenship, as I conceptualize it based on an analysis of COFA status, has three primary characteristics. First, it is *liminal*: it is an "in-between" legal status created to apply to people that occupy the spaces between metropole and colony, foreign and domestic, foreigner and citizen, and "legal" and "illegal." Nonsovereign people and places in empire are often at the margins or interstices of these constructs of inside/outside, and imperial citizenship reflects and reinforces that liminal positioning. Second, imperial citizenship is *exceptional*: it is created as an exception or a caveat to existing immigration and citizenship law. This creation often takes place through piecemeal policies, legislation, and bilateral agreements or treaties between an imperial power and its current or former territory, in other words, in legal instruments that create unique conditions for imperial subjects (subjects and populations that are colonized or formerly colonized, or in some other legally significant way enveloped into the legal geographies of U.S. empire). Finally, imperial citizenship is *exclusionary*: it creates a second-class status that, while preferential when compared with other immigrant legal statuses (such as being "fully" undocumented), nonetheless produces vulnerability, marginalization, and forms of rightlessness in its holders. Yet imperial citizenship's exclusionary effects can also foster solidaristic ties between imperial citizens and other marginalized groups, prompting activist strategies to resist shared experiences of exclusion. These three qualities of COFA legal status shape, and are shaped by, its two geographic characteristics as multiscalar and mobile, as described above.

Despite common interpretations of COFA status as a relatively privileged legal status among U.S. immigrants, or as a benefit—if not *the primary* benefit—of Marshall Islanders' envelopment in U.S. empire, my analysis of its production as imperial citizenship reveals how its partial, contingent, and revocable nature constitutes a kind of rightlessness that produces precarity and uncertainty for its holders. In other words, by theorizing COFA status *as* imperial—produced through imperial processes, using imperial logics and legal mechanisms (see chapter 2), and activated on imperial or colonized geographies—I am able to show not only the injurious effects of this legal status on COFA migrants but the central role of empire in *producing* those effects as well.

This chapter looks at the Compact's migration provisions to ask, and answer, a set of questions: What kind of legal status(es), subjectivities, and citizenship does the Compact produce? How do its effects morph when it "lands" in particular sites, such as Springdale? What kinds of effects does the Compact produce in its "beneficiaries," a group which includes COFA migrants (Marshall Islanders, Micronesians, and Palauans), as well as on citizens of Freely Associated States (FAS) living in the islands? How do residents of new destinations of empire such as Springdale make sense of the existence of COFA status and Compact migration provisions? Finally, and most importantly, how do COFA migrants experience the nature and effects of COFA status in their daily lives? As this chapter argues, each of imperial citizenship's three qualities—its liminal, exceptional, and exclusionary nature—is set into motion in the law or policy that creates it and "baked into" the particular policymaking processes that birth it. These qualities are then given meaning and form "on the ground" in the lived experiences of its holders and those who interpret, apply, and enforce it. In Arkansas, the peculiarity of COFA status plays out in both quotidian and dramatic ways, both enabling and limiting Marshall Islanders' eligibility for social programs, community advocacy, bureaucratic support, and legal protection at a number of scales. COFA status—and local actors' often partial or misinformed perceptions of it—also shapes the kinds of activist allegiances that emerge in the context of (and in resistance to) existing laws and policies.

Analyzing COFA status as a form of imperial citizenship reveals many dimensions of how imperial policies produce geography, and, in turn, how imperial geographies shape policy. For one, COFA status can tell us much about the production of U.S. citizenship on the margins of empire—where empire has, in some ways, officially ended—where legal restrictions on full U.S. citizenship expose U.S. federal anxieties about opening the door too fully to U.S. imperial subjects. Second, examination of COFA status reveals that those margins—between metropole and colony, home and abroad, citizen and foreigner—become both clarified and blurred in law and policy across scales, and that such blurring affects migrants in diaspora in prejudicial ways. Theorizing COFA status as imperial citizenship offers a clearer view of how COFA status—as a legal, political, and social status of imperial subjects who are also immigrants—manifests on the ground, providing insight into the lived experiences of imperial subjects and their encounters with receiving communities in the U.S. "metropole."

Understanding Marshall Islanders as imperial subjects is only possible by looking through the lens of the complex histories and political dynamics that gave rise to the Compact and that have modulated its impacts in various sites. As my research—garnered through multisited fieldwork conducted in diverse geographic contexts where the Compact "touches down" (Guåhan, the CNMI, Hawai'i, Arkansas, and Washington, D.C.)—makes clear, COFA status is (re)produced in Marshall Islanders' encounters with local actors in sites of resettlement, as much as it is produced through the Compact's legal and policy provisions. These encounters not only shape perceptions of COFA status in host communities but in fact *constitute* COFA status itself, giving it form and meaning.

This chapter focuses on COFA status as it materializes for Marshall Islanders in Arkansas. It is worth mentioning that COFA status take shape differently in different sites, due to state- and territory-specific legislation that determines access to certain benefits (McElfish, Hallgren, and Yamada 2015; Chiu 2014). Because COFA migrants' legal status is coproduced by policy interactions at multiple scales, their experiences with law and policy often vary widely across states. For example, while COFA migrants were rendered ineligible for Medicaid—a U.S. *federal* program—from 1996 to 2020, some U.S. states, such as New York and California, opted to provide health care services to COFA migrants using their own funds during that time, creating an uneven patchwork of health care coverage for COFA migrants across state lines. The nuances of COFA status, therefore, are not entirely generalizable across sites. For this reason, I limit my analysis to the context of Springdale and Northwest Arkansas. More importantly, such discrepancies or variations in the law reveal the complicated policy and legal landscapes that COFA migrants—and those who work with them in various capacities—negotiate as they move between sites in the wider diaspora.

To make these arguments, this chapter proceeds as follows. It begins by articulating a theory of imperial citizenship. By piecing together various primary-source legal and policy documents not commonly examined in tandem (due to their provenance at different geographic scales of law), I build my argument that COFA status functions as a form of imperial citizenship, despite the fact that the RMI and other FAS are now formally sovereign (and notwithstanding the political importance of COFA migration permissions for FAS leaders and COFA migrants). The chapter then follows this "policy on the move" to Springdale, Arkansas, to examine its production on the ground. Here, I analyze over forty-five in-depth, semistructured interviews conducted with policymakers and other key actors from Northwest Arkansas (2013–2014, 2019–2020), as well as fieldnotes from multiple site visits to court hearings, activist strategy sessions, and nonprofit agencies, to demonstrate how COFA status is produced as liminal, exceptional, and exclusionary in three respective contexts. First, I turn to Marshall Islanders' encounters within contexts of criminal and immigration law and policing to examine how COFA status as a *liminal* status materializes in those contexts. Second, I turn to the context of social services, examining how Marshallese COFA migrants, as legal subjects and as potential program beneficiaries, experience those realms, and how they are interpreted by public actors in those areas, especially in health care. Here, I argue that COFA status's *exceptional* nature results in tenuous access to social services for Marshall Islanders. Third, I look to the realm of coalitional immigrants' rights activism in Northwest Arkansas, mainly between Marshallese and Latinx immigrants. Here, I show how COFA status's *exclusionary* quality produces precarity through rightlessness for Marshall Islanders and how organizing with other legally precarious immigrants creates opportunities for coalitional and multiracial activism in Northwest Arkansas.

This chapter argues that public actors' perceptions and misperceptions of COFA status across each of these three contexts—(1) law, policing, and immigration enforcement, (2) social services, advocacy and benefits, and (3) activism and social justice organizing—causes COFA status' precarity and uncertainty to be produced unevenly across contexts "on the ground." Despite this unevenness across diverse geographic and legal landscapes, COFA status is consistently produced as liminal, exceptional, and exclusionary. COFA migrants must constantly contend with these conditions, advocating against *exclusionary* policies as well as educating public actors to counter pervasive unfamiliarity with COFA status, an unfamiliarity that results from its *liminal* and *exceptional* nature. By the same token, each of the three contexts outlined above prevents actors from seeing the *imperial* dimensions of COFA status— how it was produced through U.S. colonialism and imperialism in the RMI— dimensions which, as the chapter details, are starkly obvious to Marshall Islanders themselves. Paradoxically, in other words, imperial citizenship's (and imperial citizens') very nature *as imperial*—as proof of U.S. empire—is obscured due to the systemic and pervasive denial of the U.S. *as an empire*.

In my research across these contexts, I was interested in both how Marshall Islanders experience COFA status and how public actors in Northwest Arkansas made sense of COFA status and COFA migrants. Here, readers will note that my empirical material comes primarily from public actors, including white, Latinx, and Black as well as Marshallese and Marshallese American public actors. My choice to focus on public actors as opposed to "everyday" Marshall Islanders in Springdale was a deliberate one: early on in my fieldwork, I learned from Marshallese activists and advocates that many Marshall Islanders in the community were experiencing "research fatigue," having been the subject of many recent research projects, news articles, and grant applications. In my research with non-Marshallese interviewees, I focused on public actors who encounter COFA status in their work with Marshall Islanders, drawing on field interviews, participant observation, and informal meetings with social service providers, policymakers, legal representatives, and others whose professions put them in contact with the particularities of COFA legal status and its operationalization. By pairing a reading of the COFA migration policy's legal production on paper with its social production through COFA migrants' encounters with public actors, this chapter shows how COFA migrants' legal status as imperial citizenship manifests in *place-particular* ways in a particular new destination site.

Imperial Citizenship

Citizenship has played a crucial role in empires' management of imperial populations since the creation of the modern nation-state (Cowen and Gilbert 2008; Burnett and Marshall 2001). Although most scholarship on empire, citizenship, and migration has focused on European empires and their diasporas (Dawson 2007; Mongia 2018), COFA migrants and diasporas present a rich opportunity to examine these phenomena in the context of U.S. empire. Study of Marshallese migration under COFA status reveals that imperial citizenship can provision mobility, rights, and benefits to those who hold it while producing a precarious, conditional, and exceptional inclusion in U.S. empire. As the case of COFA migrants shows, citizenship takes on particular forms for subjects of U.S. empire, especially those who fall outside the formal protections of full legal citizenship. In this way, COFA migrants from the Marshall Islands, Micronesia, and Palau, in their "taxonomic liminality" (Baldoz 2011,

74), join residents of other former and current U.S. insular areas, such as the Philippines and Puerto Rico, who have been folded into U.S. legal status in a provisional and contingent way when migrating to the metropole (Erman 2008; Findlay 2015; Poblete 2014). These groups acquire this liminal status either simply by being born in the territories or through their migration to the United States, a process that reproduces them as second-class subjects of the nation-state with limited political, economic, and social rights.

I employ the term "imperial citizenship" here to name and analyze a phenomenon produced by the linkage of political geography (empire) and immigration law (citizenship), expanding existing understandings of citizenship as a tool used by nation-states to bestow, define, and restrict rights. Although the term "imperial citizenship" appears elsewhere in scholarship on empire (Gorman 2010; Kim 2008; Banerjee 2010; Troy 2020), it has not been used consistently or widely, nor has it been theorized for its *geographical* dimensions or its application to migrants moving within empires, as is my aim here. While concepts such as (non)citizenship (Ramírez et al. 2021), second-class citizenship (Punke 1972), and transnational citizenship (Itzigsohn 1999) shine light on certain aspects of imperial citizenship, each one on its own falls short in capturing the particular dimensions of citizenship as experienced by imperial or colonial subjects. Transnational citizenship, for example, theorizes migration *between* nations, but not *within* empires. Yet in the case of COFA migrants, their movements are both transnational—occurring between the Republic of the Marshall Islands and the U.S.—and intra-imperial, moving within the geographic entity of U.S. empire. COFA migrants' uniquely spatialized experience of rights and rightlessness thus necessitates a more geographic analysis of citizenship, which I develop in this chapter.

Arguably more than nearly any other U.S. legal status, COFA status changes as it crosses borders and is implemented and interpreted at different geographic scales. Therefore, a *geographic* analysis of this policy, as both *mobile* in its nature and *multiscalar* in its production, is crucial, as these features are part of what defines COFA status as imperial citizenship. As I argue, imperial citizenship is defined not by the possession of a particular set of legal rights, but rather by its inherent structural contingency, as well as by the imperial context—a political and geographical context—in which it was constructed. Imperial citizens are included partially, contingently, and often temporarily in the nation, through various forms of inclusion by exception. Such inclusion can occur through the piecemeal construction of imperial legal statuses—for example, through treaties, bilateral agreements, special provisions, and other exceptions to standard immigration and citizenship—and also through broader immigration laws and policies. As such, imperial subjects' citizenship or legal status often takes form, or changes form, once imperial subjects migrate to the United States. This is the case for COFA migrants, whose COFA status becomes "activated" once they leave their home countries and enter the United States. Therefore, an analysis of imperial citizenship must "follow" migrants to their sites of (re)settlement to fully grasp its effects.

Imperial citizenship takes varying forms in sites across empire. What these variations of imperial citizenship share, however, are their limitations: they are legally provisional—in other words, revocable through amendment or legislation, unlike constitutional rights—and tend to impose restrictions on their holders—restrictions, for example, on the right to vote, travel freely across U.S. borders, or pursue education or employment. Puerto Ricans' statutory citizenship, for instance, is made precarious because Congress could revoke it at any point (Perez 2008), while CHamorus born in Guåhan acquire U.S. citizenship at birth but cannot vote in general U.S. elections if or while residing in Guåhan (Bevacqua 2010). Citizens of the Marshall Islands, Micronesia, and Palau, all former U.S. territories, have the legal right to live and work in the United States but, unlike Puerto Ricans and CHamorus from Guåhan and the CNMI, can legally be deported from the United States. While almost all residents born in U.S. territories possess nominal U.S. citizenship at birth,[1] the full benefits ostensibly proffered by U.S. citizenship are not uniformly granted to residents of U.S. insular areas, which the U.S. Department of the Interior defines as jurisdictions that are "neither a part of one of the several States nor a Federal district" (2016).[2] Thus, residents of nonsovereign U.S. territories, as well as residents of former territories such as the RMI, do not enjoy the full range of legal benefits associated with formal U.S. citizenship.

The exceptional inclusion of imperial citizens may look like preferential treatment compared with that received by other immigrant groups; indeed, imperial citizens may garner a greater number of rights and benefits than certain other immigrant groups in the United States. Most notably, perhaps, imperial citizens often benefit from a heightened mobility due to their legal status (as long as they are moving within the territorial reach of the empire granting them a recognized legal status). Yet, these populations' mobility is often also *necessitated* by empire's effects, as was the case, for example, for Marshall Islanders displaced by U.S. nuclear testing during the 1940s and 1950s (Barker 2004).

Additionally, imperial populations are marked through their differential racialization as eligible or ineligible for inclusion as national subjects (Ong 2013), as seen in chapters 3 and 4. This logic of racial ineligibility—a racial logic derived from an environmentally deterministic one—formed the basis of the 1901 Insular Cases, in which the U.S. Supreme Court argued that Puerto Ricans were of an "alien race" and thus unfit for full U.S. citizenship. The Insular Cases then laid the precedent for the construction of citizenship in the U.S. territories for over a century (Burnett and Marshall 2001). As such, racial categorizations and exclusions from formal legal citizenship are central to imperial citizenship and belonging.

Migration from the U.S. territories to the mainland places in conflict the imperial desires of U.S. policy abroad and the exclusionary, xenophobic tendencies within domestic policymaking in the U.S. mainland. Imperial or postcolonial migrants expose the tension between these two tendencies, caught as they are between the foreign and the domestic, and often cause profound irritation for local and federal policymakers who might prefer to keep "over there" over there. As such, Marshallese COFA migrants to the United States, like Filipino migrants before them, embody what Mae Ngai calls the "corporeality of contradictions that existed in American colonial policy and practice" (2004, 97): these subjects were beneficiaries of the U.S. "benevolent-assimilation" approach that informed U.S. policymaking in both the Philippines and across Micronesia, yet became undesirables relegated to second-class status once they attempted to enter the U.S. mainland. A similar and more contemporary dynamic is evident in political debates about "Compact Impact," or the economic impact of COFA migrants, in Hawaiʻi and other U.S. states with large COFA migrant populations (GAO 2020). Such tensions speak to the contradictory spaces occupied by imperial subjects in the metropole and to their ambivalent reception in new sites of resettlement.

Imperial citizenship, as I define it, is a concept both specific and capacious. It encompasses the (non)citizenship experiences and legal statuses of residents of former territories, unofficially occupied sites and zones, military bases, and other spaces which might be understood as "spaces of exception" (D. Gregory 2006). While political geographers have examined the proliferation of such spaces under U.S. empire, particularly under the ongoing Global War on Terror (Minca 2015), they have focused less on the implications of these processes for citizenship (but see Pratt 2005; Mountz 2011). However, I argue in this chapter, semi- or noncitizenship for subjects of former and current U.S. territories presents a set of phenomena ripe for geographic analysis: due to imperial citizens' mobility, they carry this exceptional status with them, producing shifting and fragmented spaces of exception in their orbit in new destinations of empire (NDEs).

The Patchwork Legal Geography of COFA Status

Where in the law does COFA status originate or reside? This question, while seemingly straightforward, has a complicated answer. COFA status or Compact status—a shorthand for the status created by the Compact of Free Association and held by migrants who travel to the United States under its migration provisions—is produced at a number of different legal scales and vis-à-vis various legal and policy documents, as chapter 2 demonstrates. Together, these forms, documents, and policy statements create a paper trail that meanders unpredictably, winding back on itself and taking innumerable tangents. In my own research, I often found myself chasing from one source to another, searching in vain for one central, definitive, or authoritative definition of COFA status. However, no such document presented itself. Instead, documents on the legal status of COFA migrants, when read collectively, offer a kind of partial, jigsaw-like view of the status in law. Like other legal constructions of imperial subjectivity or citizenship, COFA status is provisional and conditional, containing many restrictions that *may* be triggered, many situations that *may* trigger its revocation and the partial benefits it proffers. It is precisely that conditionality, I argue, that produces the instability and partiality characteristic of imperial citizenship.

However, the short answer to this question—where in the law does COFA status originate?—can be found in the 1986 Compact of Free Association, the original source document for this status.[3] Article 4, Section 141 (a) of the 1986 Compact states, "Any person in the following categories may enter into, lawfully engage in occupations, and establish residence as a non-immigrant in the United States and its territories and possessions." From there, it enumerates categories of individuals to whom those benefits extend, including former TTPI citizens who became citizens of the Republic of the Marshall Islands (RMI) or the Federated States of Micronesia (FSM) with the Compact's passage.

It bears mentioning, however, that this section of the Compact does not constitute any direct pathway to U.S. permanent residency or citizenship, nor to a visa that might open the door to such legal statuses, as the text specifies: "[The Compact] does not confer on a citizen of the Marshall Islands or the Federated States of Micronesia the right to establish the residence necessary for naturalization under the Immigration and Nationality Act, or to petition for benefits for alien relatives under that Act. Section 141(a), however, shall not prevent a citizen of the Marshall Islands or the Federated States of Micronesia from otherwise acquiring such rights or lawful permanent resident alien status in the United States." The legal premise established in this short passage is a potent one, with vast ramifications for COFA migrants and their families living in the diaspora: it asserts that COFA migrants categorically have no direct legal recourse for achieving a more stable legal status, though it does not *prevent* them from pursuing permanent residency or citizenship by one of the standard legal routes available to immigrants from other countries, such as petition through marriage or by an employer. In a sense, the text above solidifies COFA migrants' status as provisional, liminal, and categorically unresolvable in and of itself—an irresolvability with significant repercussions for COFA migrants seeking public benefits and access to institutions in the United States.

While the Compact is the original legal document for Freely Associated States (FAS) citizens' U.S. legal or immigration status—meaning the legal status that virtually all FAS citizens, including Marshallese citizens, hold upon entering the United States—it interacts with other policy and legal documents to produce its outcomes, in a more complex policy framework than one might think. One such document is a U.S. Citizenship and Immigration Services (USCIS) fact sheet, titled "Status of citizens of the Freely Associated States of the Federated States of Micronesia and the Republic of the Marshall Islands." Given its concise format and easy accessibility online, it likely serves as a reference for public actors dealing with COFA status and COFA migrants in a professional capacity across a range of geographic sites.[4] This fact sheet lays out a provision that is mentioned only fleetingly but which is enormously significant: not only are COFA migrants legally susceptible to deportation (despite a common misperception among Northwest Arkansas residents), they are also technically subject to a financial-means test, sometimes referred to as the "public charge" rule, and could be deported from the United States if they become financially unable to support themselves. As the fact sheet states, "People who, following admission to the United States under the Compacts, cannot show that they have sufficient means of support in the United States may be deportable. Other grounds of deportability, such as conviction for an aggravated felony, also apply to persons admitted under the Compacts." This document also leaves open the possibility that FAS citizens will be denied entry to the United States, emphasizing that while they have the right "to travel and apply for admission to the United States as nonimmigrants without visas ... admission is not guaranteed." Whether these legal mechanisms for COFA migrants' deportability or inadmissibility are activated in any given context,[5] the fact of these provisions' existence, and thus their *potential* implementation, creates an additional layer of precarity for COFA migrants, a precarity that is integral to imperial citizenship.

To understand more about the legal construction of COFA status, beyond the information needed by immigration-law practitioners on a day-to-day basis, a little more digging is required. When digging, one might, as I did, stumble upon a Department of Justice ruling issued in the *Federal Register*, "Habitual residence in the territories and possessions of the United States" (2000), which further clarifies the derivation and legal meaning of the term "habitual resident," one of many legal terms used to describe COFA migrants' status under U.S. immigration law. This document reveals that COFA migrants' designation as "habitual residents" creates further stipulations and contingencies for their legal status (including geographic restrictions), all of which create greater conditionality for COFA status applicability and, thus, enhance COFA migrants' legal precarity.

> "Habitual resident" refers to ... an FAS citizen who has been admitted *to a territory or possession of the United States (except the* CNMI *or American Samoa as long as the Act has not been made applicable there)* ... and who occupies [there] a habitual residence [or] a principal, actual dwelling place of a continuing or lasting nature, including physical presence for a cumulative total of at least 365 days ... the term does not apply to FAS citizens whose presence in the territories or possessions is based on [another] authority, such as members of the Armed Forces of the United States ... , persons lawfully admitted for permanent residence in the United States, or persons having nonimmigrant status whose entry into the United States is based on [other] provisions of the Compacts (emphasis added).

As this ruling makes (somewhat) clear, most (but not all) FAS citizens—citizens of the RMI, FSM, and Palau—are considered "habitual residents" when living in the United States, in some (but not all) of its territories. Therefore, not all FAS citizens traveling to the United States are categorized as COFA migrants, though virtually all FAS citizens *qualify* for COFA status.[6] Habitual residency appears here as a criterion for the rights and benefits proffered by COFA status, though those rights are not enumerated here. Furthermore, the stipulations of "habitual residency" for COFA migrants do not appear consistently in other legal and policy documents regarding COFA status. This ruling, thus, adds another layer of conditionality to the legal constitution of COFA status, exacerbating COFA migrants' legal precarity and tenuousness of status, conditions which are characteristic of imperial citizenship more broadly.

COFA Status "On the Ground"

While its parameters are laid out in federal law and policy—that is to say, at the *national* scale—COFA status is also produced in meaningful ways through the Compact's intersection with laws and policies at *local* and *state* levels, which gives additional specificity to its terms. COFA status also accumulates meaning as key actors involved interpret and apply it, often in inconsistent ways. Such grounded sense-making shapes the particularities of COFA status, and its effects on Marshall Islanders' rights in practice, as much as does the formal legal definition of the status.

COFA STATUS AS LIMINAL: TROUBLING THE "LEGAL"/"ILLEGAL" BINARY

In Northwest Arkansas, COFA status is produced as a liminal or "in-between" legal status that is ambiguously located on a spectrum of "legality," ranging from fully undocumented to U.S. citizen. Many public actors I interviewed perceived Marshallese migrants as existing outside or beyond a "legal"/"illegal" binary. In Springdale, a new immigrant destination for many Latinx as well as Marshallese immigrants, discourses about immigrants' legal status fall into a "legality trap," framing legal status as more black and white than it really is. However, the "legality trap" obscures the "liminal legality" that many immigrant groups experience (Menjívar 2006). Marshall Islanders, as imperial migrants, often trouble the line between documented and undocumented, with complicated effects for their own lives in the areas of immigration, policing, and deportation. Ironically, while Marshallese COFA status often exposes the falsity of a legal/illegal line, their comparisons with Latinx immigrants, drawn by non-Marshallese public actors, often served to reproduce Latinxs as undocumented while positioning Marshallese immigrants as "more or less legal."

Local state actors must often make sense of complex and shifting immigration laws and policies (Hiemstra 2010; M. Coleman 2012; Varsanyi 2010; Wong 2012). For some actors, such as CBP and ICE agents, their work places them formally in the realm of immigration law and policy. Other actors confront the issue of immigrants' legal status in their work more tangentially; these actors include public employees (such as school administrators), local political leaders, and the police (Marrow 2011; Ridgley 2008). In my fieldwork in Northwest Arkansas, many local political figures, police, and immigration officials struggled to articulate how COFA status worked in the law and where it sat on a spectrum of "legality" to "illegality." (I did not use the terms "legal" or "illegal" to describe immigrants, but some of my interviewees did.) In one such encounter, a city official working in a legal capacity explained to me what he understood about (non-U.S.-born) Marshall Islanders' legal status.

> **EME:** What do you know about the Marshallese legal status, the immigration status that they have while they're here?
>
> **Attorney Dole:** I don't know anything other than—I've just been told they're legal. Though I've also been told—I think maybe it was [the Marshallese court interpreter based in Springdale] that told me—that they can still get deported, if they act up. I think she told me that while they're technically here "legally," [*makes finger quotes*] whatever that means—which means they can get a driver's license, they can work, they can do all these things—it's also easy for them to get sent back. By their own . . . not by ICE, but by their own . . . government, if that makes sense.

Attorney Dole then elaborated on his understanding of Marshallese deportation proceedings under U.S. immigration law.

> **Attorney Dole:** [The Marshallese court interpreter] has said, "Well, the Marshallese people, even though they're here legally, they . . . kind of police themselves," that's kind of the way it was described to me. You know, ICE checks our jail every day. If they see someone in our jail that they think, "Oh, we're not sure who they are," they'll run their fingerprints through the FBI database. And they'll put an ICE detainer on them sometimes.[7] Whereas they don't really do that with the Marshallese; it's more Hispanics that they do that with.
>
> **EME:** So, for example, ICE wouldn't come in and put a hold on a Marshallese person who's detained?
>
> **Attorney Dole:** I don't think that I've ever seen that happen.

In explaining the concept of legality, or "being here [in the United States] legally," Attorney Dole reproduced a legal/illegal binary, wherein immigrants fell squarely into one category or the other. He situated Marshallese immigrants as legal while highlighting the ambiguity of that legality—"*technically*, [Marshall Islanders] are here legally—'legally,' [*makes finger quotes*] *whatever that means*." This statement, as well as his hesitation when describing COFA status's particularities, indicates some sense that Marshallese COFA migrants fall between dominant notions of legality and illegality. Yet the legal framework in which he and other legal actors worked made it difficult to understand anything outside these binary definitions of legal status.

The concept of legality as a proxy term for immigration status was articulated frequently by Springdale public actors. In an interview with two senior police department representatives, for instance, the theme of il/legality and Marshall Islanders' complex legal status arose.

> **EME:** One of the things that I've been really curious to learn from you is how much of an issue the legal status is.
>
> **Officer McKenzie:** Well, I think even for us, because that question will often get asked by [the RMI Consul General in Springdale], she may have a concern that somebody has been deported. Well, they don't have to have a visa to come in, or they don't have to have a passport—they have to have a visa to come into the country—which is it? *[Turns to colleague to clarify; colleague shakes head and shrugs in response.]* They can pretty well come and go.... But they're not U.S. citizens. And you have to be a U.S. citizen to be a police officer. And their path to citizenship is—what's a good word—complicated. Because [the Marshall Islands are] a protectorate and not a foreign country. I don't know that we have a clear understanding [of their legal status], and sometimes I'm not sure, because they're not a problematic community. They're not here illegally. So they don't create those kinds of concerns for agencies that would be looking for those kinds of violations.

Officer McKenzie's description of Marshall Islanders' legal status issues reveals a complex range of conceptualizations of legality: legality as *not needing* certain documentation such as a visa or passport (as opposed to *having* such documentation, a more common definition of legal immigration status); legality as smooth entry or mobility across U.S. borders, or the ability to "come and go as they please"; and finally, legality as not-criminality, or as not "problematic" from a policing perspective. Like Attorney Dole, Officer McKenzie admitted that her understanding of COFA status was incomplete, and she referred me to another source who she believed would be more knowledgeable on the topic. Her response constituted a deferral of this knowledge and responsibility that, presumably, she felt her position did not require her to have or that her training never provided in the first place.

Furthermore, Officer McKenzie conveyed a perception that COFA status is not quite a "free pass" to live in the United States without conditions. As she attempted to explain, Marshall Islanders' "path to citizenship is complicated" because the Marshall Islands was "a [U.S.] protectorate, not a foreign country." While this statement is not fully accurate, it does convey her perception of the Marshall Islands' semi- or neocolonial status in relation to the United States, a perception that appeared frequently in interviews and encounters in Arkansas. This is a kind of "imperial sense-making" to which I return in the final chapter.

Despite Officer McKenzie's recognition that COFA status was not equivalent to full, unrestricted, or irrevocable legal status, and despite her awareness that Marshall Islanders with COFA status were legally deportable under certain circumstances, she eventually returned to a conclusion that Marshall Islanders with COFA status were "not here illegally" and, therefore, "not a problematic community." Simply put, Marshallese immigrants were not a concern for agencies dealing with "those kinds of violations," presumably referring to violations related to unlawful presence in the United States. While COFA status was admittedly ambiguous, the presence of immigrants with COFA status did not warrant surveillance or intervention from a policing or immigration-enforcement perspective *as compared with the situation for Latinxs*. Therefore, the Marshallese population was not of major professional concern to her.

While Marshallese immigration status is not of concern to many local legal actors, police, and immigration officials, it frequently becomes a bureaucratic (and personal) problem for its holders. This is especially true in the case of lost documentation, such as a passport or an I-94 form, as discussed in chapter 1. Furthermore, the question of deportation weighed heavy on the minds of many Marshallese community leaders and advocates by August 2019, when I returned to Northwest Arkansas. That summer, there had been a dramatic uptick in ICE raids, particularly in the U.S. South and Midwest and particularly targeting undocumented Latinx immigrants. According to several Arkansas-based Marshallese leaders, this trend had also affected the Marshallese community, with many noting an increase in deportations of Marshall Islanders, up to "hundreds in a year" (interview, Marshallese public official, Springdale, 2019). Another Marshallese community leader, when asked about the immigration climate at the time, said, "An increasing number of raids and family separations is now—I'm seeing it more often than ever before, actually. I have never seen it this. I mean, this is really bad. It's pretty bad."

Marshallese and Latinx community members I met with highlighted community members' fear of deportation amid this stressful political climate. One Marshallese nonprofit leader explained to me how Marshallese COFA migrants were being affected by the intensified immigration policing, surveillance, and deportations, despite ostensibly having greater legal protection than undocumented immigrants.

> EME: When I was here in 2014, there had been maybe two or three deportations of Marshallese [that year] across the state. The Marshallese

> Consul said [there have been] over a hundred in the last couple of years. So, is there racial profiling? It sounds like many people are getting pulled over for minor [things]?
>
> **Mary:** Here's the thing. When you're talking about immigration documents, all the Marshallese need is a passport and I-94. [But] there's a combination of things. You could be summoned to court to go for a traffic violation, and then you fail to pay your fines, and it just builds up. A little thing can absolutely build up into bigger things. Which could lead up to, you know, a deportable offense [*scoffs*].

When I asked her to elaborate on the kinds of charges for which Marshall Islanders were being deported, and whether there had been a shift in enforcement, this actor spoke to the vagueness and elasticity of the legal concept of "moral turpitude." A "crime involving moral turpitude," or CIMT, under U.S. immigration law is an act designated a crime that indicates some degree of immorality or character flaw in the person charged. While often a minor infraction, its affects can be devastating; as the U.S.-based Immigrant Legal Resource Center (2021) advises, "A single CIMT conviction might cause no damage, or it might cause a variety of penalties ranging from deportability to ineligibility for relief to mandatory detention." As such, "moral turpitude" becomes a catchall legal clause—one that interests with race, of course—that can deepen immigrants' vulnerability to deportability based on acts ranging from robbery and assault to public indecency and intoxication, or even, plausibly, housing-code violations and noise complaints, infractions for which both Marshallese and Latinx residents of Springdale are regularly reported (interviews, Marshallese and Latinx community leaders, Springdale, 2013, 2014, 2019).

> **Mary:** Yeah, [generally for "crimes involving] moral turpitude." Once again, "moral turpitude" is so vague. What is moral turpitude? It could be anything. It could be spitting on the floor.
>
> **EME:** It seems like that's exactly the power it holds. It's so flexible; it can be defined differently in different contexts.
>
> **Mary:** Yes. They can use anything to define "moral turpitude." So, yes, I think it's said in a way that it will leave the immigrant community vulnerable, for sure.

In this actor's discussion of Marshallese "deportability," including shifting applications of the "moral turpitude" clause and broader trends in deportations and ICE raids, we see how national-level political shifts in immigration-related discourses and policies led to—or at least corresponded with—a dramatic increase in Marshallese deportations during the first two to three years of the Trump administration. While COFA migrants' legal status *on paper* had not changed, the political atmosphere for undocumented migrants, particularly in terms of policing and deportation, had arguably become more punitive. This had influenced the *lived* nature of COFA status as liminal and (even more) vulnerable to deportation.

Some of the legal actors I interviewed, such as Attorney Dole, held professions that put them into regular contact with Marshall Islanders but did not require them to delve into the particulars of COFA status. Nonetheless, due to their agencies' partnerships with ICE, these interviewees still needed some basic understanding of immigration status and law. One senior legal official interviewed explained that he did not deal at all with Marshallese clients' "legal status issue." However, he clearly had a working understanding of how deportability functioned as a legal condition, particularly how certain crimes made one vulnerable to deportation.

> EME: What do you know about [the unique legal status of Marshall Islanders], and how does that come into play [in your work]?
>
> Legal official: It does not come into play at all with me. Because I don't ask them their status or anything. But I know from dealings, I understand that they've got a visa, they can get a driver's license, I mean a passport, and they can get a driver's license, and everything.
>
> EME: For Latino immigrants, or Hispanic immigrants, does their status come up in the courtroom?
>
> Legal official: No, no, I never get into that. Well, it might if they say—well, today, a Spanish-speaking prisoner said, "I'm just ready to get deported." And so, I asked if there was a hold, and there's a hold on him. But it means nothing to me at all—I'm going to treat them the same way regardless. But the Marshallese are all pretty well the same status, is what I've always heard.

Even though this legal official did not routinely ask individuals in court proceedings their immigration status, he was clearly aware that for undocumented or "out-of-status" immigrants with criminal charges, it would be common for ICE to place a hold on them to begin deportation proceedings after the criminal charges had been addressed. He also conveyed a familiarity with Marshallese legal status, albeit a vague one ("pretty well all the same status"). This legal official's vague familiarity with COFA status, despite his professional capacity as a local legal official with a high level of authority, was reflective of several legal actors and political officials I interviewed. As these interviews revealed, even actors working closely with immigration law had a superficial, and often incorrect, understanding of the legal particulars of COFA status.

Similar themes appeared in conversations with federal agents working directly in immigration. In Arkansas, I had two field encounters with Department of Homeland Security (DHS) immigration officers, one a formal interview and one an informal meeting. In the interview with Officer Anderson, a Homeland Security Investigations officer, our discussion of Marshall Islanders' legal status was brief, for the reason given in his response.

> **EME:** I wanted to get an idea of how much you work with the Marshallese population and what kind of dynamics you are seeing there in terms of legal status and their relations with other immigrant groups.
>
> **Officer Anderson:** I had limited [contact with that community], because the Marshallese, because of the agreements—well, they aren't given a green card, [but] they're pretty much looked at like immigrants, or having full immigration status, when they come in here. So unless they committed a serious offense, we really didn't have that many dealings with them.

Here, Officer Anderson used the phrase "having full immigration status" in the same way that other interviewees used the term "legal." As in previous examples, he articulated full legal immigration status as being tied to a broader range of benefits, such as employment—"[the ability] to work and everything." Furthermore, he conveyed the sense that due to their legal status, Marshallese immigrants were not a population of legal concern, unless they committed a crime that might place them at risk of deportation. In this final point, Officer Anderson again echoed a common understanding that Marshallese immigrants' legality not only *translated into* but in fact *originated from* their noncriminality as immigrants. This perception, given in a 2014 interview, is directly contradicted by the increased deportation of COFA migrants through an expanded application of "moral-turpitude" rulings, as was evident by 2019.

In interviews with police officers, immigration officers, public officials, and other local state actors, many struggled to define the il/legality of Marshall Islanders with COFA status. Quite frequently, these actors, upon assuming that Marshallese immigrants were not "illegal," assumed that they were therefore fully "legal," having full rights of a U.S. citizen or legal permanent resident. Such assumptions obscured or precluded these actors' recognition of the legal liminality of Marshallese (COFA) migrants and the restrictions on their rights and access to benefits. In this way, they shaped these actors' engagement with Marshallese immigrants in a professional capacity. As Nicholas De Genova (2002) has argued, the discursive and representational production of illegality creates a "frail ideological dichotomy of 'exclusion' and 'inclusion'" (1181). This dichotomous framing also characterized understandings of COFA status held by many law enforcement agents and policy and legal actors in Springdale.

I incorporate a focus on il/legality here because Marshall Islanders, as COFA migrants, fall between "legal" and "illegal" immigrant categories, and critiques of the il/legality dichotomy or trap can offer insights on how that trap renders COFA status illegible for certain actors. I join established critiques of il/legality: Hiemstra (2010), for example, examines illegality as a tool of neoliberal governmentality wielded at the local level, whereas Jones-Correa and de Graauw (2013) critique the analytical trap of approaching immigrant status as primarily a problem of illegality, obscuring liminal, semilegal, or contingently legal immigrant statuses. I extend these analyses to argue that imperial subjects have always been produced in the legal space—and the *territorial space*—between "foreign" and "domestic." Put differently, debates over the "legality" of imperial or (post)colonial subjects in the U.S. mainland—whether they are classified as immigrants, nonimmigrants, permanent residents, or citizens—has often been linked to debates over the legal status of nonsovereign places and populations (Joseph and Rosenberg 2001). However, such discourses about imperial migrants' legality do not always emerge in immigration debates in places such as Arkansas, which historically lack large migrant populations from U.S. territories (as do many places in the U.S. mainland), unlike, for example, Hawai'i. As a result, legal actors often do not recognize COFA status as explicitly *imperial*, or as produced by a (post)colonial or imperial political relationship between the United States and the RMI.

Instead, Marshallese immigrants, rendered illegible within a legal/illegal binary, are often assumed to be fully legal and, thus, to not pose a legal challenge, even though on paper their legal status is precarious and conditional in all sorts of ways. In Springdale, this assumption often led legal actors to disregard Marshall Islanders as potentially "unlawfully present" and to let them be in terms of immigration enforcement. This assumption may have also disincentivized these actors from looking more closely into COFA status's particular legal characteristics and to look more harshly at Latinx immigrants *in relation to* Marshall Islanders. In all these ways, legal and policy actors' interpretation and implementation of COFA status on the ground give new substance and form to categories of legal/illegal, potentially affecting the ways in which these actors chose to police (or not), monitor (or not), and respond to legal and policy issues affecting Marshall Islanders and other immigrant groups in their town.

COFA STATUS AS EXCEPTIONAL:
TENUOUS ACCESS TO SOCIAL SERVICES

While the legal and policing context generated a focus on the COFA migrants' *legality* as immigrants, the social services context was where the *exceptional* nature of COFA status was both made visible and reproduced. In the realm of social services, COFA status's exceptionality becomes starkly apparent to both to Marshallese COFA status holders seeking services and benefits and to the public actors who work with them. Let me explain what I mean by exceptionality in a practical sense: because COFA migrants have such a unique immigration status in the United States, they are neither automatically included *nor explicitly excluded* in most state-run programs, services, and benefits. Therefore, their eligibility must be spelled out somewhere in the policy, often as an addendum or a footnote of clarification. Where eligibility is not spelled out—and it is routinely not—COFA migrants fall into a dubious area of protection, neither explicitly eligible nor ineligible, resulting in an ambiguity that makes accessing (and providing) social services challenging. COFA migrants' piecemeal, conditional, and exceptional inclusion in public services and programs, therefore, creates a tenuous access to social programs more broadly. Moreover, debates over COFA migrants' eligibility for public benefits dredge up long-standing discourses and practices that exclude poor and working-class (and racialized) immigrants from state support by depicting them as dependent on the state and questioning their deservingness of state support.

During fieldwork, I encountered countless instances in which COFA status's categorical ambiguity created impediments for Marshall Islanders trying to access services and benefits. Springdale's Marshallese Consul put it to me this way:

> **EME:** I remember talking to a public housing official here [in 2014], and she was unclear about whether COFA migrants are eligible [for public housing]. That seems to be so much of the challenge: people just don't know.
> **Consul:** That's my biggest challenge here. I'm on the phone all the time, explaining what COFA is, to businesses, to government agencies.

In the social services context, both social service providers and Marshallese beneficiaries I spoke to framed COFA status through a lens of what scholars have termed "social citizenship," which "involves entitlements such as provisions for health, housing and education" (see Mann 1987, 339). This social citizenship framework enabled non-Marshallese actors in health, education, and other public sectors to see how COFA status imposed limitations on Marshall Islanders' access to benefits and services, limitations characteristic of imperial citizenship more broadly. As a result, these actors tended to have a more nuanced and thorough understanding of the *social* implications of COFA status than did the legal actors interviewed. For the Marshall Islanders I spoke with, COFA status's exceptional nature—and its resulting limitations on services and benefits—was a source of frustration, concern, and, often, anger. For Marshall Islanders, like many other U.S. imperial or colonial subjects, public benefits were kept out of reach through exclusionary federal and state policies (Riklon et al. 2010).

For a variety of reasons, health care was at the heart of much public policy and advocacy work within, and with, the Marshallese population in Northwest Arkansas. The most important of these is COFA migrants' long-standing ineligibility for Medicaid, a restriction put into place during the Clinton administration under H.R. 3734, the 1996 Personal Responsibility and Work Opportunity Reconciliation Act.[8] While Congress overturned the Medicaid eligibility restriction for COFA migrants in December 2020, the long-lasting effects of state abandonment persist: most Marshall Islanders in the United States lack health insurance, and many cannot afford basic health care. COFA migrants' long-standing Medicaid ineligibility, and the resulting limitations to health care access, has exacerbated other health concerns for Marshall Islanders, including medical issues tied to nuclear testing, such as thyroid and other cancers; diabetes and dietary issues; and communicable diseases like Hansen's disease and tuberculosis (Choi 2008).[9]

The complexity of the Medicaid ineligibility issue was heightened by the 2014 Affordable Care Act (ACA) implementation. While in some contexts, the ACA expanded coverage for previously ineligible groups, including many immigrant and low-income groups, it also created a new policy language to be interpreted. This in turn posed administrative challenges for health care providers and for populations seeking coverage. In Arkansas, practitioners, advocates, and community members, for example, spent much energy and focus on determining Marshallese COFA migrants' eligibility for coverage under the new regulations.

Marshallese community actors I interviewed—from consular staff to health care workers to pastors to educators—frequently named health care as most important issue facing their community. This strong focus on health care in

Marshallese advocacy and policy activism is evident in other sites in the Marshallese diaspora as well (Lyons and Tengan 2015). Health care activism and advocacy, in fact, has forged some of the strongest institutional and organizational connections *between* different Marshallese communities in the U.S. mainland, Hawaiʻi, U.S. Pacific Island territories such as Guåhan and the CNMI, and the Marshall Islands themselves (McElfish et al. 2015).

I was interested to learn how the shifting health care policy landscape affected COFA migrants and health care actors in Arkansas. My encounters with Arkansas-based health care advocates included several one-on-one interviews with health care providers, community-outreach coordinators, nurses, and policy specialists, as well as monthly meetings of the local group, Gaps in Services to Marshallese Task Force, "Gaps" for short), which I attended. At one Gaps meeting I attended, participants discussed strategies for addressing health care issues. Three group members, including the Task Force's founder and a Marshallese community activist and court interpreter, had just been brought on as Marshallese community liaisons for the Arkansas Minority Health Commission. They emphasized the need to advocate for Marshallese health outreach at the state level and to make the Marshallese population visible to Arkansas state legislators.

The conversation then turned to issues with the ACA, Medicaid, and Marshallese enrollment. One group member mentioned that some Marshallese people with COFA status had applied for Medicaid and been "accidentally" accepted, while others were still being rejected. Another health care provider shared that her agency had partnered with six Marshallese bilingual outreach workers to enroll at least 325 Marshallese residents of Washington County in the health plan. At that point, a Marshallese community leader mentioned that she had talked to an Independent Practice Association (IPA) representative in Little Rock, who said she was able to register about a hundred Marshallese people for Medicaid. "Obviously, [the IPA representative] had no idea what their status and eligibility was. She categorized the COFA migrants as refugees; that's probably why they qualified. They'll probably get a letter revoking those benefits later," she said, and another group member agreed. A third person chimed in: "Well, I think it was a real mistake that those benefits got taken away in 1996, that COFA residents were excluded. If we are going to raise awareness of this injustice, then we have to work with people at the federal level—who are willing and listening—to try to get them some kind of coverage." The first group member responded, "The thing is, there is some person punching the button down there who doesn't have any idea what people qualify for."

As these advocates statements indicate, even experts in health services and health care eligibility were often unfamiliar with COFA status, whose illegibility had at times made it difficult for COFA migrants to receive services (though, as one advocate pointed out, Marshall Islanders' misclassification as "refugees" could also grant them access to health care benefits for which they normally would not qualify). Thus, while COFA status did not always block COFA migrants' access to certain benefits, uncertainty around its meaning often *complicated* that access, which could have the same ultimate effect of rendering benefits inaccessible in practice.

Other Springdale-based health care providers reiterated the difficulty of getting medical coverage and care for Marshall Islanders,[10] with many expressing frustration that Marshallese youth with COFA status were not covered under ARKids, the Arkansas Children's Health Insurance Program. One provider pointed out that other immigrant children—"for example, someone from Mexico or El Salvador"—would qualify for the program after having a green card for five years. However, these benefits would not extend to undocumented children. Another advocate mentioned that despite COFA migrants' ineligibility for some health programs in Arkansas (most significantly, Medicaid and ARKids), the ACA allowed them access to certain coverage. Due to the vague wording of coverage rejection letters, she worried that many Marshall Islanders might reasonably assume that they were not eligible for *any* health care coverage: "So, if I got a letter like that—and I wasn't superfluent in English, and hadn't lived here for very long, and already didn't understand what was going on with the health care system, and didn't have health insurance, and just wasn't literate in all of that bureaucracy—then I'd just think, 'Well, that's it, I'm just not a person who gets anything with the ACA. Obamacare is not for me.' And that would be the end of that. So we were really concerned about [that]." These conversations reveal practitioners' confusion over what COFA status means in practice. Such confusion makes Marshallese more vulnerable to health issues, given the challenges and time it takes to access resources.

Many Marshallese community advocates I interviewed expressed similar concerns about coverage issues, citing the economic and social costs to migrants of a health care system that was legally restrictive and financially prohibitive. Furthermore, they expressed frustration that COFA status was often unfamiliar to advocates and policymakers, as this unfamiliarity hampered COFA migrants' access to health care. One Marshallese nonprofit leader linked the right to Medicaid to citizenship: "The only thing we need is really the Medicaid part. I think we need to re-evaluate what was taken out when they had that welfare reform. I think there need to be an appropriate term in there, the legal term 'lawful resident' needs to be part of this. Because we're definitely legal. We are . . . we're documented. We're legal. And yet, we don't have access to those things" (interview, Springdale, 2019). A Marshallese pastor I interviewed echoed similar concerns in the context of citizenship, saying, "All the Marshallese working here, they contribute to Medicare or Medicaid, but we are not on that. They take from our paycheck for Medicare or Medicaid or whatever, but we don't [get] those. They said we're not citizens" (interview, Springdale, 2019).

Similar frustrations about COFA status's exceptional and tenuous nature came up in my meeting with Marshallese English as a Second Language (ESL) liaisons for the Springdale Public School system. One administrator mentioned that many Marshallese people traveled from the RMI to Hawai'i for medical treatment, including radiation, chemotherapy, and dialysis (cancer and diabetes being two common health issues for Marshall Islanders). I commented that I had been in Hawai'i and had met with the medical referral staff there. Evangeline said that it was very overpopulated there, with so many Marshallese people going to Hawai'i for medical treatment. The Marshall Islands used to have a dialysis machine, she said, but they sold it to a neighboring island. A brief discussion ensued of which benefits COFA migrants get: free school lunches, for example, but not Medicaid or ARKids. "You know," Evangeline said, "before the amendment, we could get all that stuff. Now you have to live here five years, or something like that. So, many things happened that we didn't realize were going to take place when the original Compact was approved." Her comment echoed the frustrations of many Marshall Islanders I spoke with, who felt that the provisions originally put in place by—or concurrent to—the 1986 Compact had been eroded in the years since. Their perceptions speak again to the exceptional nature of COFA status as it has emerged in law since 1986 and in its subsequent revisions, a quality characteristic of imperial citizenship.

For other Marshallese public actors, issues of COFA migrants' health care access and health issues in the United States were directly linked not only to the Compact's (and related policies') unjust restrictions, but also to the history of U.S. nuclear testing in the Marshall Islands.

> EME: To what degree would you say people are linking health concerns to nuclear effects? Is that still something that people talk about a lot?
>
> BR: Yeah. I think sometimes it might be too much, because everybody's thinking that. And they might be right, I don't know. Everybody's thinking that all our cancers are coming from that nuclear testing.

> EME: They're high rates.
> BR: Yeah, very high rates. And all these funerals, the majority of the funerals that I go to, these people are young, like [in their] fifties. And they're dying of cancer: thyroid cancer, lung cancer.

The United States' failure to protect Marshall Islanders' health through health care and employment benefits, he felt, compounded their vulnerability, adding insult to injury.

> BR: You know, most people that come here and work at Tyson, they bring their parents to live with them. Their parents are like their [babysitters]; they take care of their kids while they're at work. And I've been trying to talk Tyson into including the parents as immediate family. It's what our culture is. Immediate family includes the parents. But they . . .
> EME: In terms of benefits, you mean?
> BR: Yes, in terms of benefits.
> EME: Yes, that would make sense. But they haven't been receptive to that?
> BR: No.
> EME: What kind of answers have you gotten?
> BR: "We'll think about it," "We will talk about it."

As many Marshallese public actors lamented, even the benefits formally proffered by COFA status are not always readily available to COFA migrants in practice. While in some instances, traveling stepwise toward the mainland—moving geographically, for example, from Guåhan and the CNMI to Hawai'i then to the U.S. mainland—enables Marshall Islanders to access necessary health care treatments, this access has been impeded by the rising costs of travel to and living in the United States, as well as Medicaid ineligibility. According to one health care advocate, Marshallese pastors in Springdale were advising people to have any needed dental work done in the Marshall Islands before migrating to the mainland because the cost was so prohibitive in the United States. Another Marshallese advocate working in legal services reflected on the health care issue in the context of the Compact, weighing the pros and cons of having migration access to the United States.

> I mean, I thank God that we can come to the United States and get a better life, but we were better off on our islands. But we come to the United States, and the thing that is the most vital to our life is our health! And we still cannot have any access to any health care or anything that they can help with, like diabetes. You have to understand that diabetes started after we were introduced

to Spam, to all those canned foods, canned vegetables, canned meats, canned fruits. And who introduced those to us? The Americans [*laughs*]!

In addition to health care, many advocates I interviewed worked in education, housing, legal services, and translation. The challenges for Marshallese COFA migrants in higher education were often socioeconomic and cultural as well as legal. Many Marshallese students at the local community college were first-generation college students and qualified as low-income; thus, they might have difficulty pursuing higher education instead of working for an income that would support other family members. Actors in higher education also pointed to the financial constraints imposed on Marshallese youth with COFA status as a result of their ineligibility for certain federal benefits. Although Marshallese citizens are eligible for federal student financial aid (FAFSA) through the Compact, they are ineligible for certain loans, making college very difficult to afford. This ineligibility points to another aspect of COFA migrants' exceptional legal status: while Marshall Islanders are *legally* able to attend college or university in the United States, their exceptional legal status restricts them from accessing the full economic support needed to do so. These restrictions, again, create a tenuous access to benefits, services, and programs for COFA migrants.

Again here, larger economic and structural issues intersected with COFA status limitations on financial aid to further limit educational access for Marshallese youth with COFA status. Limited public transportation to the local community college also created a barrier—a *geographical* barrier, exacerbated by an *economic* one—to attendance for some Marshallese young adults. Some interviewees cited the additional logistic challenge of attending Northwest Arkansas Community College (NWACC) posed by inadequate public transportation between its main campus in Bentonville and Springdale, about fifteen miles to the south, where most Marshallese students lived with their families. One NWACC employee said that she had known a few Marshallese students to take a taxi to class when they lacked other transportation options, but the cost quickly become prohibitive and the students eventually dropped out.

Marshall Islanders also struggled to obtain benefits when non-Marshallese service providers were unfamiliar with COFA status. While some social services actors were quite knowledgeable about COFA status and its benefits and restrictions, many others, working in housing or food assistance, for example, were still unaware of what COFA status entails. One advocate elaborated on this challenge.

> The Marshallese are so different because of their legal status; people don't understand that. [Marshall Islanders] are frustrated at places of employment

because their employer wants their I-94. They may have in their hand a social security card, but that employer wants that I-94, because *they're looking at them as an immigrant and they don't realize that they're nonimmigrants; they're here legally.* So it shouldn't be that big of an issue, [but] someone in an HR department in a company is not going to know those details. That's something we want to help them understand, is *the Marshallese are different.* They're here legally; they can come and go. There are no—I hate to say absolutes, I'd have to ask [the Consul] this—but *I don't think there are any illegal Marshallese in the United States. I don't think that's a legal possibility.* I think people who've committed crimes have been deported, but—and if one of those [people] came back, I suppose that would be illegal—but those are so few and far between it's not even worth talking about. (interview, Fayetteville, 2014, emphasis added)

While this interviewee discussed COFA migrants' challenges to obtaining benefits, she also positioned Marshall Islanders as fundamentally different from other immigrants. For her, the difference that marked Marshall Islanders compared with other immigrant groups was their legal presence, and moreover, their categorical impossibility of being "illegal." In framing them this way, she conflated immigrants with those who are present *illegally*. For her, being an immigrant meant possibly being "illegal." Being Marshallese, on the other hand, meant being different in an unclear register. In a sense, she was correct: categorically, as foreign entrants designated "nonimmigrants" under U.S. immigration law, COFA migrants are indeed different in key ways from other immigrant groups, such as the Latinx immigrants to Northwest Arkansas against whom Marshall Islanders are often compared (in this example, by potential employers). Her assumption that COFA migrants were categorically "undeportable" proved false: five years later, Marshallese deportations had skyrocketed, both in Arkansas and elsewhere in the United States. In other words, her assumption that COFA status offered virtually airtight legal protection for its beneficiaries would not hold true.

Another issue that had gained salience by the time I returned to Northwest Arkansas in 2019 was the public charge rule. A public charge is defined by USCIS as an immigrant who is likely to become primarily dependent on the government for assistance. The term "public charge" was first introduced in the 1882 Chinese Exclusion Act, as an effort to keep out working-class Chinese immigrants (Lee 2003). Since the late nineteenth century, political leaders have intermittently reinstated the public charge rule to effectively filter out low-income immigrants who might use public benefits, often at times of heightened national xenophobia. This history shows the long life span of this legal mechanism of racial and class-based immigrant exclusion.

At the time of my fieldwork trip in August 2019, President Trump was publicly proposing a reinstatement of the public charge rule, and many Marshall Islanders worried that by using benefits to which they were legally entitled they might be jeopardizing their COFA status. In an interview with three Marshallese nonprofit actors, I asked about how this potential public charge rule might affect their community and constituents. One interviewee responded: "The public charge issue is really scary, because Marshallese go in and out [of the United States] all the time, and most of our folks are at poverty or below. So that could potentially affect us, even though we do have this special relationship [with the United States]. Not letting people back into the U.S. because they feel like we're needy: it's so wrong on so many levels. I mean, we did not choose this. We're very angry. And people are scared." Her statement reveals the palpable anger, fear, and frustration felt by many Marshall Islanders facing this rule's proposal and the unfairness they felt at being treated this way by the U.S. government, with whom Marshall Islanders supposedly share a "special relationship." This quote also gestures to the larger logics of exclusion working against Marshall Islanders in the United States. Just as charges of moral turpitude were being used more frequently to deport Marshallese COFA migrants under the Trump administration, as discussed previously, the threat of the public charge rule was being used to discourage COFA migrants from using benefits for which they were eligible, for fear it might prevent them from accessing U.S. citizenship down the road. In other words, the logics of criminality and immorality ("moral turpitude") and dependency ("public charge"), logics long weaponized against other immigrant groups in times of intensified xenophobia, were again appearing here to exacerbate the exceptional nature of COFA status and its holders' tenuous access to social services, programs, and benefits.

In summary, then, while some social service providers' work with Marshallese clients gave them a detailed understanding of COFA status, its associated benefits and restrictions, and, often, the history of U.S. nuclear testing in the islands, their understanding of COFA status did not connect its existence to U.S. colonization of the islands, the phenomenon that produced such rightlessness in the first place. In other words, Marshall Islanders' exceptional legal status produced confusion on the part of public actors that had the effect of limiting their access to social services and benefits, even those provisioned by law.

COFA STATUS AS EXCLUSIONARY:
SECOND-CLASS CITIZENSHIP AND IMMIGRANTS' RIGHTS ACTIVISM

Finally, I turn to a third frame, one that interprets COFA status as an exclusionary status that makes Marshallese vulnerable through rightlessness. This was the frame most drawn on by activists and community organizers I interviewed, both Marshallese and Latinx as well as white and a few Black activists. Here I look at this third group—immigrants' rights activists—to examine how they understood COFA status, its characteristics, and its political significance. Activists interpreted and made sense of legal status through a rights-based framework, which enabled them to see COFA status's rights-based limitations and larger political significance. As such, this framework, and the context of coalitional activism around immigrants' rights and racial justice, offered the most potential for organizing within and across immigrant communities and with nonimmigrant allies. Most immigrants' rights activists I met with were focused on exclusions based on legal status; many of the Marshallese activists had COFA status, and many of the Latinx activists either had Deferred Action for Childhood Arrivals (DACA) status or were undocumented. Despite immigrants' legal differences—whether they were dealing with "imperial citizenship" or "no citizenship"—legal status became an opportunity for coalition building between immigrant groups, if not one without its challenges.

At the same time, as I argue in this chapter, dominant frameworks in U.S. mainland immigrants' rights organizing, which focus on the legal status–based rightlessness as experienced by fully undocumented immigrants (Carrasco and Seif 2014), do not tend to engage with *other kinds* of legal status–based rightlessness, such as those often experienced by immigrants from nonsovereign U.S. territories. As a result, non-Marshallese immigrants' rights organizers and activists in Arkansas generally did not engage with the *imperial* dimensions of COFA status and the limitations that status poses on COFA migrants' rights, limitations that were usually very obvious to Marshallese activists. The occlusion of empire here worked again as somewhat of an impediment to organizing for imperial subjects' rights, though, as I show, coalitional activism between immigrant groups in this NDE offered great potential for building awareness of, and resistance to, U.S. empire.

In Arkansas, as in many sites in the Marshallese diaspora, Marshall Islanders exist alongside other immigrant groups who have a range of legal statuses, experiences (with law, policy, and the actors who enforce them), and histories of negotiating and resisting the confines of the law (Guerrero 2017). The significance of legal status in these contexts is thus defined and given meaning in relational fashion. During my time in Northwest Arkansas—a total of five months over the course of three years—I interviewed activists and community organizers, attended weekly coalition meetings and social justice events, and examined organizational materials to examine how COFA status was understood and operationalized in activist strategies. After attending regular immigrants' rights organizing meetings for several months, I began conducting one-on-one interviews with a number of organizers and activists. In these interviews, I asked several open-ended questions about their priorities, challenges, and successes in organizing work, as well as about key issues that had come up during the previous months.

During my first extended fieldwork trip in 2014, many of the community leaders I met with were Latinx and primarily served Latinx communities in Northwest Arkansas. I also interviewed a number of Marshallese activists, who were mostly working in organizations that were not Marshallese-led. At the time, there were a few Marshallese-led activist groups in formation, and several immigrants' rights organizations working in coalitional models to connect diverse immigrant communities, but no clear Marshallese-led activist groups that I was able to identify. However, I did interview a number of Marshallese pastors; those interviews are incorporated here and elsewhere in the book. (Much Marshallese outreach and organizing happens in the context of church-based communities, and Springdale is home to at least thirty different Marshallese congregations.) When I returned in 2019, Springdale was by then home to at least two Marshallese-led nonprofit organizations that had grown significantly over the previous five years. Interviews with several Marshallese organizational leaders, administrators, and program directors at these organizations, as well as representatives at the RMI Consulate's office, are woven throughout this section. My conversations with organizers, activists, and community leaders in Arkansas covered a seemingly limitless breadth of topics, and I cannot do justice to all those conversations here. Instead, my intent is to focus narrowly on questions of citizenship and legal status and how they played out in organizing efforts among Northwest Arkansas immigrants' rights groups.

Activist groups interviewed pursued diverse strategies. Although most focused on immigrants' rights issues, their missions often overlapped with other issues: labor and workers' rights; racial justice and civil rights; voter engagement and civic participation; gender and women's rights; and economic development, among others. While many organizations I observed were Latinx-led and had largely Latinx constituents, their organizational missions were to address immigrants' social integration, service provision, legal protection, and rights in general. Many activists, thus, felt that it was key for Latinxs and Marshall Islanders to work together on these issues. A number of organizations had Marshallese employees (at least one or two) and were working with these activists as community liaisons to build outreach efforts. Often, the same person served in multiple capacities across organizations, whether as an employee, volunteer, or board member. One noteworthy example of cross-community organizing was underway at the Northwest Arkansas Workers' Justice Center in 2014, when the center's staff began to form a working group composed of Latinx and Marshallese organizers and community leaders. Through partnerships such as these, Latinx and Marshallese organizers were beginning to build meaningful links across their communities, seeing the necessity and political potential of a coalitional approach.

Immigrants' rights activists, especially those who had experienced undocumented status or another limited or conditional U.S. legal status., were more likely than other actors to understand the complexities of COFA status as something beyond, or between, "legal" and "illegal," and were more likely to see COFA-based restrictions as a form of exclusion. As many organizers and activists made clear, their focus on undocumented immigrants' issues emerged as a response to the precarity and vulnerability produced by the policing of "illegality," a precarity intensified by recent increases in immigration raids. Furthermore, many community activists were undocumented themselves (or had been previously) or had undocumented family members, and their work was thus directly informed by personal experiences of living "without papers." These experiences brought a rich sensitivity, emotional complexity, and deep integrity to these activists' work with immigrant communities on questions of legal status.

In Northwest Arkansas, many activists felt, having liminal or restricted immigration status made organizing for collective rights more difficult, both for Latinxs and for Marshall Islanders. As one Marshallese organizer put it, "[a precarious legal status] keeps us under control, or in control. It keeps us, you know, on our toes, feeling, 'I don't have the liberty to get a DUI, or I don't have the liberty to speak up about certain things. I don't have the liberty to organize.'" Her comment reflects a common analysis among interviewees of the ways that legal status was used to police immigrant communities and keep them "in check," especially to dissuade undocumented immigrants from unionizing or organizing. At the same time, this shared experience made legal status a focal point around which immigrants with very different immigration statuses could organize, bringing COFA migrants together with undocumented immigrants and DACA recipients.[11]

In many instances, a focus on rightlessness enabled Latinx and other non-Marshallese activists to gain an intimate familiarity with the "pain points" of COFA status—the conditions and terms that created the most anguish and injustice for its holders—through their coalitional activism with Marshall Islanders. In one meeting, a Marshallese community organizer articulated how COFA status produced rightlessness for COFA migrants through its various exclusions: "The legal status is definitely an issue. There are many immigration problems [for Marshall Islanders]. I can say that our status is unique, in good and bad ways. Almost all Pacific Islanders have a unique relationship to the United States. So, we're not eligible for Medicaid, or student loans, or any other benefits like that. We're also not allowed to vote, so we don't have a voice. But we do pay a lot of taxes! So it's a way for people here to take advantage of us, you know?" However, cross-community organizing was not without challenges and tensions. One issue that divided organizers, both between and within the Latinx and Marshallese communities, was 287(g), an immigration policy first discussed in chapter 4 in which local police partnered with federal immigration agencies. While 287(g) was eventually phased out in Springdale, its effects were still on the minds of many community organizers, who felt that Springdale police continued to collaborate with ICE. When 287(g) began to be implemented in 2007, it had a fracturing effect on immigrant-led organizations in Northwest Arkansas. Some groups opposed 287(g), arguing that it would increase anti-immigrant surveillance and racial profiling. Other groups eventually supported the measure, agreeing to work with local police to convey the policy to their members and larger communities. One Latinx activist shared his concerns regarding 287(g)'s implementation in the area and the divisions it produced in the area's immigrant communities.

> I was against 287(g). I spoke with the chief of police. I spoke with the mayor. I went to speak to Washington about that with the director of immigration services. I wrote letters to ICE questioning their decision to allow an area like this, with racial profiling and a lot of tension in their relations, to implement 287(g), especially when the city of Rogers had been sued for racial profiling.... Some local people were saying that it was for the good of the community, that they were after the criminals. Then, some Marshallese and some Latinos came together to support the implementation of 287(g). (interview, Springdale, July 2014)

The contentious split over how to address 287(g), several activists commented, had ruptured relations between community groups, eroding the trust and goodwill they had established. Many agreed that trust had been difficult to rebuild. Furthermore, some organizers felt that local authorities, including the police, fostered divisiveness between Latinxs and Marshall Islanders, thus weakening both communities and their potential for building solidarity. One Latinx organizer discussed the aftereffects of the 287(g) program in this way:

> Our community doesn't see it, but keeping us divided is what the city wants. It's what the government wants. They don't want us together! If we unite and we really use our power and our voice, then they're out of a job. Keeping us like this, I could even see strategically—we talk about this at the Civil Rights Roundtable[12]—with the city ordinances possibly going to our neighborhood and picking only on the Marshallese people or picking on the Latino people and not picking on the Marshallese people. What are the Latinos going to think? The city's picking on Marshallese people. Marshallese people are going to think they're only picking on us. (interview, Springdale, July 2014)

The 287(g) program and its reverberating effects created ongoing schisms and mistrust between immigrant groups, ruptures that occasionally made coalitional organizing within and across immigrant communities difficult. At the same time, 287(g) also galvanized solidarity-building efforts between Marshallese and Latinx community activists, especially during the summer of 2019, when ICE targeted immigrant communities in a series of large-scale coordinated deportation raids across the U.S. South and Midwest. While there were no large-scale raids in Northwest Arkansas, the threat of such a possibility loomed large and brought together many immigrants' rights activists from across different communities and organizations.

The 287(g) controversy also led many activists to be cautious about forming partnerships with the police, seeing such partnerships as a double-edged sword that might heighten the vulnerability for undocumented community members. Other were skeptical of policies and policing measures that would create schisms between immigrants designated as good versus bad, deserving versus undeserving, and law abiding versus criminal. In short, 287(g) created a slew of tensions within and between immigrant communities in Northwest Arkansas, just as it exacerbated precarity and rightlessness for both Marshallese and Latinx immigrants.

Misconceptions between Latinxs and Marshall Islanders about the various legal statuses held by members of each group sometimes created tensions, most frequently over employment and access to benefits. Such comparisons tended to focus on perceived hierarchies of vulnerability rather than relationally produced legal vulnerabilities (e.g., between undocumented Latinx immigrants and Marshallese COFA migrants) that impeded full coalitional organizing in some instances, and that employers, police, and ICE agents often played off one another. One organizer who had been involved in cross-community organizing summarized those tensions.

> I think the main misconception that there is that Marshallese people just get a lot of money from the government. They have everything handed to them. Latinos don't have a whole lot of things handed to them, or pretty much nothing, because of being undocumented. I think [Latinos] have that, I guess, resentment that [Marshall Islanders] got it made. "They have papers. They get money, and I don't. I work hard," is their mentality. "Why should they and not me?" Once you start talking to [Latinos] about how the U.S. experimented on their islands and all this stuff, really put it to them in perspective, they're like, "Oh, okay. I see." (interview, Springdale, July 2014)

This activist's comments touched on a recurrent theme in conversations with activists and other Springdale residents: the "mutual stereotyping" that occurred between Latinx and Marshallese communities, resulting in divisions between them. Upon closer inspection, however, these comments are not just about stereotypes but also about misperceptions of comparative legal statuses between two groups of immigrants disenfranchised due to their respective legal statuses: undocumented immigrants and COFA migrants. In the same way that long-term residents often compared anti-Black racism with anti-immigrant sentiments, activists suggested, many immigrants compared undocumented legal status with COFA status, often generating misperceptions about how each one worked.

Another Latinx immigrants' right activist critiqued what he saw as a commonly held stereotype of Marshall Islanders as lazy or complacent. He reoriented the conversation about stereotypes around the legal rights and benefits tied to COFA status, many of which were denied to undocumented immigrants. Nevertheless, while seeking common ground between Marshall Islanders with COFA status and undocumented Latinxs, he inadvertently reproduced a (false) assumption that Marshallese immigrants all receive full benefits and have less incentive to organize, a position countered by many other interviewees.

> It's hard [to build solidarity between immigrant groups]. What we can do to bring Marshallese people and Hispanics together? It's hard to come up with something right away. The thing is that Marshallese people—I don't think they're too lazy to do it. I just feel like they're satisfied with what they have. All of them get benefits. With undocumented folks, they have to fight for more be-

cause they have to pay out-of-state tuition. They can't go to Mexico, or El Salvador, or Guatemala. What do you say to Marshallese people? They get money from the government. They're not suffering now. Why would they want to fight if they have nothing to really fight for? (interview, Fayetteville, July 2014)

Despite persistent misperceptions and tensions over questions of legal status between Springdale's Latinx and Marshall Islander communities, many activists expressed a strong belief that the *possibilities* for organizing across communities and for creating solidarity between Latinxs and Marshall Islanders were potent, if not yet actualized. Several interviewees gestured to the shared experiences of exclusion or marginalization between the two communities: labor abuses (particularly at poultry plants); racial profiling by police around traffic stops, noise violations, and other city ordinances; and a shared vulnerability to police and ICE based on precarious legal status, whether immigrants were fully undocumented or had temporary, partial, or conditional legal status, such as DACA or COFA status. As one community organization leader reflected: "Both the Latinx and the Marshallese community are fearful of having the little things that they have made here stripped away, whether it's a work permit, whether for the Salvadoran [community], or for other communities, people are here with the temporary status. And so there's a big kind of fear of, 'If I get pulled over and the cop says I was drunk even though I wasn't, how do I fight back against this authority?'" (interview, Springdale, July 2014). A colleague of this activist agreed, saying that he thought that all immigrant groups, regardless of legal status, are afraid to lose whatever status they have. Immigrants do not want to put themselves at risk, he emphasized, and are afraid of repercussions. He explained that he had been working with the Arkansas Workers Compensation Commission and had learned that everyone in Arkansas, regardless of immigration status, was entitled to workers' comp if he or she had been injured on the job. "Now, at the end of the process," he conceded, "what they actually get [as compensation] may differ—if the person is undocumented, they won't get that lifetime annual payout, but they might get, for example, a $10,000 settlement all at once." The real issue, he said, was workers' fear of retaliation, exacerbated by their precarious legal status(es). This fear often prevented workers, both documented and undocumented, from speaking up about labor abuses such as withheld wages and workplace safety hazards. As this activist emphasized, his organization "wanted to help people understand that it's not about community-to-community [divisions], it's about *employer-to-employee relationships*," in an effort to build cross-community worker solidarity, both based on and regardless of legal status.

In summary, immigrants' rights activists in Northwest Arkansas pursued a range of programs, strategies, and tactics to advance immigrants' rights, many of which focused on questions of legal status. Non-Marshallese activists, however, had varying degrees of familiarity with the particulars of COFA status—its provisions, limitations, and process of acquisition by Marshallese migrants. Such gaps in knowledge and misperceptions sometimes limited the coalitional strategies that different immigrant groups pursued around legal status. Additionally, because of the way that non-Marshallese immigrants' rights activists engaged with their work based on understandings around citizenship and legality for other groups, they were generally unlikely to approach COFA status as *imperial* citizenship, resulting in a limited or partial picture of rightlessness as a result of U.S. *imperialism* beyond the U.S. mainland. In this way, immigrants' rights activists engaged a framework of rights for understanding COFA status, as compared with the frameworks of policed legality and accessing benefits and services engaged by the groups discussed in previous sections. This rights framework enabled non-Marshallese immigrants' rights organizers to see the *rightlessness* produced by COFA status. It generally left them, however, without a robust framework to identify (or resist) U.S. imperialism as the source of that citizenship-based rightlessness.

Nonetheless, there was clear potential for cross-community organizing against U.S. imperialism in Northwest Arkansas, even if that potential was not yet fully realized. One activist I interviewed, an Arkansan-based Chicanx man who had worked in coalition with Marshallese activists, drew dense and direct connections between U.S. imperialism abroad and immigration to the United States.

> [We need to look] more to the root of the problem, into what's actually causing immigration from Latin America. Because immigrants don't want to leave their families back home—they don't want to leave home if they don't have to. I think that looking at what is causing the instability back home—and then organizing towards that—would help out a lot. That's where I actually agree with the anti-immigrant groups [*laughs*]! Like, "Yeah, we need to cut down on immigration—I agree with that! Y'all want to militarize the border? I wanna get neoliberal policies out of Central American countries." (interview, Fayetteville, 2014)

This activist's point highlights the potential of social movement building in NDEs, showing how immigrant rights activists are, if in partial ways, contending not only with racial formations of the past that drag into the present but also with the violence of U.S. empire and its implications for citizenship.

Finally, Latinx (as well as white and Black) activists were well poised to continue learning from Marshallese activists and key actors in the region, people for whom the imperial dimensions of COFA status's limitations were often crystal clear. From the ESL liaisons who linked the unfairness of COFA migrants' Medicaid restrictions to Compact renegotiations, to the activist who pointed out the irony of COFA migrants paying taxes but not having guaranteed health or education benefits under the Compact, Marshall Islanders and Marshallese Americans consistently attributed COFA status's limitations to restrictions of the Compact. For many, the Marshall Islands' "unique" or "special" relationship with the United States, one born out of over four decades of direct imperial oversight, failed to live up to its promise to treat COFA migrants as special, or even as deserving of rights, in their own right.

Conclusion

Citizenship and legal status take on precarious and at times ambiguous forms for subjects of U.S. empire, especially for those who fall outside the formal protections of full legal citizenship, such as COFA migrants. On the ground, in places such as Arkansas, COFA status gains its meaning through the range of rights, benefits, and obligations that the status carries, as well as the legal and material conditions that coalesce around it. Together, such details form a constellation of rights and rightlessness, materialized through everyday encounters between COFA migrants and various public actors and institutions in NIDs such as Springdale. These encounters constitute a small part of the lived reality of COFA status. While such details—eligibility or ineligibility for a particular public benefit, or the requirement of certain paperwork for U.S. border crossing—may seem like minute or mundane administrative details, they often have life-altering effects for COFA migrants and for their U.S. citizen family members. As this chapter shows, such "mundane" details can dictate COFA migrants' ability to secure employment and affordable housing, put their children through school, and remain in the country where they have built a life.

The conditions of daily life are shaped in both mundane and dramatic ways by encounters between local actors and Marshallese immigrants in these policy areas. Such encounters generate local understandings about Marshall Islanders' relative "legality" as compared with other immigrant groups, specifically Latinxs. These ideas do not emerge out of thin air, however. Rather, local public actors make sense of COFA status as a legal category by drawing on their previous encounters with immigration law, immigrant communities, and discourses about immigrant legality and illegality. Such discourses are reflected in the way public actors discuss Marshallese migrants' legal status and have direct, and often deleterious, effects on COFA migrants' everyday lives.

Furthermore, the provision of COFA status's benefits and rights is not cut and dry. Rather, COFA status's exceptional and unique standing in immigration law spills over into other areas of law and policy, leading to ambiguity in the policy's interpretation, inconsistency in its implementation, and precarity in its beneficiaries' experiences. In each of the contexts I have examined here—law and policy, social services, and activism—COFA status is produced as liminal, exceptional, and exclusionary, enshrining it as a type of imperial citizenship for Marshall Islanders in Arkansas and beyond.

CHAPTER 6

New Transpacific Destinations and the Future of Imperial Mobilities

I opened this book with two examples of state actors' sense-making about empire's geography and its mobile subjects: first, the CBP officer in Rogers, holding the Pacific Islands chart, and second, the CBP officer at the U.S.-Mexico border in Texas, skeptical of the existence of the Marshall Islands until she found them on a map and looked up the fine print about COFA status. In the second vignette, the COFA migrants' van ride to the border for I-94 replacements also exposed the *effects* of state sense-making about empire, as it rendered precarious these migrants' legal status and right to remain in the country, at a significant financial, temporal, and emotional cost to them. This book, similarly, has aimed to make sense of empire's geography through migration. In a way, I have done here what key actors, migrants, and advocates across new destinations of empire do constantly: attempt to understand U.S. empire in the context of its mobile subjects and policies. Geographic sense-making is a significant way in which geographical imaginaries become reworked, solidified, or made anew, with powerful effects on peoples' everyday lives. When the U.S. border patrol officer looks up the Marshall Islands on Google Maps, or when the U.S. customs agent looks up an island on the Pacific Islands chart, they are not only performing the task of managing a border; they are also interpreting—and, thus, *manifesting*—the geographic bounds of U.S. empire. These acts of state sense-making, geographic imagining, and place-making on empire's different frontiers, and from its various peripheries, are integral to new destinations of empire, as they profoundly shape the experiences and reception of imperial migrants there.

In concluding this book, I return briefly to the Pacific Islands chart from chapter 1. This chart describes, but also *prescribes*, a set of geopolitical relationships and border actions, a set of rights associated with the political status of a place and the citizenship status of a people on the move. Yet across the territory this chart aims to simplify, growing calls for self-determination threaten its neat logic. In Guåhan, for example, the Guam Commission on Decolonization's latest report asserts boldly that "a fully Self-governing status is the only way to empower the people of Guam to protect our own interests and make decisions that are right for us" (2022). In Hawai'i, native Kānaka Maoli activists have led protests over the proposed Thirty Meter Telescope sited on Mauna Kea, challenging the right of U.S. American actors to construct infrastructure on sacred Hawai'ian land. These Indigenous demands for sovereignty reveal the precarious nature of imperial boundaries, showing how the geographical imaginaries from which they spring are contested by a multitude of others. In other words, that Pacific Islands chart, while a powerful form of geographic sense-making, is only one of many.

Pictured below is another. This map, first shown to me in 2013 by Springdale's Marshallese consul, Carmen Chong Gum, and later shared with me in an updated version by a Marshallese community leader in 2023, depicts the places from which Marshall Islanders had contacted the consul requesting consular services. It attests to the immense plurality of sites where Marshall Islanders live, work, and attend school in the United States and the expansiveness of their diaspora's geography. Moreover, it reveals surprising and unexpected connections between places, an evolving set of constellations coming into view that connects scattered destinations across the map. Here, again, imperial migrants disrupt Tobler's first law of geography, that "everything is related to everything else, but near things are more related than distant things." Imperial diasporas, such as the one pictured in this photograph and others sedimented beneath and atop it, map their *own* countertopographies, "link[ing] different places analytically and thereby enhance[ing] struggles in the name of common interests" (Katz 2001, 1230). In doing so, they render distant sites more related—and more connected—than might be expected, remaking the meanings of distance, remoteness, and proximity through human mobility.

As COFA migrants move to new sites—like the ones thumbtacked on this map—they also engage in geographic sense-making of their own. Pacific Islanders from across the FAS are setting out for new destinations, working to interpret, contest, and forge Pacific futures as the region's geopolitics shift under their feet. Moreover, COFA migrants, like all migrants in living in new destinations, must develop an acute geographical imaginary of the U.S. South (very different from the ones U.S. southerners may have about the Pacific Islands, except for many U.S. military veterans, as discussed in chapter 3). Where does the U.S. South—and the numerous destinations that make it up—fit into Pacific migrants' vision of a new Pacific? How does their movement

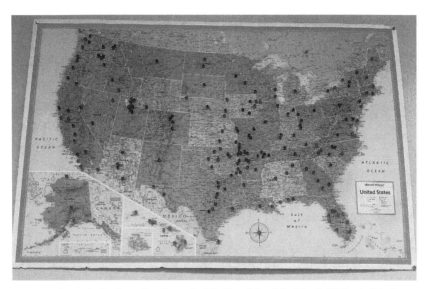

FIGURE 14. A map in the Consulate General of the Republic of the Marshall Islands (RMI) in Springdale, Arkansas, showing locations of originating requests for consular services. Photograph by Marcina Langrine, 2023.

shift the center of these "distinct yet densely interconnected political geographies" (Gilmore 2002, 261)? Where might we locate the center, for example, of Marshallese electoral politics, now that candidates often travel to Springdale from Majuro to campaign for public office? How does the ongoing dilation of diasporas remake the concept of remoteness, and experiences of remoteness or connectedness, within empires? How do imperial subjects stretch the geographic contours of empire through their mobility, and to what effect? As empire's older racial geographies—overlapping geographies of Jim Crow and sundown towns, Indigenous genocide and removal, Japanese internment, and immigrant detention—get dredged to the surface, their meanings are continually reconstituted. As they are, they produce new formations of class, social organization, citizenship, and race within which political consciousness can emerge and from which political demands can be made.

Mapping Pacific Islander Immigration and U.S. Pacific Expansion Together

The two issues this book addresses—immigration to the U.S. mainland and U.S. geopolitical influence in the Asia-Pacific region—are rarely discussed together, either in the mainstream U.S. media or in academic literature. Yet their politics are closely entwined in sites such as the FAS, where bilateral agreements still bind these nations to U.S. military priorities and where, for local residents, the United States continues to be the primary destination for migration. Given the Asia-Pacific region's centrality in U.S. geopolitical strategy and the increased political urgency of immigration and citizenship issues in the U.S. mainland, it is critical that we examine processes of U.S. empire and migration together. *New Destinations of Empire* bridges that gap, bringing geographies of immigration and U.S. empire together through a focus on the transpacific (Hoskins and Nguyen 2014) to consider the geographical dimensions of imperial migration.

The imperative for understanding human mobility in the context of U.S. global expansion is paramount in the twenty-first century. Over the past two decades, U.S. geopolitics in the Asia-Pacific region have held the attention of political scientists, diplomats, and military strategists alike. In 2019, spurred by concerns over Chinese expansion in the Pacific, U.S. secretary of state Mike Pompeo made a visit to Micronesia to meet with the leaders of Micronesia, the Marshall Islands, and Palau—all former U.S. territories now in "free association" with the United States. This visit, the first ever made by a U.S. secretary of state to the FAS, signaled the major geopolitical significance of the Compacts and of the Micronesian region to the United States.

At the same time, half a world away in the mainland United States, immigration politics were at a fever pitch under the Trump administration. National debates over immigration, driven by politician's racist rhetoric and policies, painted Mexican immigrants as "illegal" and Middle Eastern refugees as "terrorists." Appearing in these discourses were well-worn tropes—the benefit-seeking immigrant, the resource-draining refugee, and the politically threatening asylum-seeker—that acquired new meanings in the contemporary political context. These discourses also took on particular dimensions in towns with new or growing immigrant populations, shaping dynamics of immigrant reception and belonging in place-specific ways and with enduring effects. While many immigration activists were cautiously optimistic that a Biden administration would improve policies for immigrants—and though explicitly vitriolic discourses from the White House did, indeed, subside—many of Trump's restrictive immigration policies, such as Title 42, the policy that prevented asylum-seekers arriving to the United States from Mexico to enter the country, remained in place well into 2023.

At the time of this book's writing in early 2023, Pacific Island leaders are preparing to enter into negotiations with U.S. state representatives from various offices to discuss the future and terms of the Compact. The U.S.-RMI

Compact is due to be renegotiated ("or extended—the wording depends on whom you talk to," as one Pacific Islander senior government official amusedly explained to me) in 2023, while key provisions from the U.S.-FSM and U.S.-Palau Compacts are scheduled to expire in 2023 and 2024, respectively. As Compact renegotiations loom on the horizon, many questions remain about the Compacts' future. While representatives on "both sides" of the negotiating table have expressed anxieties about possible futures, the stakes are unarguably higher for the FAS and for their COFA diasporas across the United States. On the table are not only massive U.S. financial support to the FAS (and an ongoing military presence there) but also FAS citizens' ability to move freely between their islands and the United States, a mobility that, while not entirely free, has been relatively legally viable for the past several decades. Will FAS citizens, as COFA migrants, continue to be able to attend college, seek employment, and move relatively freely within the U.S. system? Once in the United States, will they be able to access affordable health care, public housing, and food assistance—all benefits that COFA migrants have seen restricted in recent years—without jeopardizing their right to stay in the country? These questions generated tense undercurrents in my most recent fieldwork visits to Arkansas and remain at the forefront of many community leaders' minds.

U.S. state actors also fret over the future of the Compacts, as they understand that the Compacts will, in large part, shape the future directions and destinations of U.S. empire. These actors know what colonized peoples everywhere know: empires always face resistance, friction, barriers, and endings. As much as empire's leaders and administrators might declare otherwise, there is always contingency in empire's destinations, as there are always political effects trickling down and scaling up, the effects of events at one scale or site reverberating at another. Across U.S. empire, from Vieques to Okinawa to Jeju, military base communities have galvanized public support to push out the U.S. military or stop its expansion in their home communities (Shigematsu and Camacho 2010). Who's to say that a similar challenge to U.S. militarism might not emerge, for example, from Ebeye, near Kwajalein (as it did in a Marshallese-led occupation of the installation in 1981), or from Micronesians living in recently proposed sites of U.S. military expansion in the FSM and Palau?

Similarly, even in places where the U.S. might perceive its foothold or alliances to be strongest, there can appear challenges to a U.S. presence. In Chuuk State, FSM, for example, a growing independence movement has advocated since 2015 to separate from the FSM and, in effect, pull out of the Compact. While the Chuuk independence referendum has been postponed repeatedly, the commission continues to hold public forums in both Chuuk State and Micronesian diasporic communities in the United States. In 2019, I asked an Arkansas-based Marshallese activist why he thought some Chuukese were pushing to leave their FAS relationship with the United States. He said, "Because they feel like everything the U.S. does is bullshit, that they make a lot of promises and then don't fulfill them. They're always on time when it's something they want, but when it's something we're pushing for, they delay, they put it off." I asked him if he felt that way. He paused for a minute, then said, "Yes. Yes, I do. Because they take advantage of us. We don't matter here. We are small, but our ocean is large. And that's what they really want." Comments like this suggest that challenges to U.S. empire are always present in nonsovereign and occupied territories. They may be shouted or hushed, may wax and wane in the public view (or fade temporarily from the sight lines of U.S. state actors), but they are never fully extinguished. Such challenges always re-emerge to question the line between dependency and protection, debt and "support," full citizenship and second-class status, and subjugation and self-determination.

As U.S. empire once again comes under threat in the Pacific, both by China's geopolitical ambitions and by Indigenous challenges from below, its actors reach for familiar geographic ideas to justify U.S. imperial expansion in territory and in the law. Secretary of State Hilary Clinton's 2011 declaration of "America's Pacific Century," for example, denotes an aspirational geographical imaginary, a destiny that she and others hoped to make manifest by naming it so, a geographic vision of a U.S. Pacific empire projected forward in space and time. This vision reappeared in a 2021 op-ed in *The Diplomat*, wherein Alexander B. Gray, former deputy assistant to the president and National Security Council chief of staff, argued for an expanded U.S. Pacific presence. His ironically titled op-ed, "How the U.S. can protect the sovereignty of the smallest Pacific Islands," advocated for the Compacts' extension to Pacific Islands such as Nauru, Tuvalu, and Kiribati, whose "exceptionally small size and geographic isolation make them especially . . . susceptible to outside coercion." Overt here, yet again, are age-old geographical imaginaries and justifications for a U.S. imperial presence, ones that closely echo the 1919 League of Nations Mandate System language that restricted Pacific Islanders' self-determination based on "the sparseness of their population, or their small size, or their remoteness from the centres of civilisation" and the 1963 Solomon Report language describing the Micronesian region as a "deficit area." Such geographic ideas, it seems, die hard. That they persist should come as no surprise, however: any politician worth their salt knows how much rides on these ideas and at what great cost to empire they are contested.

Those same geographic ideas are being contested and rewritten, as they always have been, by Indigenous Pacific Islanders in Micronesia and beyond, demonstrating that the possibilities of Indigenous sovereignty and self-determination are never foreclosed. Indeed, while many independence movements of the 1950s and 1960s were once framed as impossible—if largely from outside those movements—they were largely victorious: from 1945 to 1960, more than three dozen states gained autonomy or independence worldwide, and from 1960 to 1986, fifteen more followed across the Pacific. These gains were not only fought through military battles and insurgencies but also through *ideas*, including ideas about geography. As Edward Said wrote in *Culture and Imperialism* (1993, 7), "Just as none of us is outside or beyond geography, none of us is completely free from the struggle over geography. That struggle is complex and interesting because it is not only about soldiers and cannons but also about ideas, about forms, about images and imaginings." In the twenty-first century, which geographical imaginary will win out? That of small scattered islands in a far sea, with its inhabitants trapped in time and place, or that of a vast "sea of islands" and islanders (Hauʻofa 1994), made dynamic by their connectivity and mobility?

New Destinations of Empire and the Hinged Politics of Scale

Another set of questions looms from the other side of the Pacific, in new destinations of empire that dot the U.S. West Coast, South, Midwest, and, increasingly, the East Coast. In places such as Enid, Oklahoma, Marshallese communities continue to grow in number, creating new Pacific frontiers across the continental United States. In these sites, the future of immigrant and racial justice in the United States hangs in the balance. What will happen in these newer destinations of empire, each with its own distinct history of labor, race, and migration? Which groups will migrate there, and how will dynamics emerge among different groups? Which political affinities and organizing strategies will become salient, and which antagonisms will fester (or be fostered by employers, landlords, police, and NIMBY-ist residents)? How will new migrants be understood by receiving communities, and how will these understandings align or contrast with migrants' understandings of themselves? As these questions indicate, there is a significant degree of indeterminacy in new destinations.

Some of this indeterminacy or contingency over how dynamics emerge in new destinations of empire is produced by a kind of hinged politics at the global, national, state, and local levels, a double movement in which repression at one scale is accompanied by—and, often, spurs—resistance at others. At the scale of U.S. national politics, the Trump administration looms like a specter in recent memory, with its accompanying spate of anti-immigrant legislation, ICE raids and deportations, and xenophobic public rhetoric. With the Biden administration's disappointingly meager gains toward immigrants' rights, and the 2024 U.S. presidential election just around the corner, many Marshall Islanders and other immigrants are concerned about a rightward lurch in federal, state, and local policy that could foreclose any gains toward racial and immigrant justice.

Despite—or perhaps because of—the national rise of anti-immigrant policies and the emboldening of white supremacists, the U.S. South has recently seen major gains in coalitional and multiracial immigrants' rights' organizing. Such movements have gained major momentum in the decade since I first began the research for this book. As discussed in chapters 4 and 5, activist and nonprofit organizations have grown in size and multiplied in numbers in Northwest Arkansas since the early days of immigrant arrivals in the 1980s. Now, with dozens of Arkansan organizations dedicated to immigrants' rights, workers' rights, and racial justice, Marshall Islanders in Arkansas are well poised to fight for their rights in the coming years. They are also in good company, as their co-organizers, allies, and advocates in NDEs work to shift public opinion around, and advocate for policies in support of, their immigrant community members. In July 2022, for example, Springdale educators held a public rally against the passage of laws restricting how histories of racism are taught in schools, part of a larger nationwide backlash against what is erroneously being called "critical race theory" (Trobaugh 2022). This effort and others demonstrate a commitment on the ground in southern NIDs to advance social and racial justice.

This groundswell of social justice organizing is also visible at larger scales across Arkansas and the U.S. South. Organizations such as the Arkansas Citizens First Congress bring together movements for immigrants' rights and racial justice with focuses on prison abolition, reproductive justice, disability justice, and housing rights, among other things. This trend is accompanied by an increase in labor demands in the South and elsewhere, as unionization picks up speed across sectors, even in staunchly "right-to-win" states (Freshour and Williams 2020). These gains are also a result of Marshallese and other new migrant groups establishing their presence in NIDs over several years, seeing their numbers grow as second- and third-generation Marshallese Americans build new homes and community ties themselves. Political organizing in NIDs often grows over time, especially as those communities gain political visibility and representation and see increased voter turnout (Chambers and Williamson 2017). Yet, as history has shown, political gains toward rights for racialized, working-class, and imperial subjects must be continuously defended, as they are perennially attacked during periods of heightened xenophobia and white supremacy.

All these dynamics, occurring simultaneously at multiple interlinked geographic scales, continuously remake the landscape of COFA migrants' mobility. What are the future directions and destinations for the Compact, and for COFA migrants? What will happen on the geographic frontiers of immigrant arrivals? One thing is certain: they will forge new geographies as they continue to move. In the U.S. South and Midwest, they are already doing so, establishing new COFA migrant communities in towns such as Enid and Kansas City, towns whose work opportunities are greater and the cost of living is relatively low (compared, perhaps, with towns such as Springdale and Rogers, with their own expanding development projects and increasing cost of living). In 2023, Springdale is a town that is nearly 40 percent Latinx and nearly 10 percent Marshall Islander, where white residents will not be the majority for much longer. In addition to becoming a more racially diverse town, Springdale is now, more than ever, an *immigrant* town. However, as more and more white upper-middle-class residents move to Springdale, with its new upscale breweries, coffee shops, bike path, and relative proximity to the university, will new Marshallese arrivals and other immigrants seek different destinations? These questions and others will continue to influence the emerging geographies of NDEs.

Imperial Citizenship, Political Status, and the Limitations of Liminal Inclusion

Shifting politics at multiple scales, such as those described above, also create uncertainty about the legal status and rights of Marshall Islanders and other COFA migrants. While many U.S. state actors have expressed confidence that the possibility of the COFA migration provision disappearing or the Compact being terminated is unlikely (interviews, Northwest Arkansas, Washington, D.C., 2019, 2022), many U.S.-based Marshall Islanders are wary as COFA renegotiations loom. They have witnessed the migration provision's gradual erosion since its inception, through increasing deportations, inconsistent application of immigration policies by border agents and police, and periodic reinstatements of the public charge rule, both in Arkansas and elsewhere. Although these policies do not *eliminate* COFA migrants' legal right to migrate to the United States, they effectively *weaken* it through piecemeal restrictions and limitations. Many Marshall Islanders also recall the post-9/11 period when COFA migration permissions were almost revoked entirely due to U.S. border-security concerns. They worry that another geopolitical conflict could place COFA migration rights, and even the Compact itself, back on the chopping block.

COFA migrants and Marshallese American communities have also developed a keen awareness of how the United States has used legal liminality against other groups and how the social, political, and *spatial* exclusions (and conditional inclusions) of white supremacy and racial capitalism work against racialized migrants of the Global South. They have honed observations of these processes through their activism and coalition building with other precariously legal immigrant groups in the United States. At the same time, COFA migrants, in concert with their counterparts in other new and established destinations of empire, and in coalition with their immigrant and BIPOC neighbors, coworkers, and comrades, sharpen their political action strategies and tactics, becoming ever fiercer antagonists, and more clear-eyed critics, of injustice.

Neither political status nor the legal statuses of imperial subjects are etched in stone, much as some actors on both sides might want them to be. They are always open for contestation and renegotiation, contingent precisely because they are on the margins of empire, revealing the borders between places and people to be shifting, impermanent, constantly dissolving and recalcifying. As this book makes clear, that contingency is produced in part by phenomena taking place at different scales and the interactions of those phenomena at the hinges *between* scales. Put differently, what happens in NDEs is about place-particularity—the unique dynamics and histories *within* places such as Springdale—but also about the relationality and the scalar interlinking *between* different sites and scales.

Contingency, to be sure, poses a risk to imperial citizens such as COFA migrants. While public actors' common refrain that Marshall Islanders are not a "problem [immigrant] population" might seem to secure COFA migrants' legal status, that imperial legal status—due to its liminal, exceptional, and exclusionary nature—is never fully codified. COFA status can be, and is, frequently imperiled by shifting racial and class antagonisms, often galvanized by dog-whistling politicians. We can see this phenomenon in longer-standing COFA migrant destinations such as Hawaiʻi and Guåhan, where Micronesians and Marshall Islanders face well-established prejudices, increasing demands for deportation, restrictions of their rights, and calls for mitigating COFA migrants' perceived economic burden, or "Compact Impact." Yet these sites have also seen the emergence of multiracial coalitional organizing in recent years, indicating the undetermined yet potent political possibilities that coalesce in empire's destinations.

Across U.S. territories, there is no single consensus among Indigenous peoples about what a place's political status or relationship to the United States should be, or what legal or citizenship status its inhabitants should hold. In Puerto Rico, for example, debates and plebiscites over the island's political status vis-à-vis the United States have persisted for over a century. In American Samoa, one recent U.S. Supreme Court case, *Tuaua v. United States*, hinges on Indigenous efforts to avoid the extension of full U.S. citizenship to American Samoans, due to concerns that it might erode Indigenous governance and land-use rights. Such concerns about the costs of inclusion and recognition by an imperial state often vex Indigenous peoples on the territorial and legal margins of empire (Bruyneel 2004; Coulthard 2007). Would fuller incorporation under U.S. governance and law provide greater protections, or produce a less exclusionary status? What are the costs of inclusion?

This book's analysis, in traversing nonsovereign territories in U.S. empire, also makes visible how policies travel, connecting political projects across diverse sites in sometimes unexpected ways. Just as the Compact has traveled to NDEs, ideas about imperial policymaking continue to travel between Puerto Rico, the FAS, Guåhan, the CNMI, and the U.S. Virgin Islands and American Samoa, traversing vastly dispersed atolls and archipelagoes. In recent years, for example, Puerto Ricans have begun to consider the option of Freely Associated Statehood for their own political future vis-à-vis the United States. Although *Estado Libre Asociado*—translated into English as "commonwealth" status—was first implemented in Puerto Rico in the 1950s, Freely Associated Statehood has only recently reappeared in popular discourse as a viable option for Puerto Rican political status. That it *is* on the table, with recent articles by Puerto Rican journalists proposing a Compact solution modeled on the Pacific Compacts, recalls a long history of islanders observing keenly from the Caribbean to the Pacific, and vice versa (G. Petersen 2004). As chapter 2 explores, U.S. state administrators always observe and make comparisons between territories as they craft imperial policies, but so, too, do islanders, bringing together islands and archipelagoes across far seas.

The Future of Global Mobility

What is the future of global human migration, and how will it continue to be shaped by imperial pasts and presents, as well as movements against empire?

Three related global phenomena—border policing, climate change, and imperialism—will be instrumental in forging the contours of human mobility in the years to come. At the time of this chapter's writing in early 2023, we continue to witness a global lurch toward right-wing authoritarianism, particularly in settler-colonial nations (Jones 2016). Accompanying this trend is the hardening of national borders across the globe, as geographers of mobility and migration have examined (Sheller 2018; Jones 2016). Border policing is motivated by, and reinforces, resurgent tendencies within "immigrant-receiving" countries in the Global North to scapegoat and exclude migrants, especially racialized and working-class migrants. If the Windrush generation has taught us anything, it is that the promise of citizenship and belonging for imperial subjects is never guaranteed. Even now, nearly eight decades after the arrival of the original Windrush migrants, we witness how promises to former imperial subjects are chipped away in times of austerity or heightened xenophobia. Such political and social exclusions also take *spatial* form: they are accompanied by the fortification and increased militarization of national borders, particularly for racialized migrants of the Global South, all while empires continue to seek and break new ground, expanding their territory through new military bases, trade agreements and zones, and other spatial strategies. Yet as global "open borders" movements gain traction and enter mainstream discourses (Jones 2016), they continue to make a strong political, moral, and economic case for free movement worldwide.

As is increasingly clear, the future of global migration—especially emigration from islands, some of the most extensively colonized places in the world—will also be shaped by climate change (Miller 2017). Rapid sea-level rise renders Pacific Islanders' right to free movement a question of survival: by 2035, the U.S. Geological Survey estimates, some of the Marshall Islands will disappear underwater, while others will be left without potable drinking water due to saltwater contamination. Many Marshall Islanders and Micronesians interviewed for this book worried where that rising ocean tide would leave the political status of the U.S. FAS. What does it look like when more than a third of a country leaves? What will happen when islands and atolls disappear altogether? Will the RMI's capital move to Springdale, as a few interviewees speculated (not entirely hypothetically; already, diplomats, elected officials, and candidates running for office must visit the region)? Will COFA migrants' mobility to and within the United States always be defined by David and Goliath–like power relations, or will COFA migrants and U.S. empire's other precariously legal, mobile subjects achieve "mobility justice" (Sheller 2018)? The stakes of these questions are driven even higher by climate change, the most recent and dramatic threat to Pacific lives and livelihoods.

The third force that will continue to shape global migration is the struggle between imperialism and decolonization. The geography of global human mobility is contoured in significant ways by empires, through political alliances and treaties, trade agreements, linguistic affinities, and familial ties (Collins 2022; Mayblin and Turner 2020). When we take seriously both the histories of colonialism and the colonial and imperial present, it changes everything we think we know about how people move. This is a point I often emphasize when teaching my undergraduate seminar on U.S. immigration, empire, and race: as history shows, the construction of immigration law is not—or, not exclusively—a *national*-scale project. Rather, the project of managing outside and in, who crosses borders and where those borders are located and policed, is an inherently transnational and *global* project, a global story. Geopolitical events and "foreign affairs"—events playing out beyond U.S. national borders—have always informed U.S. decision-making and policies on immigration. This is to say that U.S. geopolitical interests *abroad* are central to immigration policy *within* the United States. U.S. nonsovereign and occupied territories, and their residents at home and on the move, straddle the interstices between home and abroad, foreign and domestic, and alien and citizen.

The urgent and weighted political contestations over the two regions centered in this book—the Freely Associated States in the Pacific Islands and Arkansas—reveals them both, once again, to be anything but remote to global politics: instead, they sit at the foreground of major issues confronting U.S. empire and the struggles for social justice within it. *How* will these two regions continue to be connected in the years to come? Where will the new frontiers of Pacific Islander immigration in the United States be? As a result, what kinds of struggles—in the social justice sense—will Marshallese and other COFA migrants face? This book has aimed to show that the edges, peripheries, and remote corners of empire are centers in their own way, intimately connected to one another and to the beating heart of movements—both *social* movements and *human* movement—within empire. As the lives and political struggles in these "remote" sites show, there is power on the edge.

NOTES

CHAPTER 1. Mapping Imperial Migrations from the Pacific to the United States

1. Sundown towns, which numbered in the thousands across the United States, "probably included more than a hundred towns in the northwestern two-thirds of Arkansas" (Loewen 2022, n.p.).

2. I use the term "immigrant town" in the informal sense in which my research participants often did, to refer simply to a town or city where many immigrants live. This is different from a "sanctuary city," a city whose policies limit local officials from assisting in the policing and deportation of undocumented migrants.

3. This is a common response to my description of this research. I discuss this sentiment and related geographical imaginaries in chapters 3 and 4.

4. When not quoting from another source, I default to the Indigenous spellings of Guåhan, CHamoru, Hawai'i, and Kānaka Maoli.

5. A port of entry is a border site at which individuals may lawfully enter a country.

6. All names given for research subjects are pseudonyms, unless noted otherwise and unless shared with explicit consent.

7. As Jodi Melamed (2015) and others have noted, Gilmore's widely cited definition of racism also appears in her 2007 book *Golden gulag*, but without the last part of the phrase: "in distinct yet densely interconnected political geographies." I include that phrase here as it articulates the multiscalar and *relational* nature of racism's geographies.

8. While I did not conduct fieldwork in the Marshall Islands, I include it in this map for reference.

9. Although I did not explicitly ask research participants how they self-identified racially, I denote some participants as white based on information they shared with me or my own perceptions of their racial presentation. While an admittedly flawed metric for racial identity, this approach allows me to characterize generally white-presenting interviewees as such.

10. Freely Associated Statehood is identified by the UN as one of the three self-determination options available to formerly colonized peoples.

11. I replace the commonly used term "American exceptionalism" with "U.S. exceptionalism" to differentiate between the United States and the Americas, a geographical entity that spans much of the Western Hemisphere.

CHAPTER 2. How Free Is Freely Associated Statehood?

1. While it does not have a singular definition under UN regulations or U.S. law, Freely Associated Statehood is a political affiliation between two political territories, one of which—historically the formerly colonized party—often functions as a minor or lesser partner to the other, historically the colonial power (Lawson and Sloane 2009). The UN defines Freely Associated Statehood as one of three self-determination options available to formerly colonized peoples. In 1952, via constitutional assembly, Puerto Rico became a U.S. commonwealth, a political status whose official Spanish name is Estado Libre Asociado, or Freely Associated State. However, the United States recognizes Puerto Rico as an unincorporated territory, a very different political status from the one held by the FAS in the Pacific.

2. The Marshall Islands, Micronesia, and Palau—the current U.S. Freely Associated States—were the last of the League of Nations mandates to become formally sovereign in the mid-1980s and 1990s. The CNMI, currently a U.S. commonwealth, is the only original Mandate without UN-recognized sovereignty as of 2023.

3. The euphemistic language of the UN, United States, and much Western scholarship to describe "transfers" and "(re)distributions" of territories between colonial powers disregards the agency and sovereignty of the occupied peoples themselves. It also erases the numerous freedom movements that challenged and prevented such "transfers." Despite what this euphemistic parlance conveys, colonial handoffs of territory were never inevitable; Indigenous movements in many colonized sites have fought for and achieved self-determination. They have indeed *needed* to fight for it.

4. In total, eleven trust territories were established at this time, ten of which had originated as League of Nations Mandates and the eleventh of which was Italian Somaliland.

5. "Administering authorities" is a term of art used by the UN to designate neocolonial powers after World War II. I use it to be consistent with the legal documents I analyze but underscore that it is a colonial euphemism for global powers operating under the blessing of the UN trusteeship system.

6. CHamorus, or Chamorros, are the Indigenous people of the Mariana Islands, which are currently politically divided between Guam and the U.S. Commonwealth of Northern Mariana Islands (Taitano 2022).

7. For discussion of the Marshall Islands' nuclear legacy, including the testing's extensive social, political, environmental, and health-related impacts on the Marshallese people, see S. Davis 2005; Barker 2004; Teaiwa 1994; Maclellan 2005.

8. The U.S. atomic bombs dropped on Hiroshima and Nagasaki departed from Tinian, an island in the Northern Marianas occupied by the United States during World War II.

9. See Hawai'i U.S. Representative Patsy T. Mink's 1970 article, "Micronesia: Our Bungled Trust," for critiques of the U.S. handling of the TTPI.

10. As chapter 5 shows, empires often use social programs and other "development assistance" as tools for maintaining control over imperial populations. COFA migrants' formal eligibility for social programs and benefits is often levied for political strategic reasons by U.S. actors, to maintain Micronesian and Marshallese goodwill toward the United States and to evade criticism from outside observers, even though COFA migrants often struggle to access many benefits in practice.

11. U.S. actors were also keenly watching political-status debates unfold in other territories. An interview I conducted with two senior U.S. officials (Washington, D.C., 2019) gestures to practices of intra-imperial knowledge transfer during political-status negotiations that have long connected the Pacific to the Caribbean and to Washington, D.C., a center of imperial policymaking.

> **Official 1:** The legal counsel for the RMI during the Carter administration (1977–1981) was also on retainer to the statehood crowd in Puerto Rico. So, he and Tony DeBrum (RMI foreign minister, 1979–1987), in fashioning the Compact of Free Association, were looking over their shoulder at the model for Puerto Rico. I think that they were thinking of the Compact as sort of a transition to statehood, or . . . I really don't know how they would concoct it.
>
> **Official 2:** You can see how Puerto Ricans could look at it as an alternative, because it does allow you a seat in the UN, getting foreign aid from other [countries]. It's nice. Free Association is a nice status.
>
> **Official 1:** In the first Compact negotiations, Puerto Rico was always in the background. It didn't impact the outcome, but I think we all recognized that what we were doing at the time could have some transfer.

12. In 1975, the Northern Marianas District voted to split from the TTPI and become a U.S. commonwealth, opting for a closer political relationship with the United States. Many Micronesians saw this move as a result of a clear "divide-and-conquer strategy" by the United States (G. Peterson 2004; interviews, Saipan, 2014, Washington, D.C., 2014), yet felt bound to support the Marianas' political-status decision, given their commitment to Indigenous political autonomy (Andon L. Amaraich, interviewed by Willens and Siemer 1997).

13. The U.S. FAS were not the first FAS in the Pacific: in 1965, the Cook Islands became a FAS of New Zealand, and in 1974, Niue, also a former colony of New Zealand, followed suit. A Micronesian delegation visited the Cook Islands after 1965 and found FAS preferable to commonwealth status, as it would proffer greater autonomy while retaining U.S. political and economic support (Willens and Siemer 1997; G. Petersen 2004).

14. For more on the U.S. militarization of Kwajalein, see S. Davis 2015; Hirshberg 2022.

15. Roth's statements allude to increasing resistance in the Philippines to the ongoing presence of U.S. bases, anticipating a need for a contingency plan should the United States lose use of that territory. In 1998, the Philippines had just marked half a century of independence from U.S. colonial rule. Nonetheless, a U.S. military presence there—principally, at the U.S. Naval Base in Subic Bay and Clark Air Force Base in Luzon—had expanded during the so-called postcolonial era. Five years later, Roth's prediction materialized, when mounting pressure from the Philippine government and civil society led to the closure of Subic, the last U.S. base in the Philippines.

16. Per Section 461(c), "'The Marshall Islands' and 'the Federated States of Micronesia' are used in a geographic sense and include the land and water areas to the outer limits of the territorial sea and the air space above such areas as now or hereafter recognized by the Government of the United States."

17. During the TTPI (1947–1986), TTPI residents held TTPI citizenship status, rec-

ognized by the United States and the UN, and traveled internationally under TTPI passports.

18. The Compact also stipulates the groups eligible for RMI citizenship: former TTPI citizens (for those born before the Compact's implementation); naturalized RMI citizens; and others able to establish lineal descent in the RMI vis-à-vis the RMI government.

19. The law stipulates that Section 141(a) "does not confer on a citizen of the Marshall Islands or the Federated States of Micronesia the right to establish the residence necessary for naturalization under the Immigration and Nationality Act... [H]owever, [Section 141(a)] shall not prevent a citizen of the Marshall Islands or the Federated States of Micronesia from otherwise acquiring such rights or lawful permanent resident alien status in the United States. (U.S. Public Law 99–239, Section 141(c), Art. IV)

20. Vine (2012) identifies "lily-pad" bases as "small, secretive, inaccessible facilities with limited numbers of troops, spartan amenities, and prepositioned weaponry and supplies" (n.p.), a base model increasingly used by the U.S. military in offshore operations.

21. Immigration and Naturalization Services (INS) from 1933 until 2003, when the agency's functions were split between the newly formed U.S. Citizenship and Immigration Services (USCIS), Immigration and Customs Enforcement (ICE), and Customs and Border Protection (CBP), all of which came under the newly formed Department of Homeland Security (DHS).

CHAPTER 3. "We Are Here Because You Were There"

1. At the time, much of the resistance to Arkansan Dust Bowl migrants in states where they headed was articulated as antipoor sentiment, framing Dust Bowl migrants as "white trash" who would usurp government benefits and pose a burden on receiving states.

2. The same J. W. Fulbright later became a U.S. senator for Arkansas and owned a summer home in Springdale that surreptitiously employed Black domestic workers (see chapter 4).

3. While white Dust Bowl migrants experienced some rejection in states where they resettled, they were often more warmly received by local populations than were immigrants and workers of color, particularly Mexicans and Filipinos. They also frequently replaced immigrant workers in sites of resettlement.

4. Sites named by interviewees, Shiloh Museum archives, and the Arkansas Educational Television Network project *In Their Words*.

5. See Wilson (2000) for a discussion of Pacific imagery in other U.S. media during the mid-twentieth century.

6. See Heisler (2007) on the contrasting treatment of German POWs and Mexican braceros in U.S. southern and midwestern towns.

7. German POWs may in fact have volunteered for this work, as the alternative presented to them was often to remain in confinement. Working in local factories and worksites afforded some POWs the ability to interact and move about, in a limited way, in the community where they were being held.

8. Chicken sexing is the method of hand-sorting young chickens by sex, a practice commonly used in large-scale commercial hatcheries.

9. The term "first-generation" is generally used to describe immigrants born in another country, while "second-generation" refers to the children of those immigrants, though there is some ambiguity and inconsistency in these terms' application. In Lana's case, her mother fell into the second category and would more commonly be understood as "second-generation."

10. Indochinese refugee populations included Hmong, Laotians, and Cambodians as well as Vietnamese.

CHAPTER 4. "Of All Places!"

1. According to informed community estimates from the RMI Consuls General in Honolulu, Springdale, and Washington, D.C.

2. Indigenous peoples native to present-day Arkansas

3. Individual's real name used with permission.

4. In early April 2014, I attended a protest march and "funeral for racism" in Harrison, in which residents, task-force members, and political leaders gathered to recognize Harrison's racialized past and assert an antiracist identity for the town. I made this trip with three activists from Northwest Arkansas; during the drive, they shared reflections on the region's racial history and present.

5. Perdue (2023) describes a similar phenomenon in Central Appalachia, another U.S. region commonly imagined as populated by "white trash," where such depictions are used to justify state abandonment, carceral expansion, and environmental degradation.

6. While this book is not an ethnography of their experiences of race in diaspora, Marshall Islanders, like other migrants, navigate shifting contexts of race and are racialized differently in the various sites where they resettle. Migrants also carry with them preexisting racial frameworks that inform their own perceptions about race as they move and resettle.

7. Almost exclusively Cherokee, they come from present-day Georgia and other East Coast regions.

8. While "federally recognized tribes" is a term used by U.S. government agencies such as the Bureau of Indian Affairs, many Indigenous people recognize the term "tribe" as offensive due to its historic usage by both colonial governments and settler anthropologists (Dunbar-Ortiz 2014).

9. Since the initial research for this book was conducted (2013–15), MONAH has developed a rich events program centering contemporary Indigenous experiences, including Cherokee-language workshops, Indigenous artist showcases, and public talks on contemporary Indigenous food sovereignty.

10. The absence of discussion about indigeneity in the context of race is not altogether unsurprising or unique to Arkansas, since race and indigeneity often work through different registers in the United States.

11. Here, I use this term to refer to people who self-identify with racial groups other than "white" on the U.S Census, while recognizing the complexity of racial and ethnic identification and self-identification that exceeds these categories and also exists within them.

12. During my visit, this staffer willingly showed me the "White Waiting Room" door and discussed other museum archives that documented Springdale's racial past. The museum staff had clearly gone to great lengths to gather and preserve such materials and share them with the community. As this staffer commented good-naturedly, "Sometimes, I think Springdale gets a reputation for being more racist historically because we do so much to showcase that history at the museum, compared to other towns." I include her point here to acknowledge the museum's effort to document Springdale's history in its complexity, and also to recognize that a relative *lack* of documentation of past racial violence in other towns is *not* indication that such racial violence did not occur.

13. See Marrow (2009) on the persistence of the Black-white racial binary in the rural U.S. South and its implications for Latinx immigrants.

14. The actual size of Northwest Arkansas's immigrant populations is likely much larger, since a large proportion of these groups are undocumented or, in the case of Marshallese immigrants, have Compact-provisioned legal status, making them difficult to count accurately.

15. Originally, Section 287(g) appeared in the 1996 Illegal Immigration Reform and Immigrant Responsibility Act.

16. Antiwelfare attitudes, which run deep in much of Arkansas, owe a strong inheritance to the anti-Black welfare narratives from the Reagan administration (Loyd 2011), as well as the Clinton administration, another local political darling. Reagan's influence appeared in multiple sites: his framed photo was even hung on the wall of a Springdale restaurant.

CHAPTER 5. "No Such Thing as an Illegal Marshallese"

1. This is except for American Samoans, who are U.S. nationals but not U.S. citizens by birth.

2. The U.S. Department of the Interior (2016) clarifies that the term "insular area . . . may refer not only to a jurisdiction which is under United States sovereignty but also to one which is not, *i.e.*, a freely associated state or, 1947–94, the Trust Territory of the Pacific Islands."

3. Until the Compact's passage, from 1947 to 1986, Marshall Islanders and other trust territory residents traveled on a TTPI passport.

4. This is the type of document that might commonly be referenced by USCIS, CBP, and ICE officials as well as others who work with U.S. immigration law. In my previous work as an immigration paralegal, documents like this were frequently referenced by both attorneys and USCIS adjudications officers when handling the cases of immigrants with uncommon legal statuses. I received an earlier version of this document at the RMI consulate in Honolulu in 2013 and from another interviewee in Washington, D.C., in 2014.

5. To my knowledge, the public charge provision has not been implemented; COFA migrants have not yet been deported from the United States based on financial status. However, the option remains in the law, and many political actors have openly considered it, including former president Trump, who reinstated the public charge rule in October 2019. At the time of this book's writing in 2023, the rule has been suspended by President Biden.

6. Under the terms of the 2003 Amended Compact, FAS citizens convicted of certain crimes are inadmissible to the United States.

7. An ICE detainer or "hold" refers to an Immigration and Customs Enforcement detainer. When an immigrant is detained by police for a nonimmigration-related charge, ICE officials may submit a request to the local jail or police department to hold that individual for an additional forty-eight hours after their release to give ICE the option of transferring them into federal custody for deportation proceedings.

8. While the 1986 Compact granted Medicaid eligibility to FAS immigrants to the United States, this eligibility was removed by the 1996 Personal Responsibility and Work Opportunity Reconciliation Act legislation, which also stripped Medicaid eligibility from many other immigrant groups.

9. Hansen's disease is also known as leprosy. However, due to the latter term's historic stigma and ableism, I use the official diagnostic term here.

10. Interviews with health care providers and health policy analysts, Springdale, April–July 2014.

11. Recipients of Deferred Action for Childhood Arrivals (DACA), a 2012 DHS provision that allows some individuals who came to the United States without legal documentation as children to defer deportation temporarily.

12. The Civil Rights Roundtable was a coalition of Northwest Arkansas social justice activists and community members focused on immigrants' rights. This group met twice a month during my fieldwork in Arkansas in 2014, meetings I attended regularly.

REFERENCES

Agamben, G. (2005). *State of exception.* Translated by Kevin Attell. Chicago: University of Chicago Press.

Aguon, J. (2010). On loving the maps our hands cannot hold: Self-determination of colonized and Indigenous peoples in international law. *UCLA Asian Pacific American Law Journal, 16,* 47–73.

An act to proclaim the City of Springdale, Arkansas, to Be the poultry capital of the world. Arkansas Senate Bill No. 949 (2013).

Anderson, W. C. (1964). Early reaction in Arkansas to the relocation of Japanese in the state. *Arkansas Historical Quarterly, 23*(3), 195–211. Another Okie. (ca. 1944). ["Arkies and Okies" poem]. Shiloh Museum of Ozark History, Springdale, Ark. Accessed March 2014.

Arkansas Democrat-Gazette. (1993). [Newspaper article discussing long-time Northwest Arkansas residents' perceptions of recent population influx and accompanying economic growth.] *Arkansas Democrat-Gazette.* Shiloh Museum of Ozark History, Springdale, Ark. Accessed March 2014.

Arkansas Democrat-Gazette. (ca. 1992). [Newspaper article presenting definitions of immigrant status]. *Arkansas Democrat-Gazette.* Shiloh Museum of Ozark History, Springdale, Ark. Accessed March 2014.

Arkansas PBS. (2022, November 14). *In Their Words* [*In Their Words* is Arkansas PBS's Education Division's Oral History Project documenting Arkansas' World War II Veterans]. YouTube channel. Accessed October 14, 2023. https://www.youtube.com/playlist?list=PL386B23DD4B16FAE6.

Armstrong, A. J., and H. L. Hills. (1984). The negotiations for the future political status of Micronesia (1980–1984). *American Journal of International Law, 78*(2), 484–497.

Atkinson, D. C. (2016). *The burden of white supremacy: Containing Asian migration in the British empire and the United States.* Chapel Hill: University of North Carolina Press.

Baldoz, R. (2011). *The third Asiatic invasion: Migration and empire in Filipino America, 1898–1946.* New York: New York University Press.

Ball, J. C. (2004). *Imagining London: Postcolonial fiction and the transnational metropolis.* Toronto: University of Toronto Press.

References

Banerjee, S. (2010). *Becoming imperial citizens: Indians in the late-Victorian empire.* Durham, N.C.: Duke University Press.

Barker, H. M. (2004). *Bravo for the Marshallese: Regaining control in a post-nuclear, post-colonial world.* Belmont, CA: Wadsworth Publishing.

Barnes, T. J., and M. Farish. (2006). Between regions: Science, militarism, and American geography from world war to Cold War. *Annals of the Association of American Geographers, 96*(4), 807–826.

Barraclough, L. (2018). Wrangling settler colonialism in the urban US West: Indigenous and Mexican American struggles for social justice. *Annals of the American Association of Geographers, 108*(2), 513–523.

Barraclough, L. R. (2019). *Charros: How Mexican cowboys are remapping race and American identity.* Berkeley: University of California Press.

Behdad, A. (1997). Nationalism and immigration to the United States. *Diaspora: A Journal of Transnational Studies, 6*(2), 155–178.

Bella, T. (2014, December 10). In Arkansas, white town is a black mark. *Al Jazeera.* http://america.aljazeera.com/articles/2014/12/10/harrison-arkansashategroups.html.

Bender, D. E., and J. K. Lipman. (Eds.). (2015). *Making the empire work: Labor and United States imperialism.* New York: New York University Press.

Berlant, L. (2014) Citizenship. In B. Burgett and G. Hendler (Eds.), *Keywords for American cultural studies* (41–45). New York: New York University Press.

Bevacqua, M. L. (2010). *Chamorros, ghosts, non-voting delegates: GUAM! Where the production of America's sovereignty begins.* PhD dissertation, University of California San Diego. https://escholarship.org/uc/item/9x72002w.

Billington, M. L. (Ed.) (1978). *The South: A central theme?* Malabar, FL: Krieger.

Blair, D. D., and J. Barth. (2005). *Arkansas politics and government.* Lincoln: University of Nebraska Press.

Bledsoe, A., L. E. Eaves, and B. Williams. (2017). Introduction: Black geographies in and of the United States South. *Southeastern Geographer, 57*(1), 6–11.

Blevins, B. (2002). *Hill folks: A history of Arkansas Ozarkers and their image.* Chapel Hill: University of North Carolina Press.

Blevins, B. (2009). *Arkansas/Arkansaw: How bear hunters, hillbillies, and good ol' boys defined a state.* Fayetteville: University of Arkansas Press.

Bolton, S. C. (1993). *Territorial ambition.* Fayetteville: University of Arkansas Press.

———. (2002). Turning point: World War II and the economic development of Arkansas. *Arkansas Historical Quarterly, 61*(2), 123–151.

Bonds, A., & J. Inwood (2016). Beyond white privilege: Geographies of white supremacy and settler colonialism. *Progress in Human Geography, 40*(6), 715–733.

Bouton, C.S. (ca. 1910). [Springdale promotional publication]. Shiloh Museum, Springdale, Ark. Accessed March 2014.

Bowman, M. (2016). World War II prisoner of war camps. *Encyclopedia of Arkansas history and culture.* https://encyclopediaofarkansas.net/entries/world-war-ii-prisoner-of-war-camps-2398/.

Broderick, M. (1968). Associated statehood—A new form of decolonisation. *International and Comparative Law Quarterly, 17*(2), 368–403.

Bruyneel, K. (2004). Challenging American boundaries: Indigenous people and the "gift" of U.S. citizenship. *Studies in American Political Development, 18*(1), 30–43.

Buesseler, K. O. (1997). The isotopic signature of fallout plutonium in the North Pacific. *Journal of Environmental Radioactivity*, 36(1), 69–83.

Burkholder, Z. (2010). From "Wops and Dagoes and Hunkies" to "Caucasian": Changing racial discourse in American classrooms during World War II. *History of Education Quarterly*, 50(3), 324–358.

Burnett, C. D., and B. Marshall (Eds.). (2001). *Foreign in a domestic sense: Puerto Rico, American expansion, and the Constitution*. Durham, N.C.: Duke University Press.

Byng, R. (2013, November 7). Arkansas town responds to controversial "Anti-racist is a code word for anti-white" sign. *Huffington Post: Black Voices*.

Byrd, J. A. (2011). *The transit of empire: Indigenous critiques of colonialism*. Minneapolis: University of Minnesota Press.

Cacho, L. M. (2012). *Social death: Racialized rightlessness and the criminalization of the unprotected*. New York: New York University Press.

Calhoun, J. (1975, November 5). The light at the end of the tunnel. *Grapevine*, 7(10), Fayetteville, Ark. University of Arkansas, Special Collections, Fayetteville, Ark. Accessed June 2014.

Camacho, K. L. (2012). After 9/11: Militarized borders and social movements in the Mariana Islands. *American Quarterly*, 64(4), 685–713.

Capps, R., E. Henderson, J. D. Kasarda, J. H Johnson Jr., S. J. Appold, D. L. Croney, D. J. Hernandez, and M. E. Fix. (2007, April 3). A profile of immigrants in Arkansas. *Urban Institute*. https://www.urban.org/research/publication/profile-immigrants-arkansas.

Carneiro, A., Fortuna, N., and J. Varejão (2012). Immigrants at new destinations: How they fare and why. *Journal of Population Economics*, 25, 1165–1185.

Carrasco, T. A. U., and H. Seif. (2014). Disrupting the dream: Undocumented youth reframe citizenship and deportability through anti-deportation activism. *Latino Studies*, 12(2), 279–299.

Chambers, S., and A. Williamson. (Eds.). (2017). *The politics of new immigrant destinations: Transatlantic perspectives*. Philadelphia: Temple University Press.

Cheng, W. (2013). Strategic orientalism: Racial capitalism and the problem of "Asianness." *African Identities*, 11(2), 148–158.

Chiu, T. (2014). Federal court upholds Hawai'i's reduction of state-funded health benefits for alien residents—*Korab v. Fink*. *American Journal of Law and Medicine*, 40(4), 470–472.

Choi, J. Y. (2008). Seeking health care: Marshallese migrants in Hawai'i. *Ethnicity and Health*, 13(1), 73-92.

Clinton, H. (2011, October 11). America's Pacific century. *Foreign Policy*. http://foreignpolicy.com/2011/10/11/americas-pacific-century/.

Coleman, M. (2012). The "local" migration state: The site-specific devolution of immigration enforcement in the U.S. South. *Law and Policy*, 34(2), 159–190.

Coleman, P. T. (1977, February 3). [Letter to Bethwel Henry]. Samuel McPhetres archives. Garapan, Saipan, CNMI. Accessed July 2013.

Collins, F. L. (2022). Geographies of migration II: Decolonising migration studies. *Progress in Human Geography*, 46(5), doi: 03091325221100826.

[Constituent letter to Senator Dale Bumpers from Jonesboro, Ark.] (1991, November 25). University of Arkansas, Special Collections, Fayetteville, Ark. Accessed June 2014.

[Constituent letter to Senator Dale Bumpers from Newport, Ark.] (1991, November 21). University of Arkansas, Special Collections, Fayetteville, Ark. Accessed June 2014.

Cook, I., and M. Harrison. (2007). Follow the thing: "West Indian hot pepper sauce." *Space and Culture*, 10(1), 40–63.

Coulthard, G. S. (2007). Subjects of empire: Indigenous peoples and the "politics of recognition" in Canada. *Contemporary Political Theory*, 6(4), 437–460.

Cowen, D., and E. Gilbert. (Eds.). (2008). *War, citizenship, territory*. New York: Routledge.

Crossette, B. (1991, December 2). Asylum policy for Haitian refugees stirs debate on fairness by the U.S. *New York Times*. https://www.nytimes.com/1991/12/02/world/asylum-policy-for-haitian-refugees-stirs-debate-on-fairness-by-the-us.html.

Daigle, M., and M. M. Ramírez (2019). Decolonial geographies. In The Antipode Editorial Collective (Eds), *Keywords in radical geography: Antipode at 50*, 78–84. Hoboken, N.J.: Wiley Blackwell.

Davis, J., A. A. Moulton, L. Van Sant, and B. Williams. (2019). Anthropocene, capitalocene, ... plantationocene?: A manifesto for ecological justice in an age of global crises. *Geography Compass*, 13(5), doi: e12438.

Davis, S. (2005). Representing place: "Deserted isles" and the reproduction of Bikini Atoll. *Annals of the Association of American Geographers*, 95(3), 607–625.

———. (2015). *The empires' edge*. Athens: University of Georgia Press.

Dawson, A. (2007). *Mongrel nation: Diasporic culture and the making of postcolonial Britain*. Ann Arbor: University of Michigan Press.

De Genova, N. (2002). Migrant "illegality" and deportability in everyday life. *Annual review of anthropology*, 31, 419–447.

Deaver, D.D. (ca. 1910). Know your home town. Shiloh Museum of Ozark History, Springdale, Ark. Accessed March 2014.

Deloria Jr, V. (2010). *Behind the trail of broken treaties: An Indian declaration of independence*. Austin: University of Texas Press.

Dentice, D. (2015). Ku Klux Klan (after 1990). *Encyclopedia of Arkansas history and culture*. https://encyclopediaofarkansas.net/entries/ku-klux-klan-2755/.

Department of Justice, Immigration and Naturalization Service (2000, September 19). *Habitual residence in the territories and possessions of the United States*. (Federal Register, Volume 65, Number 182). Washington, D.C.: U.S. Government Printing Office.

Department of the Interior. (2016). *Definitions of Insular Area political jurisdictions*. https://www.doi.gov/oia/islands/politicatypes.

Desai, J., and K. Y. Joshi. (Eds.). (2013). *Asian Americans in Dixie: Race and migration in the South*. Urbana: University of Illinois Press.

Diaz, K. K. (2012). The Compact of Free Association (COFA): A history of failures. MA thesis, University of Hawaiʻi at Mānoa. https://scholarspace.manoa.Hawaiʻi.edu/handle/10125/24265.

Domosh, M. (2023). *Disturbing development in the Jim Crow South*. Athens: University of Georgia Press.

Dunbar-Ortiz, R. (2014). *An Indigenous peoples' history of the United States*. Vol. 3. Boston: Beacon Press.

Eaves, L. (2020). Fear of an other geography. *Dialogues in Human Geography*, 10(1), 34–36.

Ehrkamp, P., C. Nagel. (2012). Immigration, places of worship and the politics of citizenship in the U.S. South. *Transactions of the Institute of British Geographers*, 37(4), 624–638.

Elkins, C. (2014). Caddo Nation. *Encyclopedia of Arkansas history and culture*. https://encyclopediaofarkansas.net/entries/caddo-nation-549/.

Erman, S. (2008). Meanings of citizenship in the US empire: Puerto Rico, Isabel Gonzalez, and the Supreme Court, 1898 to 1905. *Journal of American Ethnic History*, 27(4), 5–33.

Ewalt, P. L., and N. Mokuau. (1995). Self-determination from a Pacific perspective. *Social Work*, 40(2), 168–175.

Explore Northwest Arkansas. (n.d.). [Homepage]. http://www.northwestarkansas.org. Accessed September 2015.

Farish, M. (2010). *The contours of America's cold war*. Minneapolis: University of Minnesota Press.

Farmer, S. (2021, March 27). Walmart's Company Town of Bentonville, Arkansas. *Jacobin*. https://jacobinmag.com/2021/03/walmart-walton-family-foundation-bentonville-arkansas-company-town.

Fayetteville City Directory. (1947). [Advertisement for Ward's ice cream]. Shiloh Museum of Ozark History, Springdale, Ark. Accessed March 2014.

Fernández, G. A. (2007). Race, gender, and class in the persistence of the Mariel stigma twenty years after the exodus from Cuba. *International Migration Review*, 41(3), 602–622.

Fernández-Kelly, P., and D. S. Massey. (2007). Borders for whom? The role of NAFTA in Mexico-U.S. migration. *Annals of the American Academy of Political and Social Science*, 610(1), 98–118.

Findlay, E. J. S. (2015). *We are left without a father here: Masculinity, domesticity, and migration in postwar Puerto Rico*. Durham, N.C.: Duke University Press.

Ford, E. (2020). *Rodeo as refuge, rodeo as rebellion: Gender, race, and identity in the American rodeo*. Lawrence: University Press of Kansas.

Fort Smith Historical Society (2016). World War II Veterans History Project. https://www.fortsmithhistory.org/Oral%20History/WW2project.html.

Freshour, C., and B. Williams (2020). Abolition in the time of COVID-19. *Antipode online*. https://antipodeonline.org/2020/04/09/abolition-in-the-time-of-covid-19/

Friedlander, E. J. (1979). "The miasmatic jungles": Reactions to H. L. Mencken's 1921 attack on Arkansas. *Arkansas Historical Quarterly*, 38(1), 63–71.

Friends of Micronesia. (1973, October). U.S. blocks talks. *Pacific Digital Library*. Accessed October 2023. https://pacificdigitallibrary.org/cgi-bin/pdl?e=d-0000ff-pdl—00-2—0—010—-4———-0-1l—10en-50—-20-text—-00-3-1-00bySR-0-0-000utfZz-8-00&a=d&cl=CL1.5&d=HASH01ec0824ddf2059b8cd035a7.5.

Fujita-Rony, D. B. (2003). *American workers, colonial power: Philippine Seattle and the Transpacific West, 1919–1941*. Berkeley: University of California Press.

Fusté, J. I. (2017). Repeating islands of debt: Historicizing the transcolonial relationality of Puerto Rico's economic crisis. *Radical History Review*, 2017(128), 91–119.

García-Colón, I. (2020). *Colonial migrants at the heart of empire: Puerto Rican workers on U.S. farms*. Berkeley: University of California Press.

References

Gates, H. L. (1983). The "blackness of blackness": A critique of the sign and the signifying monkey. *Critical Inquiry, 9*(4), 685–723.

Gilmartin, M., and L. D. Berg. (2007). Locating postcolonialism. *Area, 39*(1), 120–124.

Gilmore, R. W. (2002). Race and globalization. In P. J. Taylor, M. J. Watts, and R. J. Johnston (Eds.), *Geographies of global change: Remapping the world* (261–274). New York: Blackwell.

———. (2007). *Golden gulag: Prisons, surplus, crisis, and opposition in globalizing California*. Berkeley: University of California Press.

———. (2022). *Abolition geography: Essays towards liberation*. Brooklyn: Verso Books.

Go, J. (2008). *American empire and the politics of meaning: Elite political cultures in the Philippines and Puerto Rico during U.S. colonialism*. Durham, N.C.: Duke University Press.

Gorman, D. (2010). *Imperial citizenship: Empire and the question of belonging*. Oxford: Oxford University Press.

Government Accountability Office (GAO) (2002). Kwajalein Atoll is the key U.S. defense interest in two Micronesian nations. *GAO-02-119*.

———. Trust funds for Micronesia and the Marshall Islands may not provide sustainable income. *GAO-07-513*.

———. Improvements needed to assess and address growing migration. *GAO-12-64*.

———. Compacts of Free Association: Issues associated with implementation in Palau, Micronesia, and the Marshall Islands. *GAO-16-550T*.

———. Populations in U.S. areas have grown, with varying reported effects. *GAO-20-491*.

Graham, B. (2006). Marshallese out-migration intensifies. *Pacific Island reports*. https://pidp.eastwestcenter.org/pacific-islands-report/.

Gray, A. B. (2021, May 7) How the U.S. can protect the sovereignty of the smallest Pacific Islands. *Diplomat*. https://thediplomat.com/2021/05/how-the-us-can-protect-the-sovereignty-of-the-smallest-pacific-islands/.

Greeson, J. R. (1999). The figure of the South and the nationalizing imperatives of early United States literature. *Yale Journal of Criticism, 12*(2), 209–248.

Gregory, D. (1995). Imaginative geographies. *Progress in Human Geography, 19*(4), 447–485.

———. (2004). *The colonial present: Afghanistan, Palestine, Iraq*. Malden, Ma.: Blackwell.

———. (2006). The black flag: Guantánamo Bay and the space of exception. *Geografiska Annaler: Series B, Human Geography, 88*(4), 405–427.

Gregory, J. N. (1991). *American exodus: The dust bowl migration and Okie culture in California*. New York: Oxford University Press.

———. (2006). *The southern diaspora: How the great migrations of black and white southerners transformed America*. Chapel Hill: University of North Carolina Press.

Guam Commission on Decolonization. (2022). *Guam: A territory like no other (pdf)*. https://decol.guam.gov/. Also available via the following direct link: chrome-extension://efaidnbmnnnibpcajpcglclefindmkaj/https://decol.guam.gov/sites/default/files/decolonization-newspaper-insert-digital_0.pdf.

Guerrero, P. M. (2017). *Nuevo South: Latinas/os, Asians, and the remaking of place*. Austin: University of Texas Press.

Guskin, E. (2013, June 17). "Illegal," "undocumented," "unauthorized": News media shift language on immigration. *Pew Research Center.*

Hagge, P.D. (2009). *The new Northwest: The transformation of small-town economies in Northwest Arkansas since 1960.* MSc thesis, Pennsylvania State University. https://etda.libraries.psu.edu/catalog/9652.

Halevy, D. P. (2014). World War II. *Encyclopedia of Arkansas history and culture.* https://encyclopediaofarkansas.net/entries/world-war-ii-2402/.

Hall, S. (1980). Race, articulation and societies structured in dominance. In *Sociological theories: Race and colonialism* (305–45). Paris: UNESCO.

———. (2002). When was "the post-colonial"? Thinking at the limit. In I. Chambers and L. Curti (Eds.), *The post-colonial question* (242–260). Abingdon, UK: Routledge.

Hallett, M. C. (2012). "Better than White trash": Work ethic, *Latinidad* and Whiteness in rural Arkansas. *Latino Studies, 10*(1–2), 81–106.

Haney-López, I. F. (1994). The social construction of race: Some observations on illusion, fabrication, and choice. *Harvard CR-CLL Rev., 29,* 1–62.

Hansen, T. B., and F. Stepputat. (Eds.). (2009). *Sovereign bodies: Citizens, migrants, and states in the postcolonial world.* Princeton, N.J.: Princeton University Press.

Hara, K. (2006). *Cold War frontiers in the Asia-Pacific: Divided territories in the San Francisco system.* Abingdon, UK: Routledge.

Harington, D. (1995). Over here and over there: Northwest Arkansas and WWII. Shiloh Museum of Ozark History, Springdale, Ark. Accessed March 2014.

Harkins, A. (2003). *Hillbilly: A cultural history of an American icon.* Oxford: Oxford University Press.

Harris, C. I. (1993). Whiteness as property. *Harvard Law Review, 106,* 1707–1791.

Harrison, A. (Ed.). (2012). *Black exodus: The Great Migration from the American South.* Jackson: University Press of Mississippi.

Hau'ofa, E. (1994). Our sea of islands. *Contemporary Pacific, 6*(1), 148–161.

Heisler, B. S. (2007). The "other Braceros." *Social Science History, 31*(2).

Hernandez, T. (2011, March 17). Illegal immigrant steps out: Guzman tired of "living in the shadows," takes part in forum. *Benton County Daily Record.* Shiloh Museum of Ozark History, Springdale, Ark. Accessed March 2014.

Herr, R. A. (1986). Regionalism, strategic denial and South Pacific security. *Journal of Pacific History, 21*(4), 170–182.

Hezel, F. X. (1976). Micronesia's education for selfgovernment: Frolicking in the backyard? *Pacific Asian Studies, 1*(2), 62–69.

———. (2006). Who will own business in Majuro? *Micronesian Seminar (MicSem).* https://micsem.org/micronesian-counselo/who-will-own-business-in-majuro/.

———. (2013). *Micronesians on the move: Eastward and upward bound.* Pacific Islands Policy vol. 9. East-West Center.

Hiemstra, N. (2010). Immigrant "illegality" as neoliberal governmentality in Leadville, Colorado. *Antipode, 42*(1), 74–102.

———. (2019). *Detain and deport: The chaotic US immigration enforcement regime.* Athens: University of Georgia Press.

Hills, H. L. (2004). Free association for Micronesia and the Marshall Islands: A transitional political status model. *University of Hawai'i Law Review, 27,* 1-16.

Hirshberg, L. (2022). *Suburban empire: Cold War militarization in the U.S. Pacific.* Berkeley: University of California Press.

Hoeffel, E. M., S. Rastog, O. K. Kim, and H. Shahid. (2012). *The Asian population: 2010,* C2010BR-11, U.S. Census Bureau, Washington, D.C.

Hoskins, J. A., and V. T. Nguyen. (Eds.). (2014). *Transpacific studies: Framing an emerging field.* Honolulu: University of Hawai'i Press.

Howe, K. R., and R. C. Kiste. (1994). *Tides of history: The Pacific Islands in the twentieth century.* Honolulu: University of Hawai'i Press.

Hughes, W.W. (1988, July 28). Ozark pioneers survived adventures livelier than movie. *Springdale News.* Shiloh Museum of Ozark History, Springdale, Ark. Accessed March 2014.

Igarashi, M. (2002). *Associated statehood in international law.* Leiden, Netherlands: Martinus Nijhoff.

Immigrant Legal Resource Center. (2021, June 22). All those rules about crimes involving moral turpitude. https://www.ilrc.org/all-those-rules-about-crimes-involving-moral-turpitude.

International Trusteeship System (n.d.). *United Nations.* http://www.un.org/en/decolonization/its.shtml [defunct]. Accessed April 2015.

Itzigsohn, J. (1999). Immigration and the boundaries of citizenship: The institutions of immigrants' political transnationalism. *International Migration Review,* 34, 1126–1154.

Johnson III, B. F. (2014a). *Arkansas in Modern America, 1930–1999.* Fayetteville: University of Arkansas Press.

———. (2014b). World War II through the Faubus era, 1941 through 1967. *Encyclopedia of Arkansas history and culture.* https://encyclopediaofarkansas.net/entries/world-war-ii-through-the-faubus-era-1941-through-1967-404/.

Johnson, G. (1979). Micronesia: America's "strategic" trust. *Bulletin of the Atomic Scientists,* 35(2), 10–15.

———. (1982). The Pentagon stalks Micronesia: Strategic interests vs. self-determination. *Japan-Asia Quarterly Review,* 42–50.

Jones, R. (2016). *Violent borders: Refugees and the right to move.* London: Verso Books.

Jones-Correa, M., and E. de Graauw. (2013). The illegality trap: The politics of immigration and the lens of illegality. *Daedalus,* 142(3), 185–198.

Kandel, W., and E. A. Parrado. (2005). Restructuring of the U.S. meat processing industry and new Hispanic migrant destinations. *Population and Development Review,* 31(3), 447–471.

———. (2021). Hispanics in the American South and the transformation of the poultry industry. In D. D. Arreola (Ed.), *Hispanic spaces, Latino places* (255–276). Austin: University of Texas Press.

Katz, C. (2001). On the grounds of globalization: A topography for feminist political engagement. *Signs: Journal of women in culture and society,* 26(4), 1213–1234.

Keitner, C., and W. M. Reisman. (2003). Free association: The United States experience. *Texas International Law Journal,* 39, 1–64.

Kelley, R. D. (1990). *Hammer and hoe: Alabama communists during the Great Depression.* Chapel Hill: University of North Carolina Press.

Kelley, R. D. G. (2017, March 6). Births of a nation, redux. *Boston Review.* https://bostonreview.net/race-politics/robin-d-g-kelley-births-nation.

Kim, N. Y. (2008). *Imperial citizens: Koreans and race from Seoul to LA*. Stanford, Calif.: Stanford University Press.

Kolchin, P. (2009). The South and the world. *Journal of Southern History*, 75(3), 565–580.

Kothari, U., and R. Wilkinson. (2010). Colonial imaginaries and postcolonial transformations: Exiles, bases, beaches. *Third World Quarterly*, 31(8), 1395–1412.

Labor problem aided by German war prisoners (1944, August 10). *Springdale News*. Shiloh Museum of Ozark History, Springdale, Ark. Accessed March 2014.

Lal, B. V., and K. Fortune. (Eds.). (2000). *The Pacific Islands: An encyclopedia*. Honolulu: University of Hawai'i Press.

Lancaster, G. (2010). "They are not wanted": The extirpation of African Americans from Baxter County, Arkansas. *Arkansas Historical Quarterly*, 69(1), 28–43.

———. (2014a, August 13). Harrison race riots. *Encyclopedia of Arkansas history and culture*. https://encyclopediaofarkansas.net/entries/harrison-race-riots-of-1905-and-1909-3712/.

———. (2014b). *Racial cleansing in Arkansas, 1883–1924: Politics, land, labor, and criminality*. Lanham, Md.: Lexington Books.

———. (2023). Arkansas's regional identity. *Encyclopedia of Arkansas history and culture*. https://encyclopediaofarkansas.net/entries/arkansass-regional-identity-5857/.

Lawson, G., and R. D. Sloane. (2009). The constitutionality of decolonization by associated statehood: Puerto Rico's legal status reconsidered. *Boston College Law Review*, 50, 9–19.

Lê Espiritu, Y. (2006). The "we-win-even-when-we-lose" syndrome: U.S. press coverage of the twenty-fifth anniversary of the "Fall of Saigon." *American Quarterly*, 58(2), 329–352.

Lee, E. (2003). *At America's gates: Chinese immigration during the exclusion era, 1882–1943*. Chapel Hill: University of North Carolina Press.

Lee, E., and G. Pratt. (2012). The spectacular and the mundane: racialised state violence, Filipino migrant workers, and their families. *Environment and Planning A*, 44(4), 889–904.

Leibowitz, A. H. (1976). *Colonial emancipation in the Pacific and the Caribbean: A legal and political analysis*. New York: Praeger.

Leonard, C. (2014). *The meat racket: The secret takeover of America's food business*. New York: Simon and Schuster.

Library of Congress. (2016, March 22). Library of Congress to cancel the subject heading "illegal aliens." https://www.loc.gov/catdir/cpso/illegal-aliens-decision.pdf.

Lichter, D. T., and K. M. Johnson. (2006). Emerging rural settlement patterns and the geographic redistribution of America's new immigrants. *Rural sociology*, 71(1), 109–131.

Lipman, J. K. (2014). A refugee camp in America: Fort Chaffee and Vietnamese and Cuban refugees, 1975–1982. *Journal of American Ethnic History*, 33(2), 57–87.

Loewen, J. W. (2014). Sundown towns. *Encyclopedia of Arkansas history and culture*. https://encyclopediaofarkansas.net/entries/sundown-towns-3658/.

———. (2022). Sundown towns. *Encyclopedia of Arkansas history and culture*. https://encyclopediaofarkansas.net/entries/sundown-towns-3658/.

———. (2005). *Sundown towns: A hidden dimension of American racism*. New York: New Press.

Loyd, J. M. (2011). American exceptionalism, abolition and the possibilities for nonkilling futures. In J. Tyner and J. Inwood (Eds.), *Nonkilling Geography* (103–126). Honolulu: Center for Global Nonkilling.

Loyd, J. M., E. Mitchell-Eaton, and A. Mountz. (2016). The militarization of islands and migration: Tracing human mobility through U.S. bases in the Caribbean and the Pacific. *Political Geography*, 53, 65–75.

Loyd, J. M., and A. Mountz (2018). *Boats, borders, and bases: Race, the Cold War, and the rise of migration detention in the United States*. Berkeley: University of California Press.

Lutz, C. (2009). Introduction: Bases, Empire, and Global Response. In C. Lutz and C. Enloe (Eds.), *The bases of empire: The global struggle against US military posts* (1–46). New York: New York University Press.

Lyons, P., and T. P. K Tengan. (2015). COFA complex: A conversation with Joakim "Jojo" Peter. *American Quarterly*, 67(3), 663–679.

Maclellan, N. (2005). The nuclear age in the Pacific Islands. *Contemporary Pacific*, 17(2), 363–372.

Maher, D. (2016). Indochinese resettlement program. *Encyclopedia of Arkansas history and culture*. https://encyclopediaofarkansas.net/entries/indochinese-resettlement-program-5562/.

Mains, S. P., M. Gilmartin, D. Cullen, and R. Mohammad, D. P. Tolia-Kelly, P. Raghuram, and J. Winders. (2013). Postcolonial migrations. *Social and Cultural Geography*, 14(2), 131–144.

Maki, J. M. (1947). U.S. strategic Area or UN Trusteeship. *Far Eastern Survey*, 16(15), 175–178.

Man, S. (2018). *Soldiering through empire: Race and the making of the decolonizing Pacific*. Berkeley: University of California Press.

Mann, M. (1987). Ruling class strategies and citizenship. *Sociology*, 21(3), 339–354.

Marrow, H. (2005). New destinations and immigrant incorporation. *Perspectives on Politics*, 3(4), 781–799.

———. (2009). New immigrant destinations and the American colour line. *Ethnic and Racial Studies*, 32(6), 1037–1057.

———. (2011). *New destination dreaming: Immigration, race, and legal status in the rural American South*. Stanford, Calif.: Stanford University Press.

Martin, K. (1994). Flannery O'Connor's prophetic imagination. *Religion and Literature*, 26, 33–58.

Mason, C. (2005). The hillbilly defense: Culturally mediating U.S. terror at home and abroad. *NWSA Journal*, 17(3), 39–63.

Mason, L. (1989). A Marshallese nation emerges from the political fragmentation of American Micronesia. *Pacific Studies*, 13(1), 1–46.

Massey, D. S. (Ed.). (2008). *New faces in new places: The changing geography of American immigration*. New York: Russell Sage Foundation.

Mayblin, L., and J. Turner. (2020). *Migration studies and colonialism*. Hoboken, N.J.: John Wiley.

McClain, P. D., N. M. Carter, V. M. DeFrancesco Soto, M. L. Lyle, J. D. Grynaviski, S. C. Nunnally, T. J. Scotto, J. A. Kendrick, G. F. Lackey, and K. D. Cotton. (2006). Racial distancing in a southern city: Latino immigrants' views of black Americans. *Journal of Politics*, 68(3), 571–584.

McClintock, A. (1995). *Imperial leather: Race, gender, and sexuality in the colonial contest.* New York: Routledge.
McConnell, E. D., and F. Miraftab. (2009). Sundown town to "Little Mexico": Old-timers and newcomers in an American small town. *Rural Sociology, 74*(4), 605–629.
McElfish, P. A., E. Hallgren, and S. Yamada. (2015). Effect of U.S. health policies on health care access for Marshallese migrants. *American Journal of Public Health, 105*(4), 637–643.
McGreevey, R. C. (2018). *Borderline citizens: The United States, Puerto Rico, and the politics of colonial migration.* Ithaca, N.Y.: Cornell University Press.
McKittrick, K. (2006). *Demonic grounds: Black women and the cartographies of struggle.* Minneapolis: University of Minnesota Press.
———. (2011). On plantations, prisons, and a black sense of place. *Social and Cultural Geography, 12*(8), 947–963.
McKittrick, K., and C. A. Woods. (Eds.). (2007). *Black geographies and the politics of place.* Toronto: Between the Lines.
McLoughlin, W. G. (2014). *After the Trail of Tears: The Cherokees' struggle for sovereignty, 1839–1880.* Chapel Hill: University of North Carolina Press.
McPherson, J. M. (2004). Antebellum Southern exceptionalism: A new look at an old question. *Civil War History, 50*(4), 418–433.
Melamed, J. (2015). Racial capitalism. *Critical ethnic studies, 1*(1), 76–85.
Menjívar, C. (2006). Liminal legality: Salvadoran and Guatemalan immigrants' lives in the United States. *American Journal of Sociology, 111*(4), 999–1037.
Metzler, W. H. (ca. 1940). *Population pressure in upland areas of Arkansas.* University of Arkansas.
Miller, T. (2017). *Storming the wall: Climate change, migration, and homeland security.* San Francisco: City Lights Books.
Mills, C. W. (1956). *The power elite.* Oxford: Oxford University Press.
Minca, C. (2015). Geographies of the camp. *Political Geography, 49*, 74–83.
Mink, P. T. (1970). Micronesia: our bungled trust. *Texas International Law Forum* (6), 181–208.
Mitchell-Eaton, E. (2021, May 31). No island is an island: COVID exposure, Marshall Islanders, and imperial productions of race and remoteness. *Society + Space.* https://www.societyandspace.org/articles/no-island-is-an-island.
Moneyhon, C. H. (1996). The creators of the New South in Arkansas: Industrial boosterism, 1875–1885. *Arkansas Historical Quarterly, 55*(4), 383–409.
Mongia, R. (2018). *Indian migration and empire: A colonial genealogy of the modern state.* Durham, N.C.: Duke University Press.
Mongia, R. V. (1999). Race, nationality, mobility: A history of the passport. *Public Culture, 11*(3), 527–556.
Moreton, B. E. (2006). It came from Bentonville: The agrarian origins of Wal-Mart culture. In N. Lichtenstein (Ed.), *Wal-Mart: The face of twenty-first-century capitalism* (57–82). New York: New Press.
Morris, F. (2014, May 12). Tale of two billboards: An Ozark town's struggle to unseat hate. *National Public Radio.*
Mountz, A. (2011). The enforcement archipelago: Detention, haunting, and asylum on islands. *Political Geography, 30*(3), 118–128.

Mountz, A., and J. Loyd. (2014). Transnational productions of remoteness: Building on-shore and offshore carceral regimes across borders. *Geographica Helvetica*, 69(5), 389–398.

Mullings, B. (1999). Insider or outsider, both or neither: Some dilemmas of interviewing in a cross-cultural setting. *Geoforum*, 30(4), 337–350.

Museum of Native American History website (2016). [Museum description]. Accessed April 14, 2016. http://www.arkansas.com/attractions/detail/museum-of-native-american-history/92789.

Nast, H. J. (1994). Women in the field: Critical feminist methodologies and theoretical perspectives. *Professional Geographer*, 46(1), 54–66.

National Park Service (2016). [Trail of Tears auto route sign.] National Parks Service. https://www.nps.gov/trte/planyourvisit/upload/National-Park-Service-Trail-of-Tears-Map-508.pdf.

Nelson, L., and N. Hiemstra. (2008). Latino immigrants and the renegotiation of place and belonging in small town America. *Social and Cultural Geography*, 9(3), 319–342.

Nero, K. L., M. L. Burton, and J. Hess. (2001). Creating options: Forming a Marshallese community in Orange County, California. *Contemporary Pacific*, 13(1), 89–121.

Nevins, J. (2002). *Operation gatekeeper: The rise of the "illegal alien" and the making of the U.S.-Mexico boundary*. London: Psychology Press.

Ngai, M. M. (2004). *Impossible subjects: Illegal aliens and the making of modern America*. Princeton, N.J.: Princeton University Press.

Nguyen, M. T. (2012). *The gift of freedom: War, debt, and other refugee passages*. Durham, N.C.: Duke University Press.

Niedenthal, J. (1997). A history of the people of Bikini following nuclear weapons testing in the Marshall Islands: With recollections and views of elders of Bikini Atoll. *Health Physics*, 73(1), 28–36.

Nisa, R. (2019). Capturing the forgotten war: Carceral spaces and colonial legacies in Cold War Korea. *Journal of Historical Geography*, 64, 13–24.

Nixon, R. (2011). *Slow violence and the environmentalism of the poor*. Cambridge, Mass.: Harvard University Press.

Odem, M. E. (2004). Our Lady of Guadalupe in the New South: Latino immigrants and the politics of integration in the Catholic church. *Journal of American Ethnic History*, 24(1), 26–57.

Omi, M., and H. Winant. (2014). *Racial formation in the United States*. Abingdon, UK: Routledge.

Omi, M., and H. A. Winant. (1994). *Racial formation in the United States: From the 1960s to the 1990s*. London: Psychology Press.

On the homefront: Rogers' news from World War II. (1940). Shiloh Museum of Ozark History, Springdale, Ark. Accessed March 2014.

Ong, A. (2013). Cultural citizenship as subject-making. In S. Lazar (Ed.), *The anthropology of citizenship: A reader* (79–92). Hoboken, N.J.: Wiley..

Paik, A. N. (2016). *Rightlessness: Testimony and redress in U.S. prison camps since World War II*. Chapel Hill: University of North Carolina Press

Pain, R., and L. Staeheli. (2014). Introduction: Intimacy-geopolitics and violence. *Area*, 46(4), 344–347.

Parker, S. (2011, September 25). Arkansas' hillbilly image resonates into 21st century. *Reuters*. https://www.reuters.com/article/us-hillbilly-arkansas/arkansas-hillbilly-image-resonates-into-21st-century-idUSTRE78P2C820110926.

Pearson, J. L. (2017). Defending empire at the United Nations: The politics of international colonial oversight in the era of decolonisation. *Journal of Imperial and Commonwealth History, 45*(3), 525–549.

Peck, J., and N. Theodore. (2012). Follow the policy: A distended case approach. *Environment and Planning A, 44*(1), 21–30.

Perdue, R. T. (2023). Trashing Appalachia: Coal, prisons and whiteness in a region of refuse. *Punishment and Society, 25*(1), 21–41.

Perez, L. M. (2008). Citizenship denied: The "Insular Cases" and the Fourteenth Amendment. *Virginia Law Review, 94*, 1029–1081.

Perkins, J. B. (2014). Mountain stereotypes, whiteness, and the discourse of early school reform in the Arkansas Ozarks, 1910s–1920s. *History of Education Quarterly, 54*(2), 197–221.

Personnel changes at German war prison camp. (1944). *Springdale News*. Shiloh Museum of Ozark History, Springdale, Ark. Accessed March 2014.

Petersen, G. (2004). Lessons learned: The Micronesian quest for independence in the context of American imperial history. *Micronesian Journal of the Humanities and Social Sciences, 3*(1–2), 45–63.

Peterson, H. A. (2010). *The Trail of Tears: An annotated bibliography of southeastern Indian removal*. Vol. 30. Lanham, M.D.: Scarecrow Press.

Poblete, J. (2014). *Islanders in the empire: Filipino and Puerto Rican laborers in Hawai'i*. Urbana: University of Illinois Press.

Pratt, G. (2005). Abandoned women and spaces of the exception. *Antipode, 37*(5), 1052–1078.

Prison labor necessary says Welch head. (1944, November 16). *Springdale News*. Shiloh Museum of Ozark History, Springdale, Ark. Accessed March 2014.

Public Broadcasting Service (PBS) (2014). *Banished: American ethnic cleansings*.

Pulido, L. (2017). Geographies of race and ethnicity II: Environmental racism, racial capitalism and state-sanctioned violence. *Progress in human geography, 41*(4), 524–533.

Punke, H. H. (1972). Second-class citizenship. *Social Studies, 63*(3), 127–131.

Quraishi, U. (2020). *Redefining the immigrant South: Indian and Pakistani immigration to Houston during the Cold War*. Chapel Hill: University of North Carolina Press.

Radcliff, M. (2016). Fort Chaffee. *Encyclopedia of Arkansas history and culture*. https://encyclopediaofarkansas.net/entries/fort-chaffee-2263/.

Ramírez, C. S., S. M. Falcón, J. Poblete, S. C. McKay, and F. A. Schaeffer. (Eds.). (2021). *Precarity and belonging: Labor, migration, and noncitizenship*. New Brunswick, N.J.: Rutgers University Press.

Reagan, R. (1984, March 30). Message to the Congress transmitting proposed legislation to approve the Compact of Free Association between the United States and the Trust Territory of the Pacific Islands. Ronald Reagan Presidential Library. https://www.reaganlibrary.gov/archives/speech/message-congress-transmitting-proposed-legislation-approve-compact-free-1.

Regis, H. A. (2006). *Caribbean and southern: Transnational perspectives on the U.S. South*. Athens: University of Georgia Press.

Reiss, M. (2005). Bronzed bodies behind barbed wire: Masculinity and the treatment of German prisoners of war in the United States during World War II. *Journal of Military History*, 69(2), 475–504.

Renda, M. A. (2001). *Taking Haiti: Military occupation and the culture of U.S. imperialism, 1915–1940*. Chapel Hill: University of North Carolina Press.

Rhodes, R. (2012). *Dark sun: The making of the hydrogen bomb*. New York: Simon and Schuster.

Ribas, V. (2016). *On the line: Slaughterhouse lives and the making of the New South*. Berkeley: University of California Press.

Ridgley, J. (2008). Cities of refuge: Immigration enforcement, police, and the insurgent genealogies of citizenship in U.S. sanctuary cities. *Urban Geography*, 29(1), 53–77.

Riklon, S., W. Alik, A. Hixon, and N. Palafox. (2010). The "Compact impact" in Hawaiʻi: Focus on health care. *Hawaiʻi Medical Journal*, 69(6), 7–12.

Ripped at the Seams. (2008). *Talk Business and Politics*. Accessed from the Shiloh Museum of Ozark History, Springdale, Ark.

Robinson, C. J. (1983). *Black Marxism: The making of the Black radical tradition*. Chapel Hill: University of North Carolina Press.

Robinson, D. (1993, May 20). Keeping in touch with their roots. *Northwest Arkansas Times*. Retrieved from the Shiloh Museum of Ozark History, Springdale, Ark., in March 2014.

Robinson, D. (2010). The neighbourhood effects of new immigration. *Environment and Planning A*, 42(10), 2451–2466.

Robinson, J. (2003). Postcolonialising geography: Tactics and pitfalls. *Singapore Journal of Tropical Geography*, 24(3), 273–289.

Roediger, D. R. (1999). *The wages of whiteness: Race and the making of the American working class*. Brooklyn: Verso Books.

Rogers Historical Museum (ca. 1995). [Organizational brochure]. Rogers, Arkansas.

Roth, S. O. (1999, October 1). U.S. and the Freely Associated States. Testimony Before the House Resources Committee and the House International Relations Committee, Subcommittee on Asia and the Pacific. Washington, D.C.: U.S. Department of State archive. http://1997-2001.state.gov/www/policy_remarks/1998/981001_roth_fas.html. Accessed 10 November 2014.

Rowe, A. C., and E. Tuck (2017). Settler colonialism and cultural studies: Ongoing settlement, cultural production, and resistance. *Cultural Studies ↔ Critical Methodologies*, 17(1), 3–13.

Sabo, G. (2014). Native Americans. *Encyclopedia of Arkansas history and culture*. https://encyclopediaofarkansas.net/entries/native-americans-408/.

Said, E. W. (1993). *Culture and imperialism*. New York: Vintage.

———. (1994). Edward Said's *Culture and imperialism*: A symposium. *Social Text* 40, 1–21.

Schwartz, J. A. (2015). Marshallese cultural diplomacy in Arkansas. *American Quarterly*, 67(3), 781–812.

Schwartz, M. (2010). Trucking industry. *Encyclopedia of Arkansas history and culture*. https://encyclopediaofarkansas.net/entries/trucking-industry-5062/.

Senate Bill No. 11, Act 47, "Alien Land Act." 1943. https://digitalheritage.arkansas.gov/cgi/viewcontent.cgi?article=1001&context=exhibits-online-japanese-american-internment. Accessed 19 September 2023.

Sheller, M. (2018). *Mobility justice: The politics of movement in an age of extremes*. Brooklyn: Verso Books.

Sheller, M., and J. Urry. (2006). The new mobilities paradigm. *Environment and Planning A*, 38(2), 207–226.

Shigematsu, S. and K. L. Camacho. (Eds.). (2010). *Militarized currents: Toward a decolonized future in Asia and the Pacific*. Minneapolis: University of Minnesota Press.

Shiloh Museum of Ozark History. (ca. 1903). [Newspaper article discussing Black man's alleged attempted assault on white girl and advocating for his institutionalization, lynching, and incarceration]. Shiloh Museum of Ozark History, Springdale, Ark. Accessed March 2014.

Shiloh Museum of Ozark History. (1904, January 22). [Promotional pamphlet describing Northwest Arkansas town as without "saloons, negroes, mosquitos, malaria, chills, bandy houses or other vices of this nature"]. Shiloh Museum of Ozark History, Springdale, Ark. Accessed March 2014.

Simon, S. L. (1997). A brief history of people and events related to atomic weapons testing in the Marshall Islands. *Health Physics*, 73(1), 5–20.

Simon, S. L., and J. C. Graham. (1997). Findings of the first comprehensive radiological monitoring program of the Republic of the Marshall Islands. *Health Physics*, 73(1), 66–85.

Simpson, L. B. (2016). Indigenous resurgence and co-resistance. *Critical ethnic studies*, 2(2), 19–34.

Singh, N. P. (2017). *Race and America's long war*. Berkeley: University of California Press.

Smith, A. (2015). *Conquest: Sexual violence and American Indian genocide*. Durham, N.C.: Duke University Press.

Smith, B. E., and J. Winders. (2008). "We're here to stay": Economic restructuring, Latino migration and place-making in the U.S. South. *Transactions of the Institute of British Geographers*, 33(1), 60–72.

Smith, C. C. (1986). *War and wartime changes: The transformation of Arkansas, 1940–1945*. Fayetteville: University of Arkansas Press.

———. (1994). The response of Arkansans to prisoners of war and Japanese Americans in Arkansas, 1942–1945. *Arkansas Historical Quarterly*, 340–366.

Smith, H. A., and O. J. Furuseth. (Eds.). (2006). *Latinos in the new South: Transformations of place*. Aldershot, UK: Ashgate.

Solomon, A. M. (1963, October 9). *A report by the U.S. Government Survey Mission to the Trust Territory of the Pacific Islands*. Report commissioned by U.S. President John F. Kennedy in a National Security Action Memorandum no. 243, issued May 9, 1963.

The Solomon Report: America's ruthless blueprint for the assimilation of Micronesia. (1971). *Friends of Micronesia, Micronesian Independent, and Tia Belau*. Samuel McPhetres archives. Garapan, Saipan, CNMI. Accessed July 2013.

Springdale Chamber of Commerce (2014, February 18). Northwest Arkansas adds 23 people a day. http://www.nwacouncil.org.

Staeheli, L. A., and V. A. Lawson. (1994). A discussion of "women in the field": The politics of feminist fieldwork. *Professional Geographer*, 46(1), 96–102.

Stege, K. E. (2004). Marshall Islands. *Contemporary Pacific, 16*(1),126–132.

Stevens, W. K. (1980, May 11). Pickets add to problems for refugees in Arkansas. *New York Times*.

Steward, D. R. (1995, January 29). Stunting growth: Boom rattles Fayetteville's long-open door. *Arkansas Democrat-Gazette*. Shiloh Museum of Ozark History, Springdale, Ark. Accessed March 2014.

Stoler, A. L. (2008). Imperial debris: reflections on ruins and ruination. *Cultural Anthropology, 23*(2), 191–219

———. (Ed.). (2013). *Imperial debris: on ruins and ruination*. Durham, N.C.: Duke University Press.

Striffler, S. (2007). Neither here nor there: Mexican immigrant workers and the search for home. *American Ethnologist, 34*(4), 674–688.

———. (2009). Immigration anxieties: Policing and regulating workers and employers in the poultry industry. In F. Ansley and J. Shefner (Eds.), *Global connections and local receptions: New Latino immigration to the southeastern United States* (129–54). Knoxville: University of Tennessee Press.

Stuesse, A. (2016). *Scratching out a living: Latinos, race, and work in the Deep South*. Vol. 38. Berkeley: University of California Press.

Stur, H. M. (2015). "Hiding behind the humanitarian label": Refugees, repatriates, and the rebuilding of America's benevolent image after the Vietnam War. *Diplomatic History, 39*(2), 223–244.

Swyngedouw, E. (1997). Neither global nor local: "Glocalization" and the politics of scale. In K. Cox (Ed.), *Spaces of globalization (137–166)*. New York: Guilford Press.

Tait, V. (2005). *Poor workers' unions: Rebuilding labor from below*. Cambridge, Mass.: South End Press.

Taitano, G. E. (2022). Origin of CHamoru as an Ethnic Identifier. Guampedia. https://www.guampedia.com/origin-of-chamorro-as-an-ethnic-identifier/.

Teaiwa, T. K. (1994). Bikinis and other s/pacific n/oceans. *Contemporary Pacific, 6*(1), 87–109.

Temenos, C., and E. McCann. (2013). Geographies of policy mobilities. *Geography Compass, 7*(5), 344–357.

They are more travelled. (ca. 1944). *Arkansas Times*. Shiloh Museum of Ozark History, Springdale, Ark. Accessed March 2014.

Thomas, D. R. D. (2007). *Black France: Colonialism, immigration, and transnationalism*. Bloomington: Indiana University Press.

Trobaugh, J. (2022, July 9). Springdale teachers rally to advocate for change in teaching laws. KNWA. https://www.nwahomepage.com/news/springdale-teachers-rally-in-favor-of-critical-race-theory/.

Troy, D. (2020). Governing imperial citizenship: a historical account of citizenship revocation. In E. Winter, M. J. Gibney, and E. Fargues (Eds.), *When states take rights back* (10–25). Abingdon: Routledge.

Tuck, E., and K. W. Yang. (2014). Unbecoming claims: Pedagogies of refusal in qualitative research. *Qualitative Inquiry, 20*(6), 811–818.

UN Charter, Chapter 12. International trusteeship system. United Nations.

Underwood, R. (2003). The amended U.S. Compacts of Free Association with the Federated States of Micronesia and the Republic of the Marshall Islands: Less free, more compact. *East-West Center working papers: Pacific Islands Development Series, 16.*

———. (2017, 16 November). The changing American lake in the middle of the Pacific. Paper presented for the Peter Tali Coleman lecture on Pacific public policy. Georgetown University, Center for Australian, New Zealand, and Pacific Studies.

United Nations Charter (1947). Accessed September 19, 2023. http://www.un.org/en/charter-united-nations/.

U.S. Census Bureau. (2020). *Springdale, Arkansas.* Washington, D.C.: Government Printing Office.

U.S. Department of Homeland Security: U.S. Citizenship and Immigration Services. (2015, November 3). *Status of citizens of the Freely Associated States of the Federated States of Micronesia and the Republic of the Marshall Islands.* Washington, D.C.

———. (2020). *Status of citizens of the Freely Associated States of the Federated States of Micronesia and the Republic of the Marshall Islands.* http://www.uscis.gov.

U.S. Federal Register (2000). Habitual residence in the territories and possessions of the United States. https://www.federalregister.gov/documents/2000/09/19/00-23788/habitual-residence-in-the-territories-and-possessions-of-the-united-states.

U.S. Public Law 99–239 (1986, January 14). Act to approve the "Compact of Free Association," and for other purposes.

U.S.-RMI Compact of Free Association, 1986. http://www.uscompact.org/index.php

Variety is our norm. (ca. 1995) *Arkansas Democrat-Gazette.* Shiloh Museum of Ozark History, Springdale, Ark.

Varsanyi, M. (2010). *Taking local control: Immigration policy activism in U.S. cities and states.* Stanford, Calif.: Stanford University Press.

Veracini, L. (2013). "Settler colonialism": Career of a concept. *Journal of Imperial and Commonwealth History,* 41(2), 313–333.

Villanueva, J., and M. Lebrón. (2020, February 25). Introduction: The Decolonial Geographies of Puerto Rico's 2019 Summer Protests: A Forum. *Society + Space.* https://www.societyandspace.org/forums/the-decolonial-geographies-of-puerto-ricos-2019-summer-protests-a-forum.

Vine, D. (2011). *Island of shame: The secret history of the U.S. military base on Diego Garcia.* Princeton, N.J.: Princeton University Press.

———. (2012). The lily-pad strategy: How the Pentagon is quietly transforming its overseas base empire and creating a dangerous new way of war. *TomDispatch.* https://tomdispatch.com/david-vine-u-s-empire-of-bases-grows/.

Walker, K. E., and H. Leitner. (2011). The variegated landscape of local immigration policies in the United States. *Urban Geography,* 32(2), 156–178.

Walter, M. (2003, November 16). Long ride to work. *Arkansas Democrat-Gazette.*

Ward, J. M. (2007). "Nazis hoe cotton": Planters, POWs, and the future of farm labor in the Deep South. *Agricultural History,* 81(4), 471–492.

Weise, J. M. (2015). *Corazón de Dixie: Mexicanos in the U.S. South since 1910.* Chapel Hill: University of North Carolina Press.

Whayne, J. M. (2002). *Arkansas: A narrative history.* Fayetteville: University of Arkansas Press.

Willens, H. P. and D. C. Siemer. (Hosts). (1997, March 4). Interview of Andon L. Amaraich. Northern Marianas Humanities Council. https://iyb.nrh.mybluehost.me/nmhc_archives/Oral%20Histories/Amaraich,%20Andon%20L.pdf.

Wilson, R. (2000). *Reimagining the American Pacific*. Durham, N.C.: Duke University Press.

Winders, J. (2005). Changing politics of race and region: Latino migration to the U.S. South. *Progress in Human Geography*, 29(6), 683–699.

———. (2012). Seeing immigrants: Institutional visibility and immigrant incorporation in new immigrant destinations. *Annals of the American Academy of Political and Social Science*, 641(1), 58–78.

———. (2013). *Nashville in the new millennium: Immigrant settlement, urban transformation, and social belonging*. New York: Russell Sage Foundation.

———. (2014). New immigrant destinations in global context. *International Migration Review*, 48(1), 149–179.

Wolfe, P. (2006). Settler colonialism and the elimination of the Native. *Journal of Genocide Research*, 8(4), 387–409.

Wong, T. K. (2012). 287(g) and the politics of interior immigration control in the United States: Explaining local cooperation with federal immigration authorities. *Journal of Ethnic and Migration Studies*, 38(5), 737–756.

Woods, C. (2017). *Development arrested: The blues and plantation power in the Mississippi Delta*. Brooklyn: Verso Books.

Woodward, B. (1976, December 12). CIA bugging Micronesian negotiations. *Washington Post*. http://jfk.hood.edu/Collection/Weisberg%20Subject%20Index%20Files/B%20Disk/Bugging%201972/Item%20025.pdf.

Wright, G. (1986). *Old South, new South: Revolutions in the southern economy since the Civil War*. New York: Basic Books.

Ybarra, M. (2021). Site fight! Toward the abolition of immigrant detention on Tacoma's tar pits (and everywhere else). *Antipode*, 53(1), 36–55.

Yeoh, B. S. (2003). Postcolonial geographies of place and migration. In K. Anderson (Ed.), *Handbook of cultural geography* (369–380). Thousand Oaks, Calif.: SAGE Publications.

Yoneyama, L. (2017). Toward a decolonial genealogy of the transpacific. *American Quarterly*, 69(3), 471–482.

INDEX

Italicized page numbers refer to figures

abolition, 8, 196
activism, 28, 33, 35, 54–55, 152, 155, 190, 194, 207n4; coalitional, 154, 179, 182, 198; health care, 171–172; immigrants' rights, 23–24, 30–31, 38, 118, 143, 179–188, 192, 196, 209n12. *See also* social justice
Adkins, Homer Martin, 91–92
Affordable Care Act (ACA), 171–173
Africa, 41; colonization of, 35, 39; migration from, 5, 26
Aguon, Julian, 44
"alien" discourse, 10, 90, 159–160, 201, 206n19; "illegal alien," 140–142, 192
Alien Land Act (1943), 92
"alien race" discourse, 158
Alley, Charles, 85
Allied Powers, 41, 79
American Board of Commissioners for Foreign Missions, 40
Americanness, 130, 143, 146; as whiteness, 145, 148–149
American Samoa, 161, 199, 208n1
anti-Blackness, 99, 124, 131–134, 136–137, 184, 208n16
anti-immigrant violence, 11, 24, 100, 137, 182, 184, 186, 196
Apollo on Emma Theater, *139*
archives, 21–22, 38, 79, 97, 99, 120; on Springdale, Ark., 23, 92, 94, 129, 133–134, 136, 206n4, 208n12; on U.S. empire, 18, 50, 127–128; of veterans, 74, 82, 84–85, 87

Arizona, Poston, 93–94
Arkansas: Benton County, 120, 138; Bentonville, 16, 113–115, 122, 176; Boone County, 117; Fayetteville, 24, 30, 97, 110, 113–115, 117, 121–122, 130, 136, 146–147; Fort Smith, 85, 96, 98; Harrison, 117–118, 207n4; Little Rock, 21, 24, 86–87, 91, 112, 117, 137, 172; Rich Mountain, 86; Washington County, 138, 140. *See also* Rogers, Ark.; Springdale, Ark.
Arkansas Children's Health Insurance Program (ARKids), 173–174
Arkansas Citizens First Congress, 196
Arkansas Educational Television Network, 85, 206n4
Arkansas Minority Health Commission, 172
Arkansas traveler, 81–82, 120–121
Arkansas Workers Compensation Commission, 185
Arkies, 76, 78–80, 82, 88, 121
"Arkies and Okies" (poem), 78–80, 82
assimilation, 89–90, 142, 149, 158
asylum-seekers, 29, 88, 90, 98–99, 192. *See also* refugees
atomic bombs, 48–49, 94, 102, 204n8. *See also* nuclear testing
Auto Tour Route, 127
Axis Powers, 41, 89

backwardness, 16, 74, 110, 119–120. *See also* underdevelopment
Baker shot, 48
Barraclough, Laura, 145

229

Index

Behdad, Ali, 148
belonging, 6, 24, 30, 110, 128, 143–145, 148–149, 158, 192, 200; collective, 132
benevolence, 15, 44, 46; U.S. image of, 29, 34, 53, 64, 84, 96–97, 103, 105, 158
Berg, Lawrence D., 19
Bermuda, 25
Biden, Joe, 192, 196, 208n5
Bikini Atoll, 48–49, 83, 102, 111
Blackness, 132–133, 137
Black people, 8, 24, 55, 117, 120, 131, 139, 145–146, 155, 208n13: activism of, 179, 187; in Britain, 25; exclusion of, 30, 110–111, 124; expulsion of, 109, 124, 128, 149; flight of, 134, 136; Harrison "Race Riots" and, 118; sundown towns and, 1, 132–138, 206n2; in World War I, 116. *See also* anti-Blackness
boosterism, 74, 77–91, 130–131
border control, 8–10, 31, 68–69, 141, 189, 198, 200–201
Bowman, Michael, 90
braceros, 206n6
Bravo shot, 48–49
British Nationality Act (1948), 26
Bumpers, Dale, 99–100
Bureau of Indian Affairs, 207n8
Bush, George H. W., 99
Byrd, Jodi, 14

Caddo Nation, 111, 125
California, 80, 84, 93, 140, 147, 153; immigrants from, 140; Los Angeles, 8; migration to, 76, 78–79, 88; Orange County, 2
Camacho, Keith L., 67
Cambodia, 97, 207n10
Camp Chaffee, 90–91
Camp Dermott, 90–91
Camp Jerome, 88, 89, 91
Camp Robinson, 90–91
Camp Rohwer, 88, 89, 91
cancer, 171, 174–175
capital accumulation, 111
capitalism, 4, 19, 130; racial, 17, 25, 30, 76, 109–110, 123, 198
Caribbean, 21, 29, 98, 199, 205n11; colonization of, 8, 35, 50; migration from, 25–26, 99. *See also individual countries*
Carter, Jimmy, 205n11
Castle Bravo, 48

CBP. *See* Customs and Border Protection (CBP)
CHamoru (Chamorros), 44, 157, 203n4, 204n6
Cherokee Nation, 1, 126–127, 207n7, 207n9
Cherokee Treaty (1828), 126
Chickasaw Nation, 126
chicken sexing, 93–95, 207n8
China, 144, 192, 194; Cold War and, 62; immigrants from, 177; passport debacle and, 69
Chinese Exclusion Act (1882), 177
Choctaw Nation, 126
Chong Gum, Carmen, 190
churches, 95, 106, 118, 140, 142, 180
Churchill, Winston, 44
Chuuk (Truk), Federated States of Micronesia, 46, 50, 193–194
CIA, 57
citizenship, 9, 11, 142, 156, 173, 189, 191, 199; activism and, 180, 186; British, 26; Compact of Free Association and, 60, 62–64, 68, 72, 159–160; of Freely Associated States, 28, 35, 38, 152, 160–161, 193, 209n6; Marshallese, 12, 14, 25, 37, 59, 157, 176, 206nn18–19; remaking, 1–2, 24; rights of, 3, 33–35, 56; second-class, 3, 55, 151, 158, 194; social, 171; of Trust Territory of the Pacific Islands, 45, 159, 205n17, 206n18. *See also* imperial citizenship; U.S. citizenship
Civilian Conservation Corps, 90
civil rights, 92, 180
Civil Rights Roundtable, 183, 209n12
Clark Air Force Base, 61, 205n15
climate change, 31, 200–201
Clinton, Bill, 24, 99, 104, 171, 208n16
Clinton, Hillary, 3, 194
Clinton Presidential Library, 24
coalitional politics, 23, 154, 179–183, 186, 196, 198–199; Civil Rights Roundtable, 183, 209n12
Coast Guard, 42
Code of the Trust Territory, 43
COFA. *See* Compact(s) of Free Association
Cold War, 27, 35, 37, 51–53, 61, 98; U.S. militarization and, 48, 60–63, 71
colonialism, 32–34, 36, 41–45, 47–48, 56, 65, 70–72, 205n13, 205n15; Compact of Free Association and, 2, 58–59, 67, 150, 178, 203n10, 204n1; definition of, 3; immigration and, 5–6, 8, 14, 19, 26, 35, 111, 201, 204n3;

Index

imperialism and, 18, 20, 73, 98, 101–102, 125, 151–158, 169, 171, 193; Manifest Destiny, 125; neocolonialism, 100, 164, 204n5; settler, 21, 30, 109, 123–126, 128–129, 132, 137, 145, 200; U.S. South and, 16–17. *See also* decolonization; U.S. empire
colonial present, 18, 72
Commonwealth of Northern Mariana Islands (CNMI), 2, 21–22, 64, 68–69, 153, 161, 172, 175, 199, 204n2; CHamorus in, 157, 204n6; in South Pacific Mandate, 40; as trust territory, 43, *46*, 49
commonwealth status, 27, 55, 70, 199, 204nn1–2, 205n12; versus free association, 59, 205n13
communism, 51–52, 98
Compact Impact, 158, 198
Compact(s) of Free Association (COFA; 1986), 2, 12, 192, 197; Amended (2003), 32, 38, 64, 66–69, 209n6; imperial citizenship and, 6, 14, 30, 35, 37–39, 150–160, 162–188; as imperial document, 3, 25–29, 32–33, 59, 101; Marshallese migration to United States and, 32, 35, 106–107, 138; migrant provision in, 2–4, 21, 62–66, 83, 102–104; militarism and, 47, 60–63, 69; mobilities and, 14–15, 22, 148; negotiations and, 23–24, 31, 37–38, 62–65, 71, 193; passing of, 58, 138, 150, 158, 208n3; precarity of, 10, 68, 104, 198
Compact Trust Funds, 59
Congress of Industrial Organizations (CIO), 91
Congress of Micronesia, 22, 50, 54–55, 70
connectedness, 50, 112, 180, 195, 203n7; empire and, 5, 13, 17–18, 101, 103, 178, 186, 199, 201, 205n11; of Latinx immigrants, 139; of Marshallese diaspora, 107, 147–148, 172, 190–191; of military and migration, 63, 73, 83, 99–100, 102; of U.S. South, 16, 20–21; through war, 28, 74–75, 84
containment, 14, 17, 46, 49, 51–52, 109, 111, 119
Cook Islands, 205n13
Creek (Muscogee) Nation, 126–127
crime involving moral turpitude (CIMT), 166, 168, 178
critical race theory, 196
Cuba, refugees from, 29, 88, 91; Mariel boatlift, 74, 98–99
Customs and Border Protection (CBP), 8–9, 12, 162, 189, 206n21, 208n4

decolonization, 3, 9, 18, 27–28, 30, 34, 37–41, 50–51, 57, 75, 190; migration and, 8, 26, 201, 204n3; pressure for, 35, 40, 52–53, 69–71. *See also* colonialism
Deep South, 117–119, 133–134
Deferred Action for Childhood Arrivals (DACA), 179, 181, 185, 209n11
"deficit area" discourse, 194; underdevelopment, 34, 54, 66, 120. *See also* backwardness
De Genova, Nicholas, 169
de Graauw, Els, 142, 169
democracy, 40, 46; U.S. narrative and, 29, 34, 37, 39, 46, 51, 101, 103
dependent territories, 44–45
deportation, 11–12, 141, 196, 203n2, 209n7, 209n11; grounds for, 160, 208n5; of Marshallese, 157, 162–168, 177–178, 183, 197–198
de Soto, Hernando, 125
destination, definition of, 6–7. *See also* new destination of empire; new immigrant destination; Springdale, Ark.
development, 23, 44, 128, 130, 197; aid, 52–54, 69, 204n10; economic, 20, 59, 73, 76–77, 90, 180; emigration as, 64–66, 97; U.S. military and, 47, 61–62
DHS. *See* U.S. Department of Homeland Security
diabetes, 171, 174–175
diaspora, 24, 111, 123, 191, 194, 207n6; COFA, 28, 35–36, 150–151, 153, 155, 160, 193; imperial, 4–5, 14, 19, 26, 190; Marshallese, 4, 14, 28, 33–34, 63, 106–107, 144, 147–148, 172, 179; Pacific Islander, 2
Diplomat, The, 194
disability justice, 196
displacement, 75, 90; Indigenous, 110, 125–126, 128; after nuclear testing, 49, 63, 111, 157; of racism, 118
dispossession, 1, 109, 117, 122; Indigenous, 55, 110, 124–129, 137
Dust Bowl, 76, 78, 131, 206n1, 206n3
Duvalier, François "Papa Doc," 99

Ebeye, Marshall Islands, 193
economic dependence, 51–53, 67, 69
economic migrants, 73
education, 15, 44, 52, 78, 80, 95, 120–121, 171, 196; access to, 64, 92, 187; Fayetteville and, 114;

Index

education (*continued*)
  migration and, 63, 65–66, 107, 157; political, 55; student aid and, 176, 182
Education for Self-Government (ESG), 55
Ellis Island, 96
El Salvador, 2, 173, 185
embassies, 22, 64
emigration, 35, 139; climate change and, 200; development through, 64, 97; Marshallese, 36, 63–66, 83, 104
Enewetak Atoll, Marshall Islands, 48–49, 83
England, 77, 144; Essex, 25. *See also* Great Britain
English as a Second Language (ESL), 174, 187
English language, 138, 143–144, 146–147
environment, 59, 61, 92, 207n5; deterministic logic and, 34, 41, 158; immigration and, 111, 132; after nuclear testing, 49, 65, 83, 204n7
Estado Libre Asociado (Freely Associated State), 199, 204n1. *See also* Puerto Rico
ethnography, 15, 38–39, 207n6. *See also* fieldwork
euphemisms, 92, 204n3, 204n5
European empire, 5, 26, 43, 155
exclusion, 70, 185, 199; of Black people, 1, 30, 110, 124, 133–134, 136, 138; COFA status and, 6, 14, 26, 30, 35, 151–152, 154, 158, 169, 179–188; immigrant, 122, 171, 177–178; Indigenous, 138; of Japanese and Japanese Americans, 94; military, 37, 60; racial, 88, 91, 117, 123–124, 137, 141; spatial, 111, 198, 200
expulsion, 1, 124, 136, 149

Federal Register, 161
Federated States of Micronesia (FSM). *See* Micronesia, Federated States of
feminism, 19. *See also* gender
fieldwork, 10–13, 76, 107, 132, 136–137, 153–155, 178, 203n8; with activists, 180, 209n12; in Arkansas, 23–25, 94, 113, 117–119, 127–129, 143–148, 162, 168, 170, 193; research fatigue and, 25; in Saipan, 21–22; in Washington, D.C., 22–23, 64
first-generation immigrants, 93, 176, 207n9
Fischer, Lana, 93–95
Florida, 98
foreign combatants, 73–75, 84
Fort Chaffee, 90–91, 96–99
Fort Smith Historical Society, 85

France, 26, 40, 70, 116, 126; empire of, 26; Paris, 5
Freely Associated Statehood (FAS), 10, 27–28, 36, 57, 192, 201, 203n10, 204n2, 208n2; beginnings of, 32, 38–39, 59, 150; citizens of, 2, 62, 152, 160; definition of, 204n1; Micronesia and, 50, 69; Puerto Rico and, 199, 205n11
French Guiana, 26
Friends of Micronesia, 70
Fulbright, J. William, 77, 135, 206n2
Fusté, Jose, 17

Gaps in Services to Marshallese Task Force, 172
gender, 3, 180; feminism, 19; masculinity, 146
genocide, 109, 118, 124–125, 127, 137, 191
geographical imaginaries, 10, 17, 20, 34, 62, 189–190, 194–195, 203n3; of Arkansas, 112–122; imperialism and, 36, 48; of Pacific, 86–87; of remoteness, 90; World War II and, 75, 82
George's, 106
Georgia, 207n7; Atlanta, 140
Germany, 40, 120; immigrants of, 128; prisoners of war, 29, 74, 88–93, 95–96, 206nn6–7
Gilmartin, Mary, 19
Gilmore, Ruth Wilson, 20, 124, 203n7
globalization, 19, 73, 110
Global War on Terror, 38, 68–69, 158
Goodman, R. C., 86
Government Accountability Office (GAO), 22
Gray, Alexander B., 194
Great Britain, 2, 25–26, 40, 77; England, 144; United Kingdom, 44
Great Depression, 76–77
Great Migration, 134
Guadeloupe, 26
Guåhan (Guam), 10, 21–22, 41, 55, 57, 64, 68, 153, 199, 203n4; CHamorus from, 157, 204n6; Marshallese in, 2, 107, 172, 175, 198; refugees in, 96; self-determination and, 190; Trust Territory of the Pacific Islands and, 43
Guam Commission on Decolonization, 190
Guatemala, 2, 185
Gulf Coast of Mexico, 25

habitual residents, 142, 161
Hagge, Patrick, 112
Haiti, 29, 74–75, 88, 98–100

Index

Hall, Stuart, 27
Harkins, Anthony, 120
Hau'ofa, Epeli, 7
Hawai'i, 1, 12, 41, 55, 70, 140, 190, 203n4, 204n9; Hilo, 57; Honolulu, 207n1, 208n4; migrants in, 2, 28, 106–107, 158, 169, 172, 174–175, 198; Pearl Harbor, 86; research in, 21–22, 59, 153; Waikiki, 16–17
health care, 15, 59, 102, 106, 141, 209n10; for COFA migrants, 153–154, 171–176, 187, 193; nuclear fallout and, 174–175, 204n7
hegemony, 3, 20, 36–38, 43, 51–52, 61, 68, 77
Hezel, Francis X., 55, 57
Hiemstra, Nancy, 169
hillbilly, 79–82, 119–122
Hmong people, 207n10
HMT Empire Windrush, 25; Windrush generation, 25–27, 35, 200
housing, 140, 146, 166, 171, 176; affordable, 6, 187; public, 10, 15, 170, 193; rights, 196
humanitarianism, 52, 101; military, 96–97
hydrogen bomb, 48

I-94, 12, 165–166, 177, 189
ICE. *See* Immigration and Customs Enforcement
identity, 6, 36, 80, 119, 129, 143–144, 148, 207n4, 207n11; racial, 30, 109–110, 117, 120, 146, 149, 203n9; white, 123
"illegal alien" discourse, 140–142, 192. *See also* "alien race" discourse
Illegal Immigration Reform and Immigrant Responsibility Act (1996), 208n15
illegality trap, 142, 169
Illinois, Chicago, 8
illiteracy, 54, 80
Immigrant Legal Resource Center, 166
immigrant town, 5, 114–116, 124, 134; sanctuary city and, 203n2; Springdale, Ark., as, 1, 21, 110, 138–143, 148–149, 197
immigrant tropes, 192
Immigration and Customs Enforcement (ICE), 141, 162–163, 167, 182–185, 206n21, 208n4, 209n7; raids, 11, 24, 165–166, 181–183, 196
Immigration and Nationality Act, 159, 206n19
Immigration and Naturalization Services (INS), 206n21
immigration justice, 195–196
imperial citizenship, 4, 26–28, 35, 63, 186, 192, 197–198, 200; COFA status as, 6, 14, 30, 37–39, 101, 150–159, 171, 174, 193; creation of, 59; definition of, 151, 158; limits of, 157, 159–161; marginalization and, 151–153; precarity of, 68–69, 187–188. *See also* citizenship
imperial diaspora, 4–5, 14, 19, 26, 190
imperial migrants, 3–6, 8, 13–14, 73–74, 90–92, 101–104, 162, 169, 190; from Mexico and Central America, 139–140
imperial mobilities, 5–7, 13, 36, 125, 149, 151, 156, 158, 191
imperial sense-making, 6, 16, 29, 100–101, 104, 165, 189
independence: movements, 32, 34–35, 53, 57, 69–71, 193–195; versus self-government, 43–44
Independent Practice Association (IPA), 172
India, 144
"Indianness" discourse, 125
Indian Territories, 112, 125–126
Indigeneity, 125, 127, 207n10
Indigenous geographies, 8, 112, 126
Indigenous peoples, 35, 41, 55, 109–111, 194, 207n9; in Arkansas, 116, 124–129, 137, 207n2. *See also individual nations and tribes*
Indigenous sovereignty, 190, 195
Indochina, 74–75, 88, 91, 96–98, 207n10. *See also* Vietnam
inferiority complex, 115, 120
in-migration, 131
Institute of Pacific Relations, 45
Insular Cases (1901), 158
International Trusteeship System, 43–45, 50, 204n5
internment, 29, 73–75, 84, 88–96, 105, 111, 191
invisibilization, 109, 129
Iraq wars, 145
isolation, 50, 72, 75, 112, 118, 120, 194
Ivy Mike, 48

Jamaica, 25
Japan, 42, 49, 93, 95; Hiroshima, 48, 94, 102, 204n8; League of Nations Mandate and, 40–41, 45; Nagasaki, 48, 94, 204n8; Okinawa, 87, 193; Tokyo, 22; in World War II, 78–79, 84–85, 89
Japanese and Japanese American internment, 29, 73–75, 84, 88–96, 105, 111, 191
Jerome Relocation Center, 90–91

Jim Crow era, 1, 116, 133, 191
Johnson, B. F., 78
Johnson, Giff, 52
Jones-Correa, Michael, 142, 169
Jordan, Thurman Odell, 86

Kabua, Amata, 55
Kānaka Maoli, 1, 140, 190, 203n4
Kansas, 126
Kennedy, John F., 51–52
Kiribati, 61, 194
Kissinger, Henry, 57
Korean War, 84, 99
Ku Klux Klan (KKK), 91, 117–118
Kwajalein Atoll, Marshall Islands, 17, 42, 47, 63, 83, 193; U.S. militarization of, 60–61, 66, 68, 205n14

labor, 2, 67, 109, 140; in Arkansas, 1, 24, 76, 91, 106–108, 114–115; empire and, 4, 26, 73–74, 111, 128, 195; enslaved, 109, 134; prison, 73, 92–93; race and, 17, 121–122, 124, 129–131, 134; rights, 180, 185, 196; wartime, 92–94
Lancaster, Guy, 116, 124, 134
Laos, 97, 120, 142; refugees from, 207n10
Latinx immigrants, 11, 30, 208n13; activism and, 154, 179–183, 186–187, 198–199; compared with Marshallese, 162, 165–167, 169, 177, 183–185, 187; in Springdale, Ark., 1–2, 24, 29, 106, 110, 138–141, 162, 197
League of Nations, 27, 42; Covenant, 40–41; Mandate, 36, 39–42, 45, 194, 204n2, 204n4
Lê Espiritu, Yến, 97
legality trap, 162–164, 168–169
lily-pad strategy, 67, 206n20
liminality, 14–15, 57, 63, 156, 181; COFA status and, 6, 26, 30, 35, 151–152, 154, 160, 162–170, 188, 198; taxonomic, 150, 155
Lipman, Jana, 96–97
Local Industries (mural), 108
Loewen, James W., 133–134
Louisiana, 126

Majuro, Marshall Islands, 56, 63, 83, 191
Man, Simeon, 34, 39, 75
Mandatory, 41
Manifest Destiny, 125. *See also* colonialism; settler colonialism; U.S. empire
marginality, 151–152, 198–199; geographic, 30, 112, 123

marginalization, 55–56, 123, 129, 151–152, 185
Mariana Islands. *See* Commonwealth of Northern Mariana Islands
Marianas History Conference, 22
Mariel boatlift, 74, 98–99
Martinique, 26
masculinity, 146. *See also* gender
McConnell, Eileen Díaz, 133–134
McPhetres, Samuel, 21
media reports, 52–53, 70, 191, 206n5; of Arkansans, 119–122; of Cuban émigrés, 98; of immigrants in Arkansas, 141–142; U.S. exceptionalism and, 105; of Vietnamese refugees, 96–97
Medicaid, 153, 171–174, 182, 187, 209n8
Medicare, 174
Melamed, Jodi, 203n7
"melting pot" discourse, 142
Mencken, H. L., 119
methodology of book, 13–25, 38–39
Mexico, 25, 106, 134, 145, 185; immigrants from, 2, 110–111, 138–140, 173, 192, 206n3, 206n6; U.S. border and, 8, 12, 141, 189
Micronesia, Federated States of (FSM), 22–23, 27, 34–37, 43, 50, 55, 159–161, 204n2, 205n16, 206n19; climate change and, 200–201; Compact of Free Association and, 2, 10, 15, 28, 32–33, 57–59, 62–64, 192–193, 204n10; prejudice and, 198
Micronesian Future Political Status Commission, 50
Micronesian Independence Advocates, 70
Micronesian region, 22, 32–34, 36–71, 101, 107, 192, 194–195, 204n9, 205nn12–13
Middle East, 39, 145, 192
militarism and migration, 2–4, 37–38, 58–66, 72–74, 82, 90, 105; Global War on Terror and, 68–69
militarization, 3, 19, 75–76, 82, 86–87, 91, 111, 139, 186, 200; Global War on Terror and, 68–69; of Marshall Islands, 33, 39, 58, 62, 205n14; of territories, 20, 27, 41, 47–48; U.S. empire and, 4, 6, 29, 31, 36, 45
military access, 35, 38, 51; to Marshall Islands, 2, 28, 33, 37, 60–61, 63–64, 67–69
military hegemony, 3, 36, 38, 43, 51, 60–63, 77
military imperialism, 21, 27, 29, 45, 47, 73–75, 78, 94, 100; in Southeast Asia, 51, 98
Mills, C. Wright, 45
Mink, Patsy, 70, 204n9

Miraftab, Faranak, 133–134
missionaries, 40, 42, 127
Mississippi River, 112, 126
Missouri, 140, 147; Kansas City, 197
Missouri River, 125
Missouri Territory, 126
mobilities, 3–4, 22, 27, 35, 87, 101, 115, 164; COFA migrant, 25, 28, 33, 38, 66, 148, 155, 190, 197; future, 31, 195, 199–201; imperial, 5–7, 13–15, 19, 26, 36, 125, 128, 149, 157–158, 192–193; militarized, 73, 75, 85, 80, 82, 86, 88, 105; racialized, 109, 111
mobilities turn, 14
mobility justice, 196
Moody, John, 107
multiscalarity, 13–14, 18–21, 36, 150–153, 156, 203n7
Museum of Native American History (MONAH), 127, 207n9

Namdrik Joor, 144, 146–148
National Park Service, 127
national security, 52, 68–69, 73, 194
nationhood, 144, 149. *See also* Americanness
Native reservations, 6, 111
nativism, 100, 120. *See also* xenophobia
naturalization, 71, 159, 206nn18–19; of whiteness, 124–125, 129–130, 145
Nauru, 70, 194
neocolonialism, 100, 164, 204n5
neoliberalism, 73, 169, 186
New Deal, 90
new destination of empire (NDE), 5–6, 88, 111; double movement of, 4, 19, 26, 195; imperial citizens and, 158, 179, 186, 189, 198; Springdale, Ark., as, 8, 10, 15, 20–21, 30, 72, 74, 108–109, 142, 148, 152
new immigrant destination (NID), 1, 140, 196; definition of, 4–5, 108–109, 129, 138–139; Springdale, Ark., as 4, 30, 108, 112, 162, 187
New South, 130
New World, 125
New York, 8, 22, 153
New York Times, 98
New Zealand, 205n13
Ngai, Mae, 158
9/11 attacks, 67–68, 198
Niue, 205n13
Nixon, Rob, 73
noncitizenship, 2, 156, 158. *See also* citizenship

nonimmigrants, 140–142, 160–161, 169, 177, 179, 209n7
nonsovereignty, 4, 15, 20, 47, 70–71, 151, 157, 169, 179, 201; U.S. empire and, 27, 194, 199. *See also* sovereignty
North American Free Trade Agreement, 139
North Carolina, 140
Northern Marianas District, 205n12
Northwest Arkansas Community College (NWACC), 176
nose art, *81*
Nuclear Claims Tribunal, 66
nuclear testing, 37, 47–48, 54, 101–102; criticism of, 70; displacement and, 49, 63, 66, 157; fallout from, 36, 65–66, 171, 174–175, 204n7; reparations for, 29, 59, 66, 74, 83, 101–105. *See also* atomic bombs

Obamacare (Affordable Care Act; ACA), 171–173
occupation, 6, 45, 63, 122, 129, 159, 161, 204n3; imperial, 9, 19–20, 158, 194; of Marshall Islands, 41, 193; military, 27, 36, 51, 65, 72–73, 76, 88; Spanish, 40, 125; U.S., 2, 4, 21, 35, 38, 86, 102, 204n8
Oceania, 7
O'Connor, Flannery, 122
Office of Insular Affairs, 22
Office of Micronesian Status Negotiations, 56
Okies, 78–80, 82
Oklahoma, 107, 112, 126; Enid, 140, 195, 197
Omi, Michael, 20, 123
Operation Castle, 48
Operation Ivy, 48
oral histories, 23, 39, 59, 85, 129
ordnance plants, 77–78, 90–91
Oregon, 28; Salem, 2
Orientalism, 79, 89, 100
Osage Nation, 111, 125–126
Ottoman Empire, 40
Ouachita Mountains, 112, 134
out-migration, 76, 78–79, 88, 131
overpopulation, 100, 174
Ozark: Atolls, 106; Indigenous populations and, 125, 137; Mountains, 1, 112; people of, 119–120, 125, 128–129, 132; Rodeo of the, 110, 144–146, 148; sundown towns and, 134

Pacific Islands, 7–8, 21–23, 31, 172, 182, 189–190, 204n1, 206n5; Arkansas and, 6, 17–18, 29, 73–88, 106, 139; climate change and, 200–201;

Index

Pacific Islands (*continued*)
  Compact of Free Association and, 60–71, 192–193, 199; diasporas of, 1–2, 4, 27, 35, 39, 140, 195; geographical imaginaries and, 9–10, 15–16, 33–34, 36, 41, 86–87, 206n5; sovereignty of, 39–40; U.S. imperialism in, 3, 28, 37–38, 41–46, 50–53, 57, 96, 100–104, 194, 205n11. *See also* Trust Territory of the Pacific Islands; *and individual countries and islands*
Pacific Proving Grounds, 48
Pacific Theater (World War II), 42
Pakistan, 100
Palau, Republic of (Belau), 10, 15, 32, 36, 40, 192, 204n2; COFA negotiations and, 37–38, 58–59, 61, 193; migrants of, 2, 69, 151–152, 155, 157, 161; as trust territory, 43, 46–47, 50
Papua New Guinea, 70
Paraguay, 119
Partial Test Ban Treaty, 49
passports, 22, 164–167, 205n17, 208n3; debacle, 69
patriotism, 79, 80, 82, 145, 148
Peace Corps, 51, 70
Pearl Harbor, 86, 94. *See also* World War II
Pearson, Jessica Lynne, 45
Perdue, Robert Todd, 207n5
Personal Responsibility and Work Opportunity Reconciliation Act (1996), 171, 209n8
Petersen, Glenn, 55
Philippines, 5, 35, 44, 84–86; Manila, 85; migrants from, 96, 156, 158, 206n3; Subic Bay, 61, 205n15; U.S. military bases in, 34, 61, 205n15
pioneers, 126, 128
place-making, 20–21, 111, 114, 123, 189
plebiscites, 35, 52, 58
Pohnpei (Ponape), Federated States of Micronesia, 46, 50
police, 143, 146, 162–165, 182–184, 195, 197, 209n7
policing, 146, 169, 179, 206n21; of border, 9–11, 31, 197, 200–201; of immigrants, 30, 68, 143, 150, 154, 162–167, 170, 181–186, 203n2, 209n7; racialized, 124, 129, 132, 135–136, 141
policy: administrators/enforcers of, 13, 179; analysts of, 7, 62, 64, 103; anti-immigrant, 141, 192; Cold War, 98; colonial, 33–34, 150; exclusionary, 154; federal, 23, 162, 167, 171, 196; foreign, 105; health-care, 171–173; immigration policies, 5–6, 69, 141, 150–162, 165, 169–174, 188, 192, 196–197, 201; imperial citizenship and, 30, 150–162, 157; imperial policies, 4, 13, 15, 20, 28, 70, 152, 189, 199, 205n11; managing mobility, 14–15; methodology of book and, 14–25, 36, 59; neoliberal, 186; policing and, 143, 182–183; policymakers, 15, 23, 39, 64, 154–155, 158, 173; policymaking, 20, 28, 35, 57, 152, 158, 199, 205n11; policy memos, 38; policy mobilities, 15; sanctuary city policies, 203n2; Solomon Report and, 52–54; state, 140, 150, 162, 171, 196; of strategic denial, 37; sundown town policies, 128, 132–135; U.S. Pacific imperialism and, 33–34; in U.S. territories, 68; visa-free migration and, 32. *See also individual policies and laws*
Pompeo, Mike, 192
postcolonialism, 2, 26–27, 35, 58, 158, 205n15
poultry industry, 93–95, 106–108, 185, 207n8
prisoners of war (POW), 105; German, 29, 74–75, 88–93, 95–96, 206nn6–7; Italian, 89–91
prisons, 73, 90, 92–93, 98, 167, 196. *See also* Japanese and Japanese American internment
Procter & Gamble, 114
Proposition 187 (Calif.), 140
protests, 56, 190, 196, 207n4
provincialism, 16–17, 87–88, 112, 115, 118–119
proxy wars, 51
public charge rule, 160, 177–178, 208n5
Puerto Rico, 8, 17, 55, 104, 156–158, 193, 204n1; Compact of Free Association and, 199, 205n11
Pulido, Laura, 123

Quapaw Nation, 111, 125

Race Riots in Harrison, Ark., 118
racial capitalism, 17, 25, 30, 76, 109–110, 123, 198
racial cleansing, 109, 122, 124
racial diversity, 115–116, 120, 129
racial formations, 20, 89, 122–124, 149, 186, 191
racial geographies, 30, 115–117, 119, 122–138, 140, 148–149, 191, 203n7; in Arkansas, 108–149; definition of, 122; imaginaries, 138
racialized labor, 17, 121–122, 124, 129–131, 134
racialized mobility, 111
racial justice, 24, 30–31, 179–180, 195–196
racial present, 30, 109, 122, 137
racial profiling, 166, 182, 185

racism, 16, 34, 88, 98–100, 196; anti-Black, 99, 124, 131–134, 136–137, 184, 208n16; anti-Japanese, 79, 84, 89–95; in Arkansas, 30, 112–123, 134–136; definition of, 20. *See also* white supremacy
racist towns, 109, 114–116, 135
razorback hog, 81–82
Reagan, Ronald, 144–145, 148, 208n16
Reconstruction, 130
redneck stereotype, 121
refugees, 73, 192; in Arkansas, 74–75, 88, 90–91, 96–99, 105; Marshallese seen as, 29, 74, 101, 103, 172–173. *See also* asylum-seekers
relocation, 26, 103, 105, 147; of Indigenous populations, 1, 109, 111, 126, 137; of Japanese and Japanese Americans, 88–91; nuclear testing and, 49, 63, 66; of refugees, 91, 97–98, 101
remoteness, 31, 50, 53, 102, 190; of Arkansas, 30, 74–75, 77, 90, 105, 109–110, 112–113; empire and, 4, 7–10, 13–18, 33, 36, 41, 70, 72, 191, 194, 201; nuclear testing and, 48–49; racism and, 117–119, 122
removal, 49, 75, 97, 100, 128; of Indigenous populations, 109, 111, 124–128, 191
reparations, 29, 59, 66, 74, 83, 101–105
reproductive justice, 196
research fatigue, 24–25, 155
resettlement, 88, 101, 105, 111, 140–141; empire and, 5, 19, 90, 96–98, 148, 153, 158; of Marshallese, 2, 24–25, 29, 48, 65, 102, 107, 110, 138, 147; racialized, 1, 99, 109, 128, 139, 206n3, 207n6
Réunion, 26
rightlessness, 15, 154–155, 178–179, 182–183, 186–187
Robb, Thomas, 118
Robinson, Cedric, 109
Rodeo of the Ozarks, 110, 142–146, 148
Rogers, Ark., 8, 12, 80, 93, 120, 135, 182, 189; compared to Springdale, 113–115, 122, 131, 143, 197
Ronald Reagan Ballistic Missile Defense Test Site, 61
Rongelap Atoll, Marshall Islands, 49
Rota, Commonwealth of Northern Mariana Islands (CNMI), 22
Roth, Stanley O., 61, 205n15
ruination, 73
ruralism, 5, 112, 121, 132

Said, Edward, 195
Saipan, 21–22, 39, 51, 59, 84–85, 107
Samoa, 70
sanctuary, 74, 88, 101; cities, 203n2
Saudi Arabia, 144–145
second-generation immigrants, 106, 142, 196, 207n9
self-determination, 27–28, 34, 37, 39, 51, 59, 70; calls for, 8, 41, 190, 204n3; Freely Associated Statehood and, 203n10, 204n11; UN Charter and, 43–44
self-government, 27, 51, 54, 62, 190; capacity for, 16, 28, 33–34, 36, 41, 52; definition of, 43–45; transition to, 37, 39
Seminole People, 126
settler colonialism, 21, 30, 109, 123–126, 128–129, 132, 137, 145, 200
settler romanticism, 128–132, 145, 149
Shiloh Museum of Ozark History, 23, 78, 80, 87, 126, 133, 136, 206n4, 208n12
Singh, Nikhil, 34
Sioux People, 127
slavery, 109, 134
slow violence, 73
Smith, C. Calvin, 79
social citizenship, 171
social justice, 21, 30, 154, 180, 196, 201, 209n12
social services, 15, 30, 154, 170–178, 182–183, 186–188, 193, 204n10, 208n8
soft power, 37, 52–53, 60
Solomon, Anthony, 51
Solomon Report, 50–55, 57, 65, 194
Somaliland, 119, 204n4
South Asia, 4, 25; India, 144; Pakistan, 100
southern exceptionalism, 119
southern trope, 121
South Korea, 99, 120, 145; Jeju, 193
South Pacific Mandate, 40–42
sovereignty, 2, 34, 36, 50–51, 57, 62, 68–69, 204n3, 207n9, 208n2; Indigenous, 190, 195; Marshallese, 14–15, 20, 28, 32–33, 38–49, 58–60, 67, 154, 204n2; U.S. empire and, 194. *See also* nonsovereignty
Soviet Union, 48, 51, 61–62
Spade, John, 83–85
Spain, 40, 125, 145
Spanish (language), 120, 143, 167, 204n1
Springdale, Ark., 4, 8, 10, 15, 63, 20–21, 72–74, 106–108, 152, 187; archives, 23, 92, 94, 129, 133–134, 136, 206n4, 208n12; demographics

238 Index

Springdale, Ark. (*continued*)
of, 1–2, 29–30, 109–110, 117, 129–132, 138, 140, 148, 197; as immigrant town, 1, 21, 110, 138–143, 148–149, 197; Indigenous history and, 125–128; as provincial place, 112, 115; racism and, 112, 114–117, 121–138; remoteness of, 30, 75, 112–113; as sundown town, 111, 132–138; as white town, 124–126, 128–131, 138, 141, 149
Springdale County Court, 23–24
Springdale News, 128
Springdale Public School, 106, 174
Stege, Kristina, 4
Stoler, Ann, 18, 73
strategic denial, 37, 60–63
Striffler, Steve, 108
sundown towns, 1, 128, 191, 203n1; definition of, 124, 133–134; lore of, 135; Springdale, Ark., and, 111, 132–138
surveillance, 14, 69, 90, 109, 165, 182

Tennessee, 86; Nashville, 140
Texas, 80, 131, 189; Austin, 117; Copperas Cove, 140
Thailand, 97
third-generation immigrants, 106, 196
Thirty Meter Telescope, 190
Thomas, Roger, 84–85
Tinian, 21, 204n8
Title 42, 192
Tmetuchl, Roman, 55
Tobler's first law of geography, 190
Tonton Macoutes, 99
tourism, 145; in Hawai'i, 16–17; in Micronesia, 54; in Northwest Arkansas, 113
Trail of Tears, 1, 126–127
transnational citizenship, 156
transnationalism, 15–16, 27, 35, 122–123, 139, 148, 156, 201
transpacific, 2, 20, 29, 74, 192; making of, 75–76
"tribe," as term, 207n8
Trinidad, 25
tropes: hillbilly, 79–82, 119–122; immigrant, 192; southern, 121
Trump, Donald, 24, 167, 178, 192, 196, 208n5
Trust Territory of the Pacific Islands (TTPI), 3, 27, 35–37, 39, 42–45, 47–58, 60, 63, 65, 71; citizenship, 62, 205n17, 206n18; creation of, 2, 27; criticism of, 52–53, 70, 204n9; headquarters of, 21; map of, *46*; passport, 208n3
Tuaua v. United States, 199
Tunica, 125
tutelage, 27, 44, 55
Tuvalu, 194
287(g), 143, 182–183, 208n15
Tyson Foods, 16, 106–108, 111, 175

underdevelopment, 34, 54, 66, 120
undocumented immigrants, 141, 151, 165, 167, 173, 179, 181, 183–185, 203n2, 208n14; illegality trap and, 142, 162
unincorporated territories, 22, 204n1
unions, 91, 130, 181, 196
United Kingdom, 25–26, 44. See also Great Britain
United Nations (UN), 20, 22, 38, 41, 56–57, 99, 204nn2–3, 204n5; Charter, 40, 43–45, 47–48, 54; Freely Associated Statehood and, 203n10, 204n1, 205n11; Trust Territory of the Pacific Islands and, 2, 27, 35–36, 39, 42–43, *46*, 52–53, 70, 205n17
University of Arkansas, 77, 81, 104, 114–115; Special Collections, 23, 97, 99
University of Hawai'i at Mānoa, 22
U.S. Army, 42, 85, 98
U.S. Atomic Energy Commission, 48
U.S. census, 1, 106, 126, 138, 207n11
U.S. citizenship, 22, 89, 93–94, 152, 168–169, 178, 208n1; forms of, 157–158, 199; path to, 62–64, 142, 159–160, 164. See also citizenship
U.S. Citizenship and Immigration Services (USCIS), 160, 177, 206n21, 208n4
U.S. Civil War, 126, 128, 134
U.S. Defense Nuclear Agency, 48
U.S. Department of Defense, 50, 66
U.S. Department of Homeland Security (DHS), 12, 141, 168, 206n21, 209n11
U.S. Department of Justice (DOJ), 161
U.S. Department of State, 50
U.S. Department of the Interior, 50, 66, 157, 208n2
U.S. empire, 10, 17–19, 25, 29, 32–33, 43, 51, 70, 193, 199–200; diasporas and, 14; expansion of, 34, 36, 48, 71, 194; imperial citizenship and, 30, 101, 104, 150–152, 155, 158, 171, 186–187; Manifest Destiny, 125; militarism and, 3, 60, 67, 75–78, 82, 94, 100; mobilities

of, 4–6, 22, 68, 72–74, 90, 103, 111, 139, 156, 189, 192; racialization through, 20–21, 84, 109–110, 122; remoteness in, 15–16, 105; resistance to, 179, 193; violence of, 125, 128, 186. *See also* colonialism
U.S. exceptionalism, 16, 29, 72, 74, 82, 97, 101, 104–105, 203n11
U.S. Geological Survey, 200
U.S.-Mexico border, 8, 12, 139, 141, 189
U.S. military bases, 3, 6, 27, 43, 59–60, 67, 158, 193, 200, 206n20; in Arkansas, 73, 77, 90, 96, 99; expansion of, 45–47, 200; in Pacific, 61–63, 80; in Philippines, 34–35, 61, 205n15. *See also individual bases*
U.S. Navy, 43, 86
U.S.-Palau Compact of Free Association, 47, 193
U.S. permanent residency, 63–64, 89, 159–161, 168–169, 206n19
U.S. Supreme Court, 158, 199
U.S. territories, 2, 10, 22, 50, 53, 55, 67, 192, 199; formal citizenship and, 157–159; migration from and within, 4, 14, 62–63, 66, 72–73, 161, 169, 179. *See also individual U.S. territories*
Utrik Atoll, Marshall Islands, 49

Vanuatu, 61
Veracini, Lorenzo, 128
veterans, 29; of Vietnam War, 97; of World War I, 91; of World War II, 74–75, 82–88, 102–103, 190
Vieques, Puerto Rico, 17, 193
Vietnam: language of, 120; refugees from, 29, 74–75, 88, 91, 96–98, 100, 105, 207n10
Vine, David, 67, 206n20
voting, 56, 91, 152, 157, 182, 197, 205n12; in plebiscites, 35, 52, 58; rights, 157, 182

Wake Island, 96
Walmart, 16, 24, 106, 114–115
Walton Family Foundation, 114
War Relocation Authority, 89
Washington (state), 78, 146
Washington, D.C., 100, 182, 207n1; fieldwork in, 21–23, 39, 59, 64, 67, 153, 208n4; policymaking and, 50, 57, 205n11

Watkins, Kenneth, 92–93
Weise, Julie, 17
Welch Grape Juice Company, 92–93
welfare, 174, 208n16
West Africa, 5, 41
West Indies, 5
West Virginia, 119
white identity, 123
whiteness, 21–22, 111, 139–140; Arkansan stereotype and, 80, 120, 122; construction of, 123–125, 128; Springdale, Ark., and, 129–134, 136–138, 145–146, 148–149
"whitening," practices of, 21, 129
white settlement, 110, 112
white space, 124, 129
white supremacy, 8, 20–21, 24, 79, 88, 95, 111, 196–198; in Arkansas, 91–92, 100, 110, 117, 124, 130, 141; settler colonialism and, 123, 129. *See also* racism
white towns, 29, 114, 124–126, 128–131, 133, 138, 143, 149
Williams, F. Haydn, 56–57
Winant, Howard, 20, 123
Windrush generation, 25–27, 35, 200
women's rights, 180. *See also* gender
Woodward, Bob, 70
World War I, 27, 33, 39–40, 53, 116
World War II, 20, 27, 32, 37, 39, 41–42, 61, 70, 145, 204n5; Arkansas and, 75–88, 90–91, 105; atomic bombs, 48–49, 94, 102, 204n8; detainees, 29, 88–96, 105; Kwajalein Atoll and, 42, 83; Pacific Theater, 42; postcolonial migration and, 26, 28, 73–74; veterans of, 29, 74–75, 82–88, 102–103
Wright, Gavin, 16

xenophobia, 137, 158, 178, 196–197, 200; in Arkansas, 20, 99–100, 120, 143; of Asians and Asian Americans, 90–91, 95; in Britain, 25

Yap, Federated States of Micronesia, 46, 50
Young Micronesian, The, 54

Zeder, Fred M., II, 58

GEOGRAPHIES OF JUSTICE AND SOCIAL TRANSFORMATION

1. *Social Justice and the City*, rev. ed.
   BY DAVID HARVEY

2. *Begging as a Path to Progress: Indigenous Women and Children and the Struggle for Ecuador's Urban Spaces*
   BY KATE SWANSON

3. *Making the San Fernando Valley: Rural Landscapes, Urban Development, and White Privilege*
   BY LAURA R. BARRACLOUGH

4. *Company Towns in the Americas: Landscape, Power, and Working-Class Communities*
   EDITED BY OLIVER J. DINIUS AND ANGELA VERGARA

5. *Tremé: Race and Place in a New Orleans Neighborhood*
   BY MICHAEL E. CRUTCHER JR.

6. *Bloomberg's New York: Class and Governance in the Luxury City*
   BY JULIAN BRASH

7. *Roppongi Crossing: The Demise of a Tokyo Nightclub District and the Reshaping of a Global City*
   BY ROMAN ADRIAN CYBRIWSKY

8. *Fitzgerald: Geography of a Revolution*
   BY WILLIAM BUNGE

9. *Accumulating Insecurity: Violence and Dispossession in the Making of Everyday Life*
   EDITED BY SHELLEY FELDMAN, CHARLES GEISLER, AND GAYATRI A. MENON

10. *They Saved the Crops: Labor, Landscape, and the Struggle over Industrial Farming in Bracero-Era California*
    BY DON MITCHELL

11. *Faith Based: Religious Neoliberalism and the Politics of Welfare in the United States*
    BY JASON HACKWORTH

12. *Fields and Streams: Stream Restoration, Neoliberalism, and the Future of Environmental Science*
    BY REBECCA LAVE

13. *Black, White, and Green: Farmers Markets, Race, and the Green Economy*
    BY ALISON HOPE ALKON

14. *Beyond Walls and Cages: Prisons, Borders, and Global Crisis*
    EDITED BY JENNA M. LOYD, MATT MITCHELSON, AND ANDREW BURRIDGE

15. *Silent Violence: Food, Famine, and Peasantry in Northern Nigeria*
    BY MICHAEL J. WATTS

16. *Development, Security, and Aid: Geopolitics and Geoeconomics at the U.S. Agency for International Development*
    BY JAMEY ESSEX

17. *Properties of Violence: Law and Land-Grant Struggle in Northern New Mexico*
    BY DAVID CORREIA

18. *Geographical Diversions: Tibetan Trade, Global Transactions*
    BY TINA HARRIS

19. *The Politics of the Encounter: Urban Theory and Protest under Planetary Urbanization*
    BY ANDY MERRIFIELD

20. *Rethinking the South African Crisis: Nationalism, Populism, Hegemony*
    BY GILLIAN HART

21. *The Empires' Edge: Militarization, Resistance, and Transcending Hegemony in the Pacific*
    BY SASHA DAVIS

22. *Pain, Pride, and Politics: Social Movement Activism and the Sri Lankan Tamil Diaspora in Canada*
    BY AMARNATH AMARASINGAM

23. *Selling the Serengeti: The Cultural Politics of Safari Tourism*
    BY BENJAMIN GARDNER

24. *Territories of Poverty: Rethinking North and South*
    EDITED BY ANANYA ROY AND EMMA SHAW CRANE

25. *Precarious Worlds: Contested Geographies of Social Reproduction*
    EDITED BY KATIE MEEHAN AND KENDRA STRAUSS

26. *Spaces of Danger: Culture and Power in the Everyday*
    EDITED BY HEATHER MERRILL AND LISA M. HOFFMAN

27. *Shadows of a Sunbelt City: The Environment, Racism, and the Knowledge Economy in Austin*
    BY ELIOT M. TRETTER

28. *Beyond the Kale: Urban Agriculture and Social Justice Activism in New York City*
BY KRISTIN REYNOLDS AND NEVIN COHEN

29. *Calculating Property Relations: Chicago's Wartime Industrial Mobilization, 1940–1950*
BY ROBERT LEWIS

30. *In the Public's Interest: Evictions, Citizenship, and Inequality in Contemporary Delhi*
BY GAUTAM BHAN

31. *The Carpetbaggers of Kabul and Other American-Afghan Entanglements: Intimate Development, Geopolitics, and the Currency of Gender and Grief*
BY JENNIFER L. FLURI AND RACHEL LEHR

32. *Masculinities and Markets: Raced and Gendered Urban Politics in Milwaukee*
BY BRENDA PARKER

33. *We Want Land to Live: Making Political Space for Food Sovereignty*
BY AMY TRAUGER

34. *The Long War: CENTCOM, Grand Strategy, and Global Security*
BY JOHN MORRISSEY

35. *Development Drowned and Reborn: The Blues and Bourbon Restorations in Post-Katrina New Orleans*
BY CLYDE WOODS
EDITED BY JORDAN T. CAMP AND LAURA PULIDO

36. *The Priority of Injustice: Locating Democracy in Critical Theory*
BY CLIVE BARNETT

37. *Spaces of Capital / Spaces of Resistance: Mexico and the Global Political Economy*
BY CHRIS HESKETH

38. *Revolting New York: How 400 Years of Riot, Rebellion, Uprising, and Revolution Shaped a City*
GENERAL EDITORS: NEIL SMITH AND DON MITCHELL
EDITORS: ERIN SIODMAK, JENJOY ROYBAL, MARNIE BRADY, AND BRENDAN O'MALLEY

39. *Relational Poverty Politics: Forms, Struggles, and Possibilities*
EDITED BY VICTORIA LAWSON AND SARAH ELWOOD

40. *Rights in Transit: Public Transportation and the Right to the City in California's East Bay*
BY KAFUI ABLODE ATTOH

41. *Open Borders: In Defense of Free Movement*
EDITED BY REECE JONES

42. *Subaltern Geographies*
EDITED BY TARIQ JAZEEL AND STEPHEN LEGG

43. *Detain and Deport: The Chaotic U.S. Immigration Enforcement Regime*
BY NANCY HIEMSTRA

44. *Global City Futures: Desire and Development in Singapore*
BY NATALIE OSWIN

45. *Public Los Angeles: A Private City's Activist Futures*
BY DON PARSON
EDITED BY ROGER KEIL AND JUDY BRANFMAN

46. *America's Johannesburg: Industrialization and Racial Transformation in Birmingham*
BY BOBBY M. WILSON

47. *Mean Streets: Homelessness, Public Space, and the Limits of Capital*
BY DON MITCHELL

48. *Islands and Oceans: Reimagining Sovereignty and Social Change*
BY SASHA DAVIS

49. *Social Reproduction and the City: Welfare Reform, Child Care, and Resistance in Neoliberal New York*
BY SIMON BLACK

50. *Freedom Is a Place: The Struggle for Sovereignty in Palestine*
BY RON J. SMITH

51. *Loisaida as Urban Laboratory: Puerto Rico Community Activism in New York*
BY TIMO SCHRADER

52. *Transecting Securityscapes: Dispatches from Cambodia, Iraq, and Mozambique*
BY TILL F. PAASCHE AND JAMES D. SIDAWAY

53. *Non-Performing Loans, Non-Performing People: Life and Struggle with Mortgage Debt in Spain*
BY MELISSA GARCÍA-LAMARCA

54. *Disturbing Development in the Jim Crow South*
BY MONA DOMOSH

55. *Famine in Cambodia: Geopolitics, Biopolitics, Necropolitics*
BY JAMES A. TYNER

56. *Well-Intentioned Whiteness: Green Urban Development and Black Resistance in Kansas City*
BY CHHAYA KOLAVALLI

57. *Urban Climate Justice: Theory, Praxis, Resistance*
EDITED BY JENNIFER L. RICE, JOSHUA LONG, AND ANTHONY LEVENDA

58. *Abolishing Poverty: Toward Pluriverse Futures and Politics*
BY VICTORIA LAWSON, SARAH ELWOOD, MICHELLE DAIGLE, YOLANDA GONZÁLEZ MENDOZA, ANA GUTIÉRREZ GARZA, JUAN HERRERA, ELLEN KOHL, JOVAN LEWIS, AARON MALLORY, PRISCILLA MCCUTCHEON, MARGARET MARIETTA RAMÍREZ, AND CHANDAN REDDY

59. *Outlaw Capital: Everyday Illegalities and the Making of Uneven Development*
BY JENNIFER LEE TUCKER

60. *High Stakes, High Hopes: Urban Theorizing in Partnership*
BY SOPHIE OLDFIELD

61. *The Coup and the Palm Trees: Agrarian Conflict and Political Power in Honduras*
BY ANDRÉS LEÓN ARAYA

62. *Cultivating Socialism: Venezuela, ALBA, and the Politics of Food Sovereignty*
BY ROWAN LUBBOCK

63. *Green City Rising: Contamination, Cleanup, and Collective Action*
BY ERIN GOODING

64. *New Destinations of Empire: Mobilities, Racial Geographies, and Citizenship in the Transpacific United States*
BY EMILY MITCHELL-EATON

Printed in the United States
by Baker & Taylor Publisher Services